DEVELOPMENT OF PRIMITIVE TRIBAL GROUPS IN INDIA

DEVELOPMENT OF PRIMITIVE TRIBAL GROUPS IN INDIA

Dr. P.K. Mohanty

PUBLICATIONS

KALPAZ PUBLICATIONS
DELHI - 110052

DEVELOPMENT OF PRIMITIVE TRIBAL GROUPS IN INDIA
[*Anthropology, Tribal Studies*]

Rs. 790

ISBN: 81-7835-024-6

Published in 2015 in India by
Kalpaz Publications
C-30, Satyawati Nagar
Ashok Vihar-III, Delhi-110052
e-mail: kalpaz@hotmail.com

Laser Typeset at: Alphabet, Delhi
Printed at : Chawla Offset Press

Dedicated to
My Daughter (PRATITI)
and
My Son (PRASANJIT)

Contents

Foreword

Broaching the subject of what is spoken of in official and even academic parlance as "primitive tribal groups" is fraught with an element of slight to one's sensitivity towards fellow human beings. It invokes in its immediate implication, what a sensitive mind perceives implied in the stereo-typical relationship between a member of the non-tribal society and a member of remote tribal society, i.e., a feeling of superciliousness, an attitude of superiority, a sense of noblesse oblige.

Should one unravel in our mind the genesis of the state in which various primitive tribal groups are placed today we may have to put the "civilised societies" in the dock. Those endowed with a degree of sensibility would begin suffering from a sense of guilt. For, not very long ago, most of these "primitive tribal groups" could neither have been considered "primitive" in terms of the norms and notions then prevalent, nor could they have been treated disdainfully. They lived in their very own nature-rich encysted world, engaged in evolving their own systems of social and political organisations, culture, language, ethos, in fact a whole way of life in harmony with the environment in which they were placed. Which is saying much more than we can say of our own warring, plundering world. But over centuries the avaricious and predacious "civilised societies" have been raiding their resources, encroaching on their ecology and maiming their minds. This history has elongated into contemporaneity.

But who are the "primitive tribal groups"? Recent chroniclers trace the appellation to Dhebar Commission Report of 1961. The chairman of the Commission, Shri U.N. Dhebar in a forwarding letter to the President of India, wrote that amongst the tribals the Commission was "able to notice four different layers..... We feel that at the base of these four layers is the class of tribals which is in an extremely underdeveloped stage and at the topmost level amongst the tribals is a layer that can well afford to forego any further help. We feel that this lowest layer needs the utmost consideration at the hands of the Government.....".

The Dhebar Commission had embarked on a mission - that of writing a report for the good of the country's tribal population, as could be and should be undertaken by government agencies. Not to miss the point, their perspective was tribals relative to the rest of the society. Considering that, that Commission and a number of its successor-bodies charged with a similar charter, did remarkable jobs. Further, if I may strike a personal note, in drafting the Sixth, Seventh, Eight and Ninth Plan Working Group Reports for Scheduled Tribes a privilege in which I had a full share, not only was due concern for primitive tribal groups expressed, but prescriptions were liberally spelt. But it is one thing to diagnose and inscribe prescriptions, but another to nurse an ailing member of the family. Even now, it looks that unless radically different approach is adopted, the predominantly bureaucratic process would continue to do reverence merely to the established ritual.

The problem is intensely human. Being aware that we live no longer in the era of "noble savage" of Bronislaw Malinowski's Trobrianders of the Pacific, R.B. Lee's Kung Bushmen of Kalahari, E.E. Evans Pritchard's Nuer of Sudan, Harold Conklin's Hanunoo of the Philippines and being alive to the general underestimation of the dynamics of the time-dimension, there are risks involved in overlooking or by-passing groups in our subcontinent, which should more appropriately be designated as "primary". For, the serious anthropologist may live to rue a lost paradise. The most outstanding among them are the Bay Islanders i.e. the Sentinelese, Jarawa, Shompen, Onge and the Great Andamanese of the Andaman and Nicobar Islands, since for them time has stood centuries-still. In a sense, they represent the perenniality of human species and time's transience. A member's end does not erase the group; the group lives on eternally. Not far behind, though not as redoubtable when up against the formidable change-inducing time are the Muria and Madia of Bastar, Madhya Pradesh, the Bondo and Saora of Orissa, the Chola-Naicken of Kerala and a few others. That they have survived ravages owes not a little to their sequestered habitat concealed from the gaze of the depredations of their fellow-men. It could also owe to a conscious or unconscious intrinsic philosophy of sustainable consumption, in any event a negation of mindless exploitation of nature extracting the maximum and returning the minimum. Clarke and Hindley (1975) put it pithily when they wrote that a member of this group has neither been a detached observer nor an exploiter of nature - he was of it, and in it. The critic might well say that the then small population made in possible. Let us not forget that, as Gandhiji said, if properly managed, the resources of this earth are enough for everyone's need, but not for greed. To this day, the largely untrammelled ecology of the primary groups yields enough. Some conservation measures today might help for more ease.

But it is erroneous to believe that all or even most of primary groups are ensconced in plenitudinous environs. Once a thriving tribe a century ago, the Great Andamanese have now been reduced to a double-digit figure. They face a situation of near-extinction; so do some other lesser known groups. One would like to think that, on the whole, the holistic world of the primary primitive living totally away encompasses facets which have remained in shadow for long and which can be illumined through deep and empathetic studies.

We may now turn own attention to those groups and communities that dot the fringes of the "civilised" society.

While the primary groups just discussed located generally in far recesses may impinge subliminally on the national consciousness, (one Lt-Governor of Andaman and Nicobar Islands having a military background wanted to conduct a flag-march in Jarawa territory to teach them a lesson!), we now need to turn our attention to others. There are certain groups and communities that dot the fringes of the "civilised world". They have arrived at a stage of considerably depleted and degraded environment. Yet it is perfectly conceivable that their forest and eco-system were, at one time, as well-endowed as are presently those of the primary groups we have spoken of. Adversity may have struck in many ways. It is not improbable that repeated depredations of many non-tribal sections of people who would have dealt jolts through a mixture of aggression and subterfuge to the balanced eco-system. Colonial over-runs led to further deprivation and debasement. It is also possible that some mismanagement on the part of certain communities and acts of God upset ecological and demographic equilibrium. But the most potent factor seems to have been the expansionist designs and tendencies of the neighbouring communities which might have themselves been in the grip of population pressures and economic stresses. In the Chota Nagpur and Santhal Parganas tract, many small tribes like the Maler and Pahariya were pushed deeper and deeper into the forest, which was very nearly wiped out. Thus, the more numerous and powerful peoples geographically marginalised the smaller tribal communities. Concomitantly, the resources of the latter were annexed to an ever-increasing degree.

Next we may consider a group even in a more pathetic state. Their environment has been stripped mostly by external agencies. It is notable that their poverty and want arise not from isolation, as could be a possible surmise in respect of the two foregoing groups, but mainly on account of the fact that they live within close reach of agricultural villages and bigger centres of population. At one time, they might have occupied themselves in hunting wild life, fishing, gathering honey and collecting minor forest produce. But their natural eco-systems have shrunk, having been acquired for some "development project" or otherwise depleted for extraction of forest, minerals, ores or other resources. Numerically small, non-vocal and undemanding, they have been left to fend for themselves, having been set afloat like flotsam and jetsam. Being hardly educated, possessing few skills and rudimentary technology, robbed of command over their resources, they are poised precariously on the brink of historical disaster. Suspended in a time-space frame, they are condemned to semi-existence. The examples are too numerous to be quoted, but the instance of the Korba is a case in point.

There are groups in some other different categories. The hill Kharia and Gadava of Orissa, the Chenchus of Andhra Pradesh and the Baiga of Madhya Pradesh are examples of shifting cultivators with varying interaction and confrontation with neighbouring population, but not of a magnitude which would throw them overboard. But other shifting cultivating groups like the Birjia of Palamau and Bharia of Patalkot have had to abandon even shifting cultivation more and more to depend on wage-labour and whatever little is available of minor forest produce. The hill Kharia of Purulia district of West Bengal seem to have almost lost control over forest resources, while the Kolga and Kotwalia of Gujarat have taken to bamboo-matting and cane-work as artisans. The Asur of Bihar have turned to iron-smithy also. The state of some solitary groups and segments of some other solitary groups located between the core and neighbouring populations like the Kathodi, Didayi, Raji and Jenu Kuruba is particularly hapless since they have lost their lien on their original natural resources and have not been able to strike a new base in the alien ambience. These socio-cultural islands marooned in surrounding seas of exploitative aggrandisement and population pressures are in the process of losing heart. Invoking the poet, one may have to say that all these communities live between "two worlds, one dead, the other powerless to be born.

At this juncture when distinctions among the different tribal groups here concerned have been made for the purpose of understanding them, three common, perhaps esoteric, features invite attention. First, that almost all these groups identify themselves powerfully with forest "within and with which they live". Their perception of the natural objects around them e.g. forest, trees, hills, rocks, animals differs from ours. These objects are for them "moral agents in their local sense as relatives and kins". Secondly, among them, they share their lives with other human beings as well as their predecessors-in-spirits in time and space. Relations among the dead, living and relatives and kins are important for determining the health and well-being of the members of the community. It may involve conversation with the spirits, which shamans among them hold routinely. Thirdly, among the living a strong communitarian spirit and ethos bind the members of the community.

It will be noticed that in the broad and differing conceptual frame of the various groups described above, I have mostly avoided the use of the term "primitive tribal groups." This pejorative term does violence to sets of people who are evolved with reference to the environment in which they are placed. Till the moments in history when external intrusions shattered the carefully composed man-nature harmony, each facet and dimension of their world blended into the other. For them, divinity was "the ultimate matrix of the world and man's experience in it." But the harsh modern winds will it otherwise. In the first instance, as emphasised repeatedly above, their eco-systems have been under enormous invasive strain. Then their own life-styles have been dealt such body blows as make the prospect of recovery beyond the realm of possibility. In the circumstances, would not the question of restoration of their pristine state be a pure fantasy? Or can at least conservation and consolidation become a possibility? These are poignant questions though one may wish that the small groups, for whom the appellation "primary" seems more apt, could return to that blissful dawn.

For many, one may realise that the ambrosial fragrance of the dawn has been lost for ever, for most of these groups. They have to join the mass who, again, in the words of the Poet

> ".......in the sun's hot eye,
> With heads bent o'er their toil, they languidly
> Their lives to some unmeaning taskwork give."

To reconcile ourselves with reality, it appears that for each group the unique taskwork, it is suited for would have to be diagnosed and devised. In plain words, the first step would be to investigate each group specifically for the gestalt to include engagement with (a) natural environment (b) mode of sociality, a new ethos and (c) their imbibal and practice of the new environmental perception and ideology. It is difficult to imagine that this could be brought about by methods and agencies which have heretofore been assigned to work for and among the officially-labelled 75 primitive tribal groups, as Dr. Mohanty, refers to them in this work. A priori, even the criteria of pre-literacy, pre-agriculture, pre-industry and smallness of numbers would need to be turned over and over again, not only because of their initial inherent inadequacy but even more on account of the fast-moving changes taking place all round. Further the agencies entrusted with the task of the investigation, leading to preparation of holistic profiles and goals desiderata need to be imbued with deep insights, empathy and vision for the future course of action. Having undertaken the task of completion of the profiles and action-oriented project reports, agencies which can be relied upon to implement the programs need to be identified. The horizon for their search should be scanned far and wide, up and down and in all cardinal directions. Constraints such as their being in public or private sector, institutions and individuals, should be broken loose, focusing largely on the capacity to deliver goods.

Lest it be thought that this is a tall order and utopian expectation, it should not be forgotten that even now we have shinning islands in this country sending out beacon-signals of selfless service which ought to be picked up by idealistic and high-minded individuals and institutions, of which there is no dearth. The Ramakrishna Mission, the Bharathiya Adimjathi Sevak Sangh, Dr. Sudharshan's Vivekananda Kendra in Karnataka, to name a few, have been doing splendid substantial unobtrusive work. They crave little publicity. One may have ideological differences with them, but their devotion and dedication leave no room for doubt. One cannot help observing in this context that they offer a refreshing contrast to the bureaucratic machinery, though even among the official organisations it is not rare to come across individual gems who not only merit recognition but should also be held up as role models.

Dr. Mohanty is one of them, committed to the cause of tribal development. In the present work, he demonstrates his dedication to those segments of tribes which need priority delicate and perceptive nursing. By university training an anthropologist, he has decades of service and experience behind him in the Government of Orissa and the Government of India which he attempts to bear on the present work.

Amidst the razzle-dazzle of fast technological transformations and luxurious life-styles emerging more and more in emulation of the West, the impoverished and marginalised have been receding more and more from the view of the public and particularly the ruling political classes, now intensely pre-occupied with themselves. Further, market economy and globalisation may perhaps be good in India's long-term interest, but as of now they are likely to push these sections further back. This has implications for future, which different sections may interpret differently. What we need to remind ourselves in the welter of the present conditions is that it will be a grave error to be oblivious of the vast multitudes in a state of unrest today in our own murky backyards. It does not presage well for the future. Individuals like Dr. Mohanty set the tone of the imperatives of the day.

While reiterating that each action blue-print has to be specific to the milieu and ethos of the particular group, two questions arise. First, how this can be effected and ensured. Luckily, the 73rd and 74th amendments inserted as Article 243 in Part IX of the Constitution and the Provisions of the Panchayats (Extension to the Scheduled Areas) Act 1996 have lately empowered the tribal communities to take charge of their own destinies through the panchayat hierarchical system. Secondly, the direction set for future of scheduled tribes in general and primary and related ST groups in particular, is a matter of huge debate. It appears, however, that, considering everything, they may tend to follow the course of development of the larger neighbouring non-tribal communities. Should this occur to the logical end, a time may come when the distinction between ST and non-ST might disappear except, perhaps, to the extent of physiognomy. Nevertheless, one cannot fail to notice a current of pride in preservation of tribal cultures and individuality. Ethnicity the world over, has been asserting itself during the past two decades. It is not the purpose here to indulge in speculation over which will get the better of the other. But there is no doubt that obliteration of tribal cultures generally and tribal character and values will be a great loss to the humanity. There is a need for positive action in this regard.

January 2002 **Bhupinder Singh**

Preface

Planners and administrators have been aware of the special problems of Scheduled Tribes. Reference to these problems is contained in the plan documents right from the beginning. The attempt has been to fashion policies and programmes in accordance to the Constitutional provisions as well the Panchsheel of tribal development evolved by the first Prime Minister of India, Shri Jawahar Lal Nehru. According to 1991 Census, STs numbered 8.08 per cent of the total population of the country excluding the State of Jammu and Kashmir.

After independence, we set out to building a sovereign, socialist, secular, democratic republic in which all citizens are assured social, economic and political justice. Two important means for shaping such a society were to (a) engage in nation building and (b) bring about socio-economic development of the people.

It is our perception that while we have achieved some degree of success in socio-economic development, particularly, through the planning process, our attention to nation building activities should be given priority. The building bricks of the nation, i.e., the different constituents like religious, linguistic, ethnic communities have not been cemented together adequately into a strong national edifice. There has been copious talk of national integration, there is little to show it on the ground. That perhaps explains why these five decades after Independence have been increasingly marked by internal conflicts and even violence. Social, political, psychological and other steps are necessary to weld the diverse groups in the country into an emotionally cohesive and united polity. In this context, it is well to remember that about one-fourth of the total population of the country comprising scheduled castes and scheduled tribes has been kept at the society's margin. There is need for integrating them into the mainstream of the society as equal and rightful members; failing which, the caste and the ethnic divisions will persist and even deepen. As far as we can see, the injustice done to them during the course of history.... has to be undone and the denial and deprivation has to be replaced by equitous socio-economic order. This calls for protective discrimination as well as affirmative action. Through protective legislation and socio-political activism, they have to be assured equality and dignity. Through socio-economic planned development, their social and economic status has to be raised to a level equivalent to that of others.

It was thoughtful of the Government of India to have constituted several committees to suggest measures for the welfare and development of the Scheduled Castes and Scheduled Tribes being implemented during different Plan periods. To Baba Saheb Dr. B.R. Ambedkar, nothing was dearer than the welfare of the downtrodden. The abolition of the practice of untouchability, "Beggar", special provisions for protection and promotion of the interests of the SCs and STs were incorporated in the Constitution as a conscious decision of the nation to ensure justice to all. All is well-known, Baba Saheb was the chief architect of the Constitution.

Development planning is essentially a mechanism to achieve improvement in the quality of life of the people. Apart from accelerating economic growth, planning aims at distribution of development benefits tending towards creation of an equitous polity. It is axiomatic that economic growth without distributive justice leads to accentuation of social and economic disparities and inequality. It has been observed that scheduled castes and scheduled tribes and similarly placed groups may not be able to meaningfully avail of the benefits of growth process unless the state intervenes to protect and promote their interests. It is in this context that special constitutional provisions for these groups have to be viewed and considered.

The Constitution enshrines a number of important provisions for the safeguard as well as promotion of the interests of scheduled tribes. Broadly speaking, it envisages a tripod schemata comprising (a) policy goals and objectives in the shape of Directive Principles in Article 46, (b) the legislative and physical infrastructure in the

Fifth and Sixth Schedule and (c) financial support in Article 275 for funding schemes of tribal development and welfare. It is clear from Article 46 that stress has been laid on (i) promoting the educational and economic interests of scheduled castes and scheduled tribes and (ii) prevention of their exploitation. Both are important goals, but in the context of the acute exploitation to which they are subject, prevention of exploitation should be given primacy of attention as such measures are like to lead to immediate accrual of benefits to tribal families. Nevertheless, both the measures, anti-exploitative and positive socio-economic development should be treated on complementary basis.

The Fifth Schedule of the Constitution relates to the administration and control of Scheduled Areas of 9 States, while the Sixth Schedule relates to the administration of some tribal areas in the north-east in the States of Assam, Meghalaya, Mizoram and Tripura. The Fifth Schedule particular covers the central Indian tribal tract, but its scope and amplitude are vast. Witness, for instance, the first clause para 5 which confers on the Governor the power to render inapplicable any Act of Parliament or the Legislature of a State or modify a legislative measure. That, this provision has not been brought into use is a different matter; its potential has to be conceded. Apart therefrom the Fifth Schedule contains several measures of importance like promulgation of regulations in regard to the land of scheduled tribes, proper conduct of the business of money-lending, functioning of a Tribal Advisory Councils and so on. It is pertinent to notice that it authorizes the Union to issue directions to a State as to the administration of Scheduled Areas in it, though, to our knowledge, no such directions have been so far issued.

As indicated, the provisions of the Sixth Schedule of the Constitution cover some tribal areas of the north-east. It enables autonomous district councils and regional councils to be constituted in those areas with a fair amount of legislative and executive powers.

If a comparison of the Fifth and Sixth Schedules were to be made, broadly speaking, it could be said that the Fifth Schedule tends to be protective and even paternalistic, while the grain of Sixth Schedule veers towards self management. It is possible to reconcile the apparently antagonistic thrusts of the two Schedules by taking the help of the Fifth Schedule to create and strengthen legislative and administrative infrastructure which is directed more and more towards self-management and self-reliant proclivities of the tribal people. The tribal areas in central India in the States of Madhya Pradesh, Chhatisgarh, Orissa and Jharkhand specifically stand in need of provisions of both the Schedules. We would, therefore, urge that in the Central Indian tribal heartland autonomous district councils should be constituted on the pattern outlined in the Sixth Schedule, while simultaneously receiving the benefits of the Fifth Schedule.

The North Eastern Council, created through an Act of Parliament, has been performing a useful role in regional planning. We feel that an institution of this type is necessary for the central tribal heartland to coordinate and integrate the planning process for STs in several contiguous States.

Taking an overview, it would appear that the Constitution provides an elaborate framework for (a) policy goals and objectives, (b) legislative and physical infrastructure and (c) financial support. It is now felt that the provisions of the Constitution have not been operationalised adequately to the benefit of scheduled tribe people. There is need to work on these provisions more closely and even intensively.

Though number of efforts have been made for over all development of Scheduled Tribes it was visualized that some groups are still in very backward stage. As such 75 groups have been identified as Primitive Tribe Groups which need special attention. In 34 years of my involvement in planned development, it is ascertained that these groups have not reached to the desired level in spite of various efforts are made both by State and Central Government. During the visits to the different remote tribal areas of the country, one will be pleased to see the traditional institutions of these groups but no efforts have been made to preserve these rich cultural heritage. However, efforts are being made for overall development of these primitive tribal groups in the country. My work among the most primitive groups, *viz.*, Chenchus of Andhra Pradesh, Lodhas of West Bengal and Orissa, Totos of West Bengal has given me sufficient insight with regard to their problems both in economic terms and social aspects. My work among the other tribal groups of the country has given me enough scope to compare the social development indicators among the primitive tribal groups and other developed tribal groups in the country.

I am indebted to Dr. Bhupinder Singh, Ex-Special Commissioner, Tribal Development, Government of India, Professor P.K. Bhowmick, Ex-Dean, Department of Anthropology, Calcutta University and Professor A.B. Saran, Former Head of Department of Anthropology, Ranchi University who have given me adequate guidance for this publication. I am thankful to my wife Mrs. Kalpana Mohanty who has given me full cooperation even if I could not attend to my family due to my absence during my long field work. Due to her such cooperation, I am able to complete this work. I record my thanks to Mrs. Bina Suri, Research Officer, Ministry of Tribal Affairs who has helped me in compilation of various data and presentation of issues pertaining to primitive tribal groups in spite of her official and domestic engagement. I am also thankful to Shri Sanjay Kumar Sharma of Ministry of Tribal Affairs who has taken keen interest to type out valuable work in computer for this publication. I record my appreciation to Miss Anuradha Thakur who has given assistence in proof reading.

New Delhi
Date: 26.1.2002

Dr. P.K. Mohanty

One

Introduction

I

Men in all times and climes are to adjust themselves with varied geographical, geo-physical settings and also with other groups of people with whom they come in contact. Some times, these interactions take place with varied degrees of friendliness. At substantial period of time, we find changes, by which we mean 'transformation', i.e., departure from one point of time to another with distinctive changes in the material life as well as in socio-religious institutions. Whenever we consider such a situation, we have to think of these as' acculturation', or 'assimilation' which are nothing but the various aspects of interaction when these groups of people are involved. This is the reality of life and all people of different status are the subject of such situations.

In this connection it can be said that the people or a groups of people of the same stock behave differently due to these backgrounds such as the locale, the socio- economic background and the nature of involvement either to reject or to accept the processes of change in the circumstantial exigencies. In general we may equate the sole life-pattern with a bio-cultural triangle, man being in the centre. The arms of the triangle represent three important aspects of adjustmental situations. The base is the geophysical setting, and the interaction with the same provides their material life, one side represents the man describing social interactions, and other one is the man with the world of supernatural indicating the growth of magic and religions. But, when a man loses his capabilities in a bewildering situation to understand the cause and effect, he depends on supernatural powers of different entities, supposed to reflect in magical performances. Their hard core-religious beliefs and practices develop with all these background; so we have to consider a group of people, their culture and the nature of transformation from a certain point of time. It is generally believe that people at a static rather than a less communicable area are more conservative, as they have to depend on traditional cultural heritage which are nurtured on the decision of the elderly persons of the community. They are encapsulated by intricate webs of rituals and belief patterns prevailing among them. Under such situation, the nature of transformation or the degrees of transformation might be of low rate, whereas the people at more communicable areas or interactional zones have to accommodate quickly as they are subjected to more changes. As result, the transformation process an the result of the interaction will be of a different type in their case.

A careful examination has been made here about the nature of transformation of some groups of people belonging to the three important language groups and inhabiting three different geo-political diversities. These groups of people, as per our present administrative term, are known as a 'tribe' or rather a 'Scheduled Tribe' or a 'Primitive Tribal Group' (PTG), and are entitled to certain constitutional benefits from the administration because our country is a 'welfare state'. Under such circumstances we have to consider the geo-physical background and the population structure of India and also many other attributes of some groups of people, as these are very common and in vogue, while describing or describing or designating them. It may be stated that in the interaction with the geo-physical setting one ethnic groups differs forum another with regard to their intricate traditions which envelope them from their birth. The degrees of interactions will undoubtedly be visible to reflect their life style; and not only the social scientists but, also the administration urgently need to study these things.

II

India has its typical geo-physical setting where we get snowcapped mountains preventing the biting could from the north. This Himalayan tract give rise to many more rivers, streams and rivulets which practically kept the country fertile with a contact supply of fresh water. Ultimately, these flow to the dancing bay-allowing the coastal belt tapering and get fresh deposition of silt keeping the landmass sandy and saline. This condition has the advantage of plenty growth of certain types of trees and plants. Again, we find rocky areas' sometimes rivers criss-crossed the landmass at different places to reflect a new scenario. Then we find rocky mountainous strips in the Deecan trap, and again in the western region we find waves of sand to give the place an ever thirsty desert. Naturally, this geo-physical background reflects all the physical setting of the earth and, as such, it is popularly known as the 'epitome' of the world - a replica of the world in a miniature from. There are dots of island in the south and as well as in the west which constitute the political boundary of our country. Though India has been partitioned on political ground, still we find similarity and dissimilarity and these factors bind the people together to have an Indianess.

These geo-physical settings have a profound impact on its population and on the life-style, house-making, dress and ornaments and also on many of their economic activities. But very recently transport facilities have cut across the isolation and it has developed a new spirit of accommodation in the life-style of the people, even those who live in the sylvan jungles. Naturally, all these have a profound impact on the population structure of the people.

In this connection it can be said that the history of India dates back to the prehistoric times of civilization, for we get the examples of Paleolithic culture signifying the group of people who were food-gatherers and hunters. These old-stone-age industry has many more evidences at different places. We have to believe that these old-stone-age culture has resemblance with that of African stone-age culture, indicating a possible interaction of the people during the bygone ages. Neolithic culture flourished at many places where we can see the beginning of agriculture as the tool types indicate. With all this background we are to believe, that acculturation an accommodation of the prehistoric people was a continuous process which has changed the life-style of the earlier population. These undoubtedly transformed their way of life. .

The Indian society is a caste-ridden society. Population groups are designated as caste, having a high of low status. Typical occupational pattern is attached to a 'specific caste groups'. These are originated long ago and have a colourful mythical background, and people both educated and uneducated had to surrender subconsciously, though now-a-day due to the growth of industry and scientific education these strong caste-based attitudes have begun to erode in some places. Even the so-called tribals or 'Bhumiputras', who are also influenced by the Varna-caste model of,hierarchy and occupation. So, the tribal groups have gradually been acculturated at different contact zones and even the same groups of people behave differently. Industrialisation, communication facilities etc. have made a profound impact. A typical example be given. The Oraons (ST) are basically from the Chotanagpur region. But they in circumstantial exigencies had to migrate from their homeland to other places, such as the Sunderban areas of Bengal for cutting and felling trees to bring forest land under cultivation. Some groups have been brought by the Britishers for indigo plantation and some and some to Himalayan slopes for tea cultivation. Thus, these groups have to adjust themselves with different situations though they belong to the same stock. Naturally, we have to believe that entire population of our country portrays different scenarios, and thus, the population structure is also variable. Table-1 reflects the population structure of our country as per 1991 census even though we do not get the distinctive figures on specific tribal groups here.

TABLE-I
INDIAN POPULATION (1991)

	Total	*Scheduled Castes*	*Scheduled Tribes*
T	846302688	138223277	67758380
R	6286191676	112343797	62751026
U	217611012	25879480	5007354

IV

If we carefully trace the historicity of the concept of tribal we have to go even to legendary times when we find certain groups of people who were different from the others. All these groups were designated by different names like, 'Anarya', 'Kirata', 'Kalla', 'Malla' etc. Later, we get a very clear idea of these groups as they are, as fringe or marginal, or as they live or subsist on a collection of edibles such as roots and tubers, sometimes supplemented by hunting. Their generation might have been depicted by different names or identities and, as such, we get some groups or people as *Adivasis* or early settlers, or autochthons or *Bhumiputra*, i.e., the original settlers of our country. In a way, these groups of people were not disturbed by the administration and another non-tribal groups also had no hostility towards them. As we find many important sacred or holy places of the Hindus are located in deep forests and those deities are considered to be the original deity of those adivasi groups too. Examples can be given from the Lodhas who claim that Lord Jagannath of Puri was the original deity of the Savara group of people. The Lodhas of Orissa or Bengal assert this. Such is the case of the Narasimha, i.e., the lion incarnate is the deity of the Chenchus. This Narasimha had the advantage of marrying Chenchita or Chenchu girl. This deity is installed at the Srisailam temple on the bank of the river Krishna.

In this way, we get a very clear amalgamation of the so-called Hindus and the tribal events in the ancient times. But after many changes in administration we gradually see the so-called tribal communities had to face many averse situations, indicating certain changes in their socioeconomic life and position. The Muslim administration did not disturb the tribals though sporadic examples are available when some Muslims tried to cell horses in the tribal land of Chotanagpur. But the British administration had a very bad impact on the tribal life. They disturbed the tribals in many way and as a result we get a very painful picture of them even from the hands of some who belonged to the British administration. Dr. H. Hutton gave a very lucid description:

"Far from being immediate benefit to the primitive tribes, the establishment of British Rule in India did most of them much more harm than good. It may be said that the early days of British administration did very great detriment to the economic position of tribes through ignorance and neglect of their rights and customs-many changes have been caused incidentally by the penetration of the tribal country, the opening up of communications and protection of forests and the establishment of schools, to say nothing of the openings given in this way to Christian Missions. Many of the results of these changes have case acute discomforts of the tribes" - (Hutton from U.N. Dhebar, page 21: 1961).

We have a series of discomforts like the Santal Rebellions (1855-1857), Sardari agitation (1887), Birsa Movement (1895), Tana Bhagat Movement, etc. indicating the discontent of the groaning tribals against the administration. However, ultimately the British Administration began to follow a 'policy of isolation' which put them in a still more uncomfortable position.

However, after Independence we find drastic changes and thus the so-called tribal people were given special privileges. The Indian Constitution placed the responsibility for the welfare on the popular Governments through the President or the Governors. In this context Article 46 of the Constitution can be quoted:

> The State shall promote with special care the educational and economic interests of the weaker sections of the people, and, in particular, of Scheduled Castes and Scheduled Tribes, an shall protect them from social injustice and all forms of exploitation:.

Naturally, developmental work for the benefit of the weaker section, especially the tribal groups, were assured by the Constitution as it is considered a part of normal routine work of the Government. Again, Article 339 of the Constitution says:

> The President may in anytime and shall at the expiration of ten years from the commencement of the Constitution by order of appoint commission to report etc."

This clearly indicates that the Government is very careful to look after the so-called tribal communities and also suggest remedial measures from time to time which is deemed to be essential in this regard.

V

Though the Constitution initially categorised the weaker section of our total population, those who were practically considered to be lagging behind and were not in a position to complete with their stronger brethren those were nothing but some castes and tribes. But for this purpose a term was used, viz. 'Schedule', just to signify or categorise the group as 'scheduled' to have constitutional benefits. However, the total number of such Scheduled Tribes is 635 (Singh, 1992). Most of them have distinctive lifestyles of their own which are sometimes symbolised through their language and culture. It is often said that some of them have been pushed back to the remotest parts of unhealthy terrain of our country just to enable them to eke out their existence. When these groups of people were faced with an extinction the government under Article 342 of the Constitution, declare that the tribes are entitled to have development benefit, provided they are 'Scheduled'. The President by his special powers specifies some groups as 'Scheduled Tribes', or Tribes or tribal communities or the parts of groups within the tribes of tribal communities, by a public notification.

All these Scheduled Tribal groups are entitled to have many benefits directly from the Government, along with many other opportunities in respect of economic development, educational facilities, improvement of basic requirement in connection with health, communication etc. The tribes are not to be exploited an some of their traditions are to be respected, especially in the areas where the Sixth Schedule is operative. There is a provision for reservation for them, not only in Government service but also in the Legislative Assembly and the Parliament. Many of them live below the poverty line, having no job facilities or any source of income due to lack of proper education and training. It is desired that they should be pulled out of their present situation without any disturbance to their traditional life style or basic philosophy, namely, the one which kept them from unseemly greed from material possessions. It is of course a fact that these groups of people have been cheated outright by many, especially during the British Rule so much so that their discontent had burst out in the form of armed revolt and insurrections as mentioned before. There were various instances revolts from all parts of the country and naturally, the then British Government in power maintained a policy of *laissez faire* about them. However, it has been unmistakably proved that these people live at widely different stages of development; some of them have a specific economy and a primitive technology but very little acquaintance with the wider spectrum of the society in and around them. Generally, many more plans and projects for their welfare and many more programmes for their development were initiated not by the Government but - by some voluntary organisations with a view to ameliorating their condition on the one hand, and to raise their standard of living from poverty to prosperity and from illiteracy to modern scientific education. At the same time, ill-health and malnutrition due to lack of good drinking water and absence of communication facilities causing difficulty of access into the tract where the people live were given special importance while considering the question of their development. It is also thought that through education the people will get white cellar jobs; all these together will hope them shake off their traditional shyness and bring the people to a standard for integration. With all these views, the Government had to sanction money in various plan-periods and thus development was given the utmost importance by all.

VI

In this context, various commissions were set up to assess the actual condition of the people. How far these groups of people have actually benefited or whether these ameliorative measures were at all helpful or not requires a probe. For that purpose, mention may be made of various reports and most of these are available for they are considered to be a part of the development activities. Annual Reports of the commissioner of Scheduled Castes and Scheduled Tribes, Reports of many Study Teams, Report of the Scheduled Areas and Scheduled Tribes (1961) by U.N. Dhebar and some other like Shilu Ao, or Renuka Ray are very noteworthy. After Independence successive Five-Year Plans have been implemented all over the country for the overall betterment of the so-called tribal communities, because ours is a welfare state.

In this connection, it may be mentioned that the first attempt to list 'Primitive Tribes' in the country was made during the Census of 1931. It has being reiterated that these tribal people are in a state of extreme poverty; many of them are exposed to hostile external situations which subjected them to exploitation of a different nature. They are t the lowest level of literacy. Their lands were cultivated and are passed into the hands of aliens. Naturally, the important areas which needed attention were:

(i) education,
(ii) economic uplift.
(iii) health/housing/providing good drinking water, and
(iv) removal of social disabilities etc.

First, a commission was known as the Scheduled Areas and Scheduled Tribes was formed under the Chairmanship of U.N. Dhebar (28th April, 1960). Popularly it is known as Dhebar Commission Report. The Report ultimately found that there were some groups of people who lived in the lowest ladder of development.

Shilu Ao became chairman of another committee (Constituted on 26th October 1966). However, many committees were of the opining that there were some groups of people who all the belonged to the lowest strata and these groups of people are included in it. However, a clarification in this regard was made later (Report of Working Group on Development of Scheduled Tribes during Seventh Five-Year Plan (1985-90) in respect of the Primitive Tribal Groups. As per Dhebar Commission 72 Scheduled Tribe communities have been identified by the Ministry of Home Affairs on the basis of low growth rate criterion mentioned and the following two additional criteria:

(i) Pre-agricultural level of technology,
(ii) extremely low level of literacy.

The ecological conditions practically have a profound impact on the life-style of the people; at the same time, their capabilities to interact with nature through technology can be justified. As a result, we get such groups of people. However, during the Fifth-Five Year Plan period the Ministry of Home Affairs identified 52 tribal communities Primitive Tribal Groups (PTG). During the Sixth-Plan period 20 tribal groups were added and their estimated population was about 14 lakhs. Later, another 2 groups have been added recently. Though as per the circular of the Government the number of such Primitive Tribal Groups is 74, but in reality it will be 60, as some groups of people live in two or more States. Example can be given considering the case of the Birhors. They are designated as Primitive Tribal Group in Bihar, Madhya Pradesh, Orissa and West Bengal. In the same way the Dongria Kondhs live in Andhra Pradesh as well as in Orissa. Hill Kharias live in Bihar, West Bengal and Orissa. The Kathods/Katkarias live in Gujarat, Maharashtra and Andhra Pradesh, the Koragas live in Karnataka and Kerala, the Kurumbas live in Kerala and Tamil Nadu, the Kutia Khonds in Andhra Pradesh and Orissa, the Kuttu Naikans in Kerala and Tamil Nadu, the Lodhas live in Orissa and West Bengal. Any way a Table is given as per the Ministry of Welfare (T.D.).

However, some think that prolonged habitation in remote enclaves in which these groups have been entrenched, has been responsible for their insulation, perhaps breeding in them an indifference towards change an advancement. The apparent shell of apathy has put off many a change agent working among them. Considering all these problems and in order to bring the people to the national standard, the Government of India (Ministry of Welfare, T.D.) has been making available to the State Governments financial assistance on cent percent basis for development of Primitive Tribal Groups since 1975-76. Naturally, it is expected that during these years the condition of the Primitive Tribal Groups will be improved and they will have a legitimate share of the national resources to come on a par with their stronger brethren.

VII

Before selecting three tribal groups, the researcher places his justification for selecting them. In India there are many languages with numerous dialects. Out of these three language groups, i.e. the Tibeto-chinese family, one tribe has been selected. They are the Totos, who live in Sub-Himalayan region of West Bengal. The next group is the Lodha - belonging to the Austric language family. They are found in the lateritic jungle-covered regions of Bengal-Orissa-Bihar. This practically has been selected from the Mayurbhanj district of Orissa. The third one is the Chenchus who speak Dravidian language and live mainly in the forests and plateaux region of Andhra Pradesh on both sides of the river Krishna which is full of forest.

Recent reports on these three tribal groups and a monograph at length are available and as such the researcher, has to depend on the reports for his basic data. Besides, the researcher by way of his profession was in charge of a Research Division (T.D.), Ministry of Welfare. These three tribes belong to primitive tribal groups. The Totos are basically gardeners doing horticultural work as they live in slopes of a hills. In the same way, the Lodhas were earlier treated as a criminal tribal group later denotified (1952), and later on treated as P.T.G. after 1982. They live mainly in jungle-covered rugged terrain having very little idea about agriculture. They prefer to collect edible roots and tubers from the jungle and hunt in the jungle region. To them settled, agriculture is yet to be accepted. The third tribe selected is the Chenchus. They are also food-gathers and hunters. Settled agriculture has to be introduced yet if they are provided justifiable land for plough cultivation.

With this background the researcher has attempted to portray the ethnographic features of the tribes and consider the gradual welfare measures needed for them. He also tries to examine the nature of transformation of these groups from the development point of view It is true that no tribal group can be kept in isolation, but all attempts should be made to bring them nearer to the other counterparts, for it is only by this way that they can share in the nation-building processes, overcoming their tribal coyness and timidity. Following this way they will be gradually associated with the ideas of integration and sharing them with other groups of people.

However, basic ethnographic materials will be discussed in the subsequent chapters in respect of each tribe. We apprehend resistance which might arise from various culture traits creating hindrances. Sometimes they constitute angularities and constraints which create resistances while accepting new welfare programmes. As a result, the researcher, through placing the ethnographic materials, will be able to show the nature of acceptances of these three tribal communities and at the same time to interpret the basic resistance inherent in their cultural life. Thus, through the ethnography of these three primitive tribal groups of different physical, political and linguistic background will we be able show the entire developmental phenomena along with the gradual process of transformation. In this connection we may refer to Lucy Mair (Anthropology of Development, 22: 1984) who described a situation in the contest of development:

> ...And norms and values that may indeed sometimes

engender resistance to beneficial innovations but on the other hand, if they were better understood, might be harnessed to development policies instead of causing disillusion and disappointment. It is of such difference in social structure that a development agent most to be aware.

VIII Research Methodology

The basic assumption of a development strategy is to explore the present situation and plan a programme accordingly. The social sciences provide the methodology of data collection which helps formulating a scheme of development. This is the appropriate step for formulating a plan, specially in case of tribal India. So far as PTGs are concerned, their specific scenario vary most. Hence, each tribal group has to be studied in detail to visualize the need of their life.

Therefore, the first step was taken to collect extensive data from the written records. The three PTGs Toto, Lodhas, Chenchus- have been studied by different social scientists, who provide preliminary glimpses of their life and culture. The Administration, specially the census operations, have recorded ethnographic notes from time to time. Historically speaking, each of the three tribes have their baseline data from variable length of time but it has served our purpose by providing a foot hold for analysing development.

As the second step, one has to look into the history of tribal development in India, right from First Five Year Plan. Therefore, a long discussion on the subject has been taken up next. One will be able to see the change in direction and emphasis with the passage of time and understanding of tribal ethos.

The field area for data collection has been limited keeping in view the location of the tribe as well as development schemes in the region. That is why Totopara (Dt. Darjeeling, Kukai in Midnapur district, and Burlutiguden & Viarabad in Mahboobnagar districts were selected for the studies of the three tribes - Toto, Lodhas and Chenchus respectively.

The hypotheses formed during the preparation of the outline of this research were tested and ideas were later modified. For example, it was presumed that all PTGs can be brought under one process of development, but one observed special schemes and programmes for each of the three tribes. Similarly, it was observed that ecology was playing a very important role in the development process. It was also interesting to note that population concentration viz-a-viz development is more applicable for PTGs. A programme could work well and show some results where the PTG is located in comparatively large number, as compared to the sparsely populated habitat. It was also very interesting to record that the works of the voluntary agencies are virtually absent from PTGs (with exception of one at Bidisha among Lodhas), and it has been left for the government to work among them.

For field work, the most important tool for data collection was schedule, which was used to record data on each scheme. The Govt. personnel, social and political leaders, tribal folks and social scientists were interviewed to know their views on PTG's development. As usual the state of affairs were closely observed (non-participant observation). The selected field area was thoroughly studied, both through recorded data & field analysis. As the main objective of the study was to have an overview of PTG Development through detailed scrutiny of the development programmes among the three tribes, the analysis in the following chapters have been generalized. This has enabled the author to draw conclusion and submit specific recommendations.

IX

The Organisation of chapters have been done with great care. The first four chapters have been tilted as introduction as they enumerate the theme of this dissertation, along with research methodology; followed by introduction of the three PTGs under study - the Totos, the Lodhas and the Chenchus.

The next chapter deals with detailed analysis of tribal development programmes and policies in Historical perspective. Thereafter, the welfare programmes for the three PTGs have been taken up, which forms the basis of analysis & scrutiny of the programmes. These has enabled the author to draw a pinpointed conclusion showing transformations and change in PTGs. Lastly, a few suggestions and recommendations for the benefit of future policy and programmes for PTGs have been proposed.

Two

The Totos

I

The Totos are one of the little known communities living in the Himalayan hill slope in the district of Jalpaiguri, West Bengal. The Madarihat Police Station touches Bhutan where stands a hill popularly known as Tading. The village Totopara is nestled in the hill slope. The height of the hill varies from 750 ft. to 1, 500 ft. above the sea level. The Northern and Western sides of the village are guarded by the hill whereas the eastern side is bathed by a gargling river popularly known as Torsa, whereas the south-western side is curved by a small rivulet known as *Hauri*. The western side of the Hauri, full of thick jungle, is popularly known as *Titi*. This is under the western Duars. The forest belongs to West Bengal. There are many more trees in the jungle and the scenic beauty of this region is very attractive. Very recently a morrum road connects Madarihat to Ballalguri, but from there a man has to walk or travel in a jeep to proceed to Toto para, and this distance is about 51 kms.

As records indicate, this area was under the 'Bhutan territory'. But the British administration, in course of their imperialistic invasion occupied the tract. Ultimately a treaty was signed in 1869 which was known as Bhutan-Duars Act. But the British permanently took possession of it; but in later periods Elurin's suggestion of 'Leave them alone' might have influenced the administrators and so the place was not disturbed by the outsiders except the unlawful Nepalese migrants. The entire area possessed by the Totos might be 3.12 sq. km. and this area has a record of 1, 196, 76 acre of land to be inhabited only by the Totos, but in actual case it is not. Very little is in their possession. It is recorded that one Dhanapati Toto - the Chief of the Totopara had to pay a token of rent of Rs.120.00 for this possession where the Totos stay. However, the village has six hamlets and each of these hamlets have its own name like, Panchayat hamlet, Subba hamlet, Mitrang hamlet, Dhumdri hamlet and Puja hamlet. Besides, there are four villages known as Pukha gaon, Mangar gaon, Poar gaon and $Kabrabati. The village has been gradually penetrated by the scheming Nepalese and they began to settle permanently in all these gaons. Hasimara is the nearest Rly. Station which is about 12 km. from Totopara. The Madarihat Rly. Station or Block office is about 16 km. away.

The earliest history of the Totos is lost in obscurity. Some of the older generations say that the forefather of the Totos had come to this area probably seven or eight generations ago. Possibly the ancestors of the Totos used to collect medicinal plants and herbs as well as skeletons of the dead wild animals which might be of use for overcoming the spirits and ghosts, considered to be prevalent in the living memory of the rural people. Besides, they used to collect available Copper or gold ores from the river side. Regarding the name "Toto" there are certain speculations. Somebody reported that Totos used carry the bullets of the soldiers during wars. This bullet is locally known *Tota*; hence, they are called *Toto*. Others are of a different opinion. According to them, these people used to roam about without any aim; hence they are known as Toto. Whatever may be the reality, they are known as Toto and they themselves have accepted it'.

II

The physical features of the Toto are yellowish skin, short but well-built body, hair almost straight; very few persons have facial hair. Women are flat-chested but apparently are very unclean. Their language is Tibeto-Burmese. Professor S.K. Chatterjee asserts this; but when they speak with others they use a kind of broken Bengali and Hindi. But in actual sense they belong to the Mongoloid strain. Some think that the Toto dialect has many more mingled words. Some of them are well versed in Nepali. As it is a small group their total number is given in Table-2:1.

TABLE 2.1
POPULATION

Year	*Source*	*Households*	*Population*
1901	Census operation	35	171
1911	Census operation	60	255
1921	Census operation	80	271
1931	Census operation	-	321
1941	Census operation	-	321
1951	Census operation	68	395
1961	Census operation	109	616
1962	I.S.I.	88	650
1971	Census operation	95	675
1979	C.R.I.	123	-
1981	Census operation	137	761
1989	Bhowmick	163	852

TABLE 2.2
FAMILY SIZE

No. of individuals	*Family*
1	4 -
2-3	29 (24.37)
4-5	37 (31.09)
6-7	23 (19.33)
8-10	23 (19.33)
11-13	7 (5.88)
Total	123: 100

Source: D.N. Dhali (1987)
Toto - Cultural Research Institute, Calcutta.

III

The Totos have a very neat clan organization. All the Totos have been affiliated with particular types of clan. They are given in table 2:3. The males are recognised with a particular type of clan. After marriage, the woman has to be affiliated with the clan of her husband's family. Marriage never takes place in the same clan.

TABLE 2.3
DISTRIBUTION OF CLAN

Sl. No.		*Family*
1	Danko-Be	26
2	Dandra-Be	25
3	Bouder-Be	17
4	Bongyo-Be	10
5	Nubi-Be	9
6	Nuringchako-Be	8
7	Bader-Be	7
8	Mangko-Be	7
9	Longkaji-Be	5
10	Mandro-Be	4
11	Diring Chako-Be	2
12	Mangching-Be	2
13	Pisuchangko-Be	1

Source: Dhali (1987) Toto Cultural Research Institute, Calcutta.

IV

Regarding the house-type and settlement pattern of the people it can be said that the Totos have to construct their huts in the slope of the hills. As a result, houses are built on bamboo platforms with walls of split bamboos. There may be uncovered bamboo platforms attached to the huts which is known as *dui*. Both wooden and bamboo poles are used to make the house strong.

In general the hut possesses one room and this is generally divided into three portions for specific purposes. These are:

(i) a sleeping space, popularly known as Siri;
(ii) a sleeping space of the guests, popularly known as Daichiko-Siri; and
(iii) a place of the household deities known as *Jiri*.

Besides these there is a separate sleeping place locally known as *Merring*. It is generally located at Siri. Outsiders are strictly prohibited from entering into or touch the merring at Siri. Sometimes small rectangular windows are found conveniently in some houses. Below the platform of the house, domesticated pigs, goats, fowls and other livestocks are kept. With these arrangements they have no provision for latrine; the floor of one side of the sleeping room is used as a latrine and the fallen excreta on the ground is consumed by the pigs and swines. In many house-complexes there is 'tungsa', *i.e.*, an 'auxiliary' hut which is used for guests or some persons of the family. This structure is generally in an area located in the cultivable plot. A few families maintain kitchen gardens.

They do not have sufficient bedding. A canvass is stretched on the dried grass just to give it a little softness which severe as a bedding.

They have a few household implements - like baskets, and small traps for keeping some earthen pots for storing water as well as rice beer or other types of drink. During winter they collect some local variety of blankets. In respect of dress and ornament, a very small sized piece of cloth is used by the males which is tied in front and allowed to hang up to the knee. Sometimes a separate piece of cloth is used to make a pocket where betel nut, lime etc. were kept for occasional use. The females use four pieces of cloth; one is worn in waist, one is used to cover breast and back, while another is tied in the waist tightly. Married women use another piece on the head like a turban. Now-a-days, many girls and women use blouses like the Nepalese women. The Males began to use pants and shirts in imitation of the local Nepalese. It has been already mentioned that they remain very unclean. Rarely do they take bath. Nothing is used on their hair - no oil or any other thing. One interesting fact is that both males and females consume plenty of tobacco, and they chew betel nuts. They never wash the teeth; as a result, their teeth appear dark. Even they have no idea of washing after evacuation. Simply dry leaves or pieces of stones are used to clear the rectum. Because of this unclean habit, they suffer from various skin diseases and a very bad smell often comes out of their body. Almost all the persons suffer from skin diseases.

V

Their educational advancement has been due to the involvement of a voluntary organisation viz. the Lutheran World Service which started a primary school. The Bharat Mahajati Mandali also did some welfare work among the Totos. But recently the Tribal Welfare Department has built residential hostel for Toto students. The school has been elevated up to Class VII standard. There are teacher's quarters also.

VI

In respect of the details of the economic activities of the Totos it can be said that most of them were involved in orange trade. Orange is abundant in Totopara as well as the adjoining areas of Bhutan. But suddenly the orange trade began to die out and it is surprising that there is not a single orange tree in the village now. But the Totos engage themselves as portars for carrying orange from the gardens of Bhutan wherefrom these are marketed to the various places of West Bengal by the traders. Some suggest that the land has been cleared for other agricultural purposes. Due to this type of deforestation some changes took place in ecology and environment. Naturally their maladjustment began as a consequence of this changing situation.

TABLE 2.4
AGRICULTURAL ACTIVITIES

	Types of crop	*Starting month of cultivation*	*Harvesting*
1.	Maize	Ashard (June-July)	Bhadra (August-September)
2.	Marua	Sravan (July-August)	Kartik (October-November)
3.	Gundi	Sravan (July-August)	Kartik (October-November)
4.	Kaoni	Fulgun (February-March)	Sravan (July-August)
5.	Paddy	Sravan (July-August)	Kartik-Maisore (October-November)
6.	Kalai (Pulses)	Bhadra (August-September)	Kartik (October-November)

It is to be understood that the Toto families possess little land for domestic purposes or for cultivation. The largest size of land possessed by two persons viz. Dipa Toto and Dinesh Toto is 17.48 acres and about 16 acres respectively. Others have very small fragments of land. It is seen that 34 families have no land at all. This indicates that they are facing considerable difficulties to maintain themselves. This is considered to be the most vital problem of the people. This factor is pushing them to many other areas and activities just to maintain their livelihood.

These landless people do not prefer to go outside to maintain their livelihood. This is due to their psycho-emotional factor which interlaced them to the economy and environment. Only a few are found to work as labourer during the orange collection season. This psycho-emotional attachment of the people is so strong that they can not go out of their narrow geographical boundaries and, as such, poverty reigns supreme among these, hapless people struggling to keep their body and soul together.

In this context it can be said that the market economy has been introduced among them, but they are quite ignorant of the complicated market economy. Naturally, their daily problems slowly multiplied and the people could hardly adjust themselves with the changing situation.

As a result, we find examples of indebtedness which gradually penetrated into the life of the Totos. In their circumstantial exigencies they have take loans for consumption purposes and also for socio-religious purposes which are a must with the tribals. The money-lenders come from different places during the weekly market day and tactfully enter into various terms and conditions with the Totos. An example is given just to explain the situation.

> 'One of such common terms is known as *thika system* in which when Toto takes loan in advance from a Mahajan to meet his daily necessities, and in exchange he repays the loan with qua (areca nut), bamboo, maize, millet etc. which they grow on their land and invariably the prices of the commodities are fixed at a very lower rate. This is a kind of sever non-monetised exploitation through a kind of burter transaction (Sarkar: 1993:15)'.

VII

In respect of social organisation the Totos are split into several groups and all those groups have their own clan/totem organisation. Besides, the Totos of the six hamlets are also territorially divided into two groups knows as:

(i) Waiying ting bei and

(ii) Wareng bei.

These two divisions have hamlets of their own. For example, the waiying ting bei has three hamlets viz. Puja gaon, Dhumschri gaon and Mitrang gaon. All these are under the former territorial division while the remaining three gaons are with the next territorial division viz. Wareng bei. These territorial divisions practically have some duties and obligations in times of ceremony or festival.

VIII

These groups of people like any other simple folk have their duties and obligations in respect of life-cycle rituals, and these are a must with them.

The Totos generally do not consult a physician at the time of pregnancy or delivery; rather they accustomed to consult a pan - who is medicine man. In times of complication during a pregnancy they perform magical rites to drive away the evil spirits supposed to cause harm. As per suggestion a pig or a fowl is sacrificed to appease the spirits as well as to have his blessing. The umbilical cord is cut with the strip of a bamboo piece. There is also the name-giving ceremony. There are many more other rituals which are associated with birth and caring of the babies. Children are generally named after their grand parents. Mahakal is all the time worshipped. This might have been due to their constant involvement with Nepalese.

Marriage takes place when the girl attains puberty. There is no bride-price or dowry. But it is important to note that during childhood days the betrothal ceremony takes place. But when the girl attains puberty then she is allowed to go to her husband's place and a ceremony takes place. If the community festival had not taken place during marriage then it is a must when the wife is pregnant and carrying 5, 7 or 9 months. As per the customary rule all the invitees come to attend the ceremony with a bowl to consume rice beer as well as to take beef. The sacrifice of an ox or a cow is essential and the blood is taken by the priest known as Kaji and he sprinkles the blood on the forehead of the bride with the spell to seek blessing from Mahakal. It is to be understood that there is no taboo for mixing between the sexes. Marital relation with the mother's sister's daughter is however avoid.

Death is attributed to the malevolent spirit entering into the body. Evil spirits are required to be propitiated by the village magicians. It becomes such that an individual has to pay high price for the same. Dead bodies are generally buried in their respective clan ossuary which is near the Torsa. The dead body is buried and there are certain formalities. It is placed keeping its head towards the north. Some offerings are made when used utensils are kept near the burial. They take bath after the burial. The funeral party is provided with rice beer. Again on the 5th day after the death all those persons are served with rice beer. On the 5th or 6th day after burial the senior members of the deceased family offer prayer by lighting incense. Through this the house is purified. Thus, the life-cycle rituals are over.

All these clearly indicates that these rituals and social systems are so inextricably mixed with this group of people that they have formed angularities and bendings either to receive or to reject any new plan for development. Naturally, the ethnography must be known to the planner and this is social anatomy which is meant for any sort of changes.

It has been mentioned that to bring any change for the betterment of a tribe the planner must go through the details of their customs, that is to say, he must be well-versed in their social anatomy for making a full analysis of the cultural background to find out the various forces operating in them.

However, some welfare activities for the betterment of the Totos were started sometime in 1951 when a centre of welfare by the Bharat Mahajati Mandali was set up with the financial assistance from those who were in charge of development. The work was initiated by Sarkar who began to stay at the Totopara and in course of time he was successfully in overcoming the people's suspicion. The following lines of activities were started by hum:

(i) Imparting primary education among the Totos and the Nepalese.

(ii) Persuading the Totos to practice cleanliness.

(iii) Protection of land against encroachment.
(iv) Introduction of improved agricultural practices in co-operation with officers of the Agriculture Department.
(v) Persuading the Totos to take vaccination and inocultations against preventive diseases.
(vi) Protection against exploitations through bamboo rade.
(vii) Encouragement to wearing clean clothes.

—*(Das: 1969:115)*

But Sarkar's stay for about 2 yrs. at Totopara brought remarkable changes among the Totos. It is estimated that due to interaction with him the Totos gradually began to shake off many of their beliefs and prejudices. In this way, they began to accept the changes. Important changes of the life pattern of the Totos are those related to their material life; they began to take bath, if needed, once in a week. The use of soap also become common. He requested the government to provide the Totos soap free of charge from the Government or Welfare Organisation. Children began to consume milk which was never seen before. Some of them also began to use mustard oil for cooking.

In 1955, the Tribal Development Centre at Totopara was taken over from the Bharat Mahajati Mandali and was placed under the direct control of the Government. Sometime in 1955, D. S. Rana was employed as Social Worker on behalf of the Government Department. His work was mainly :

(i) To hold regular class with the Toto and Nepali children.
(ii) Enquiring about various socio-economic problems.
(iii) He has to work just a liaison officer to contact the Totos and the outsiders.

Gradually the Lutheran World Service came into the picture and they began to construct school buildings, health centres. The Tribal Welfare Department of the Government of West Bengal also came forward and through their activities began to bring about changes; teacher's quarters etc. were constructed and roads became accessible by car or jeep. The recent development work in respect of the Totos will be discussed later on when they are treated as member of the P.T.G.

Three

The Lodhas

I

The Lodhas, a gathering and hunting tribe, originally lived in the jungle-covered rugged terrain of Orissa, West Bengal and Bihar. Due to marathan axing by many other land-grabbing people they had to migrate in search Bengal where other groups of people are basically settled agriculturists. Naturally, they are exposed to a new environment with new environment with new socio-cultural forces. Regions of West Bengal especially the southern bank of the river Subarnarekha cannot be distinguished from the Mayurbhanj region of Orissa, for no clear geophysical boundary can be established. However, the political boundary is quite appreciable and all these are subject to different political administrations and managements. The total number of Lodhas in Mayurbhanj does not exceed 4,000 souls, and they are concentrated in some villages where they live along with other groups of people. Sometimes isolated, the Lodhas are described by different scholars by different names. Sometimes they are considered as Savara. Rishy (1891) considered them as a caste. However, it is clear that they are reluctant to work for agriculture. Due to their clinging to the forest habitat they adjusted themselves to the forest economy, and as such they do not like to take part in any sort of agricultural activities. In the 1991 Census the Lodhas numbered about 8,000 only in West Bengal as a caste. But they were categorised as a criminal tribe, not even Scheduled, to enjoy facilities from the Government, because they were not included as weaker section. Their criminal activities created problems to the administration and ultimately they were declared as Criminal Tribe sometime in 1876.

In this context it is said that:

"The Criminal Tribes Act was passed by the British

Government of India as early as 1871 and applied against some of the aboriginal tribes of certain special communities of British India. The Law empowered the local governments to define any community or tribe or any part of tribe, gang or class indulging in systematic commission of non-bailable offences as a criminal tribe. Various amendments were made in this Act in course of time. In 1876, the application was extended to lower Bengal. An amendment was made in 1897 in which enhanced penalties for repetition of offences and breaches of laws were provided for in 1911. Further amendments were made which provided for maintenance of a Register of Persons considered criminals for detailed information of their whereabout. Registered members of their communities who came under this Act were compelled to give finger-prints and to report changes of their residence to the Police even it is was just for one night. Members of such tribes had to suffer punishments for alleged crimes even on suspicion. By a further amendment it was applied to the whole of British India in 1924. An individual of any community who was considered to be a habitual criminal or who committed systematic crimes came under the purview of criminal tribes act for constant surveillance. Eventually in 192 this law was repealed".

It is true that a gathering-hunting tribe lacking any kind of agricultural skill may have a tendency to commit crime. When the Lodhas were gradually pushed back to the forest they have no other alternative but to commit any sort of crime for their existence. In this context Bhowmick says: "However, the basic causes of crime of the Lodhas still persist. The economically displaced Lodhas could not adapt themselves to the changing situation which further drove them towards a precarious existence and growing needs of an expanding family clamped in a small territory could not be met with a lower income. Enduring frustration and lack of self-reliance brought in its train a perpetual stagnation in their collective life and subsequently turned them into a inveterate criminals with every work of waves of changing circumstances". With this background we have to consider the Lodhas and their life-styles especially of those living in the jungle environs of Mayurbhanj in Orissa. But in West Bengal these groups of people were treated as a Scheduled Tribe sometime in 1952. Earlier, in 1951 there were only 7 Scheduled Tribes, later the number was increased to 28 due to changing circumstances. Such was the case at Orissa. They became Scheduled after 1961 in Orissa.

The Lodha after the repeal of the criminal tribe act in 1952 were treated as a denotified tribe and later as a Scheduled Tribe, and again as a Primitive Tribal Group (PTG) sometime in 1981.

The term 'Lodha' might have originated from the word Lubdhaka - i.e., 'trapper' or 'fowler'. It is true, this gathering-hunting people depended on the beauty of forests. Collection of edioble roots and tubers, small games etc. was their main occupation, but after the enactment of the "Permanent Settlement Act" (1793) by the then British Administration, the entire region of the forests was given to the landlords and in this way their right over the forest was given to the landlord. Ultimately, they became paupers from the level of poverty. Helpless as they are, they were flooded with all sorts of criminal activities. True or imaginary, being goaded by the pangs of hunger and the tryranny of the rich receivers belonging to varied political parties practically they have no other alternative than to fall back on various crimes for a living. Territorial and economic displacements made them real pagans. The housetype and settlement pattern of the Lodhas bear the works of poverty. Houses are clustered near the fringe of the jungle or other habitat. Other groups of people do not like these people. As a result this created some sort of isolation which is conceivable if anybody happened to visit their settlements. Cottages with single rooms and walls rarely mud-build, rather split bamboos or branches of the trees plastered with mud constitute their hut. In one corner of the hut there is a heart and an elevated rectangular mud alter which is considered to be the seat of the departed persons. In emergency or on last day of the year Chaitra (March-April) some offerings are made to the dead spirits who are supposed to work after the family. There is no clear-cut rule for the entrance of the huts. In a particular place all huts are handled together. However, the household utensils are kept there and persons sleep there at night when they use only palm leaf mats. Now-a-days, they also use blankets of local variety during winter. A Lodha man or woman can be recognised simply by seeing their dress. Very old persons use a piece of cloth which passes through the thighs. Halfshirts are even worn by them, women in earlier times used only a piece of cloth. Now-a-days due to the impact of other groups of people they use female garments in bodered cloth, petticoat etc. It is true that their dresses are extremely dirty and a bad smell comes from their body.

II

Regarding household implements they have the axe, spade some cutting implements and various baskets. Traditionally, they use earthen pots and pitchers, but now-a-days aluminium utensils are found in their huts. Male persons go to collect roots and trees and the females sometimes accompany them to collect fuels which are made into bundles and sold in the market or to other caste-Hindi villages. By selling these they usually get, little cash money and these are immediately used for purchasing their daily requirements. These are up to the capacity of the earnings of the people. Bhowmick (1954:51) described that they grapple with their abject poverty year in and year out in two stages (a) a period of feast and (b) period of fast.

During the rainy season, they get a little employment in the houses of the neighbouring communities as agricultural labourers and also collect various fishes, molusca, but when these are exhausted they face a semi-famine condition. Their societies are grouped into several classes.

TABLE 3.1
CLASS-TOTEMS

	Class	*Totem*
1.	Mallik	Salfish (oplicaphabus marulices)
2.	Kotal	Moon
3.	Layek/Laik/Nayek	Makar or salfish
4.	Digar	Porpoise
5.	Paramanik	A type of bid known as Manik
6.	Dandapath or Bag	Tiger
7.	Ari or Ahari	Chanda fish

They do not marry in the same class. But the class Bhugta or Bhakta has been grouped into two Bara Bhakta or Chota Bhakta i.e., inferior Bhakta. Their marriage takes place even in the same class. The masses of the Bara (superior) Bhakta can take lives from the Chota, i.e., junior Bhakta, not vice versa. This sort of rigidity is being decreased now-a-days. Some of the caste group of people also have Lodha woman as concubines and this is accepted by the neighbouring communities. But class and totem male among the Lodha is very strong. Family is the basic unit of their society. In very rare cases joint family is seen. Even the sons after their marriage abandon their family of origin and keep away from their old and infirm parents. After marriage, the couple lives for a short time and then they start their own small family. Sometimes they live in the parents village and construct a small hut in the village of the wife's father. However, the size of the family can be grouped into three categories.

1. Small-size family (1-3 members),
2. Medium-size family (3-7),
3. Large-size family (more than 7 members).

But this type of family is very rare among the Lodhas. This is due to their economic condition. As this group of people is basically non-agricultural, so involvement of other members in all matters especially during the agricultural activities is rare. In this way, whole relationship becomes less strong and we ascribe this as brittle due to lack of involvement of the people in day-to-day life. Still family exercises some formalities: division of labour in the economic sphere and participation in other social activities, both in social are religious levels. In these cases, identity of the family is maintained. The family has to function many more activities in day-to-day life. In all ceremonial activities, political issues especially those dealing with the cases of disputes and the quarrels, the heads of the family have a distinctive role. Even religious activities or functions head of the family must participate and come to a decision for smooth running of the society.

It has been mentioned that some classes have a special duty in respect of socio-religions activities. In the same way, some families, especially those holding important positions in outer spheres of social life and have to take the advantage of special prestige when the total villagers are considered. Thus in the patriarchate societies it happens that heads of the families exercise very important roles for the smooth running of the society and have external contacts when it faces some problems. Thus, the Lodha family has to follow a typical patriarchate family with a male domination. Marriage as defined as a relation of one or more men with one or more women, sanctioned by the society customs or laws and involves certain duties and obligations in the case of the parties entering into the union. Thus Lodhas, as the case study shows, has almost all these functions to perform. Leaving the life cycle activities, the marriage in the Lodha society has a definite role to play. Practically not a single case has been found where the Lodha remains unmarried or maintains celibacy. However, the marriage forms in the Lodha society are: monogamy as well as polygamy. But it is very peculiar that two married wives never stay together. There might be formal divorce but these formalities do not conform any ceremonies as we find it in many other tribal societies. There is no formal divorce. Simple the wife refuses to stay with the husband. Earlier, there was infant marriage, i.e., when the bride did not attain maturity. But now-a-days, this form of infant marriage is not in vogue. It is to be noted that all the persons, males and females, have to work together; even the children have to take part in many of the day-to-day affairs. Sometimes they are to keep the younger children when both parents are away in economic activities.

The life cycle rituals of the Lodhas are colourful. Birth, pregnancy and death rituals have very significant roles to play. After birth, the placenta after birth are buried in the corner of the house. This is done to avert the evil powers. It is believed that if it is exposed to a particular magician or a man of evil potentialities, this may cause harm to the newly-born baby. Thus, this type of preventive measures are taken. The young babies have to depend on breast milk. Care is taken by which no one can do harm to the lactating mother. There is ceremonial rice-eating ceremony for the babies. On this occasion a Bhog or Khir is prepared with milk, coarse sugar, sun-dried rice, a piece of ginger and all these are cooked in the form of gruel. The village priest prepares this in the compounds of the Sitala shrine. This is a ceremonial offered to the baby. In most of the cases the hair of the baby is removed and then a ceremonial bath is given to him. In this way, the ceremony is over. Then slowly the girls attain puberty, and some rituals are associated with it after the first menstruation. Marriage takes place sometime when the girls attain puberty. There are elaborate wedding ceremonies. Formal vigil or seeing the bride or the groom is necessary. Then a go-between, locally called Sambar, is fixed up who negotiates and after that the marriage takes place. Marriage is linked with a chain of rituals. There are five more phase in such a ceremony. After negotiation and during marriage there are the preliminaries of selection of bride, fixation of bride price and its mode of payment, fixation of the date of marriage, i.e., logan and its formal intimation and, finally the reception or welcoming of Lagan articles as well confirmation of the date of marriage; and then the marriage is solemnized.

The chain of rituals associated with wedding preparations include 'Gae-halud', i.e. anointment of turmeric paste accompanied by worship and ceremonial bath, erection of 'Chhamra' or wedding booth, construction of an earthen platform or alter, dressing of the bridegroom and Sambar who is the chief conductor of the marriage ceremony and reception which is known as 'Luli mather'.

The marriage ceremony proper is performed by tying of her or wedding knot followed by the ceremonial farewell of the couple and their feeding.

On the next morning the send-off of the bride is performed. The newly-married couple along with the bridegroom's party start for the bridegroom's village and they are cordially received there. However, before the entrance to the house several persons including the bridegroom's sister stand at the door and want some payment before they allow the married pair the entry into the house. As soon as the payment is made the way is opened. The ceremony is known as 'Batghera' or blocking the road. The bride and the bridegroom are then taken to the family alter. According to the direction of the 'Sambar' to the forehead and hair-parting of the bride. The iron bangle is then handed over to the bride. The later also touches the bareface of the bridegroom with the vermilion on her bangles. This is repeated three times and at last the bridegroom slips the iron bangle on to the left wrist of the bride. The ceremony is known as 'Kharu paramo' or wearing the bangles. The other rites proceeding the same are undoing the wedding-knot and the sacred thread on the wrist of the groom, throwing away the basket and ceremonial bethey, presentation of the couple or 'Bandhapan' and auspicious eighth day return of the bride.

'Punarbibaha' is arranged when marriage takes place at the tender age of the bride. It is also seen that often prior to the marriage ceremony proper the bride formerly marries a 'Mohua' tree, while the bridegroom marries a mango tree.

Remarriage or 'Sanga' is the second marriage of a widow or a divorcee wife. The marriage ceremony costs less than the usual one. There is no fixed date or ritual for the same. The bridegroom simply pays a visit to bride's residence, hands over the royalty in cash to the village headman and takes the bride.

There are two traditional ways of disposing of the dead body. One is cremation and other is burial. The method of disposal is determined according to the nature of death. If the death is caused by snake bite, attack by wild animals, drowning, epidemic diseases or if death occurs during pregnancy or delivery and during childhood then the dead bodies are buried. Corpses of natural death are cremated. After burning or cremation work, all the persons assisting in the burial/cremation work assemble near a waterbody and take there bath and shout thrice 'Haribal, haribol, Haribol' and the handle used in the burial or cremation work is thrown into the water. The mourners before entering the village of the deceased person embrace a 'peepal tree' when they come back, and then a fire is lighted in front of the entrance. The party sits around the fire and they place their palms on it to warm themselves up. The person whose turn comes last throws the bid away. The womenfolk of the family inspite of their non-participation in the funeral procession, take their bath after the arrival of the party which participated in the funeral, procession. Afterwards, all the persons who join at the funeral rite take some puffed rice. The hearth is not lighted on that day for cooking from the next day to the ninth day; daily offering of food to the dead is made. This is arranged by means of 'Telpanja' which is a sort of a-oil divination. Death also creates uncleanliness for a period of ten days when certain restrictions are imposed in the matter of food and activities. On the tenth day the 'Sradh' ceremony is performed early in the morning of that day. Class members, villagers and persons taking part in funeral rites in some way or other including taking part in the funeral procession assemble near the bank of the stream or river. The barber shaves them all latter on a fish is kept in a leaf cup and the rice is kept in an earthen pot. Then the nails of the female kins of the deceased and a few locks of hair are collected by the barber and put inside the cooking pot. Then heaped-up dried leaf cups are used to boil rice, fish, hair and nails together. The ritual is called shurhanri or Ghat. Two rice balls are prepared out of the boiled rice, fish, hair and nail. A smell quantity of mud is also mixed with the ball. Then a ceremonial immersion of the rice balls in the name of the departed soul of the deceased marks the end of the death pollution. The used clothes of the mourners are then taken away by the washerman for washing. Later on the 'Kand Katua' or 'Gurupule' that is the 'Men who helped in the burial or cremation services are entertained with a feast. In the next morning all the used pots and leaves are thrown into the jungle; on that day a Vaisnava is burnt dried mango twigs with clarified better on the spot where the person had breathed his last. This is called the 'Sraddha' ceremony. On that day foods are cooked in new earthen pots and a feast is given to the villagers and relatives as well. On the next day, the food offered to the spirit of the dead is thrown into the stream or river. It terminates funeral rites.

III

The administration of justice, settlement of disputes amongst individuals families and sometimes even villages, maintenance of peace and promotion of social welfare are some of the functions of the tribal council of the Lodhas, popularly known as 'Panchayat'. There are three important office-bearers of the Lodha caste panchanga. They are: Mukhia - the headman of the village, Dakua or Atgharia the village messenger or bailiff, and Paramanik - the village cook for the ceremonies. All the adult male members of the Lodha village constitute the village panchayat. It sits when an aggrieved person lodges a complaint or when some break the customary rules. When a complaint is lodged with the Mukhia, he consults some of the important members of the council and asks the Dakua to convene a meeting at the village shrine of the goddess sitals or at his own residence, if that might seem convenient. The persons involved in the case are summoned and the trial is held by the panchang. The Mukhia holds the highest post and is unquestionably obeyed by others. But if he himself commits on offence he may be dismissed by the panchaga. However, the panchayat after trial can impose a cash fine or physical punishment or social boycott if the person is found to be guilty. Often compensation is given to the aggrieved party from the fine collected from the person declared as guilty by the panchayat. However, with the introduction of statutory panchayat system the secular power of the traditional Lodha panchayat has been curtailed to a considerable extent.

The religious and ceremonial officials among the Lodhas are (i) Dehari or village priest, (ii) Talia or Charidar, i.e., assistant to the village priest, (iii) Hantaker or official sacrifices, (iv) Gunni or the medicememan, (v) Byakra or Shaman or the spirit possessed man who is supposed to be able to forecast future events. The Gunni and Byakra generally solve supernatural problems requiring supernatural blessing through direct communication, while Deheri, Talia or Chharidari and Hantakar deal with religious problems requiring supernatural sanction.

According to the beliefs prevalent among the Lodhas, supernatural spirits are generally invisible though they might become visible when they wish. Spirits may be classified according to their attributes. Some of these are of benevolent nature such as Basumati (Mother Earth), Dharam Devata (God of righteousness) etc., while others are malevolent. The Goddesses Sitala and Chandi are held in apprehension; but they can be beneficient when appealed to with proper prayers, offerings and sacrifices to Baram or Garam, the tutetary deity of the village. The malevolent deities are Yugini and Bhuts like Chirguni, Pretsin etc. Bhagawan is the supreme being. He created the universe and all things which live in the earth. He never demands any sacrifice or worship. According to a few Lodhas, Ramachandra of the Ramayan and Srikrishna of the Mahabharata were incarnations of Bhagawan in different ages. Basumati or Mother Earth is considered to be a very important deity, though she has no recognised anthropomorphic form. She is propitiated with simple prayers at the time of a marriage ceremony.

Some of the Lodhas identify her with the earth and propitiate her with offerings, prayers and flowers as a mark of gratitude. Dharam Devata or God of righteousness is worshipped and involved in all the ceremonial occasions by the Lodhas. He lives in heaven and observes all the deeds of man and animals. He rules over the destinity of the world. He is thus invoked during the marriage ceremony or before the worship of any particular deity or spirit. He is also invoked before a ceremonial dance. There is no temple or sacred place for the Dharam Devata. No animal sacrifice or food offerings are made to him. During ceremonial bath of marriage, sand or mud is piled near the water. One betel leaf is placed near the sand grains and a betel nut is placed on it. This represents Dharam Devata.

Sitala is the chief deity of the Lodhas. She is worshipped with awe and fear since she is the controlling deity of the epidemic diseases such as Cholera, small-pox and the like. Even the prayers, offerings and sacrifices make her pleased and she proves to be benevolent. The deity resides in the shrine. Sitala has go six sisters, named after six epidemic diseases, viz. Koda Basanti, a type of small pox; Lodha Goria, a kind of betal small pox which makes the body black; Bainch, chicken pox; chalta phulie, a type of betal pox with oedema; Milmila, measles, olaytha or asiatic typical cholera. During the invocation of the goddess Sitala all her sisters are invoked and prayers are offered to them. Baram or Garam is the tutelary deity of the Lodhas. IT is thought to be a powerful deity of the weeds.

Chandi is also considered as a mighty deity of the Lodhas. Eymologically, 'Chandi' means the terrible one. In Chandi Mangal Kabya, she has been referred to as the Goddess worshipped by the Vyadha chieftain named Kalketu. A myth depicts that Kalkety was the ancestor of the Sevaras (Lodha). In certain places of Mayurbhanj they are known as Baram Chandi.

Yugini, one of the kinds of the Goddess Sitala, is considered to be a dreoded spirit. Yugini retains the souls of those who die during an epidemic. She is ever changing in shape. Elaborate worship with sacrifices is required to pacify her anger. Each Sitala worship is followed by the worship of Yugini.

Kundras Chirguni, Pretsini, Kelpurus, Baghoa, Gomua etc.

are some of the vicious spirits. They are the souls of those died in accidents or unnatural causes like, suicides, snake-bites, attacks of wild animals'etc. The souls of women who died during pregnancy or in cause of child-birth or those who are killed by evil spirits also enter their number. These spirits do not have any special shape and reside in unclean places like cremation grounds or places for disposal of carcasses or burial grounds etc. They also reside in large ancient trees or desolate haunts.

Four kinds of Kundras, viz. Kalipat Kundra, Desi Chandi Kundras, Dhana Kundra and Sonamukhi Kundra are the mischievous ghosts or spirits. The Lodhas are animists and believe that death is caused when should leaves the body for good. The Lodhas take the help of the sorcerer who is the spirit-doctor or spirit-binder and is known as 'Gunin' or 'Ojha'. Daen is the witch who indulges in anti-social activities. The 'Byakra' is their shaman and practise divination, while snake charming is done by the Savaras or a section of the Lodhas. During the month of Vaishak (mid April-mid May) the Lodhas worship Sitals, Yugini, baram, Chandi and Manasa on Communal or individual bases with goat and fowl sacrifice. Deheri assisted by other religious officials conduct this festival. It has already been stated that Sitala and Yugini are worshipped to escape from the scourage of epidemics while Baram and Chandi are worshipped for welfare of the village and protection of the village from depredation of wild games. Manasa is worshipped in the month of Jaistha (mid May-mid June) by the medicineman only to appease the deity of snakes and to make snakes lose their poison. The medicine man along with his disciples worship manasa with goat or pigeon sacrifice.

Ashari is observed in the month of Ashar (mid June - mid July) on communal bases for good harvest and general welfare of the community. Deheri performs Shari rarely W.H. big sacrifice. The Lodhas organise Jalhel in the month of Sraban (mid July - mid August) as communal festival before the transplantation and first collection of tussen cocoons from the forest. Asthami and Manasa are worshipped in the month of Asvin (mid September - mid October) on communal or individual basis. Asthami, i.e. eighth day of the worship of Durga is celebrated with worship of Sitals for the general welfare. Jathel and Bandana is observed during

Kartick (mid October - mid November). Head of the family assisted by elderly female members perform Bandana for the welfare of the cattle. During Bandana cattle are bathed and garlanded. In Agrayan (mid November - mid December) Bari and Lekshni are worshipped on family basis. Bani and Sar are worshipped during the first last reaping of grains; Lakshmi, the goddess of wealth, is worshipped by the female members of the family. In Paush (mid December - mid January) Muchri, an agricultural worship and worship of Baram, is done. Muchri is connected with agricultural operations. Head of the family propitiated it with a few sacrifices. The festival observed during Chaitra (mid March - mid April) includes offerings of Natun Hanri to the Manas and worship of Baram, Sitala and Yugini. During Sraddh 'Natun Hanri' is offered to the Manasa for the welfare of the family. Sometimes the first fruits are offered, and occasionally fowls are sacrificed.

Sports and games are conspicuously few in the Lodha society. Ha-do-do, Telkati Ekir-Mikir, Ubur-Dubur, Dudh de Gur de, Kanamachi, Dera Dang or Tipcat etc. are their traditional sports and games. Besides this, they also play cards, football, cricket etc.

Dancing and music form an important aspect of the recreation of the Lodhas. These are generally monopolised by men and are performed on festive occasions. They use musical instruments like Changal or Kundali, Madal etc. The communal song, of the Lodhas are composed in corrupt Bangali; some Oriya words can also be recognised. The songs may be classified into four categories as follows:

(a) Prayers or songs of Invocation- These songs are generally sung before the commencement of any dancing of musical performance.

(b) Baramasi songs or songs of Twelve-month cycle- Bengal shows a varied picture of natural scenery during the twelve months of a Bengali year. It was a custom with the ancient Bengali poets to point out changes in the feelings of nature during these months. The heroes and heroines were generally personages from the Purana and epics like Ramchandra, Sita, Radha, Fullara and so on. Baromasi songs usually begin with a narration of the miserable lot of the hero or heroine and end with a hope of better times.

(c) Jhumur songs are generally sung in honour of Srikrishna while he was engaged in pasturing his herd to cattle. Jhumur songs are generally sung during Kathi nach, i.e., stick dance.

(d) The Lodhas also sing miscellaneous songs, *viz.* songs sung during Bandana festival, songs about Shyama (a deity like the Goddess Kali) songs and so on.

The Lodhas also dance 'Katchi Nach', i.e., stick dance and 'Pita nach', i.e., leaf dance.

Four

The Chenchus

I

The Chenchus are one of the most backward tribes in Andhra pradesh and its population figures as per 1981 Census is 28,297, out of which Adivi Chenchus account for 23,277. The Chenchus though inhabit in almost all districts of Andhra pradesh, their main concentration is in Nallamalai is hills and Amrabad plateau. The Nallamalais are the parts of the Eastern Ghat Hills which have been penetrated by some rivers like the Godavari, the Krishna and some of their tributaries. The hill terrain have an elevation varying from 2000 to 4000 feet above the main sea level. These consist of very old rocks, popularly known as Khondabites (gneisses and schists), whereas the northern portion of the Nallamalai is constituted by Archean gneisses. The northern side of the river Krishna has a steady height varying from 1600 to 2500 ft. and the entire area is known as Amrabad plateau. It lies in the present-day Mahbubnagar district of the Telengana region which is the main adoble of the Chenchus.

Both sides of river Krishna are full of forest. Forests on both sides of the river are of deciduous type, the important trees being Pachari (Dalbargia paneiculata), Chirumanu (Anegeissus latisolia), Chikerni (Albizzie amara) etc. There are other types of vegetation growth comprising a good number of different varieties of timber reed and innumerable types of grass which cover the region so widely that the Nallamalai, i.e. black forest, seems to be a fitting appellation. These forests are infested with wild animals of which most important are the bear, tiger, samber, spotted dear, four-horned antelope, wild pigs, peacocks, wild fowls, snakes, lizards, scorpions etc. Mosquitoes carrying malarial protozoa are plentiful in the forest. They have often caused epidemics of malaria. Climate vagaries like storm, heavy rainfall affect the life of the forest. Dry summer lasts from the middle of February to the end of May, and a stormy monsoon follows with occasional cyclone accompanied with fitful rains having an average annual precipitation of 53.50 cm. Rain and storms carrying dry leaves of the trees for along time have changed the soil type and caused thick layers which are characterised as 'Black cotton' and red and brown sandy layer. The chief crops grown in the Chenchu habitat are castor, groundnut, jowar, bazra, tobacco, ckellies, horse-gram, green-gram, black-gram, rice miger, mango and citrus.

The Chenchus live in a small settlement, locally called Guden or Parts Previously they used to roam in the forest and return to familiar to place in the evening. It was observed in the Census of India 1961 (Monograph on Byrlutigudem in village survey Monograph No. 33 of Census of India 1961 p.6) that their habitation, fixed at one place bearing a proper name of the place, must have been a later development. Now-a-days, every Chenchu-gudem consist of several clusters of colonial huts dispersed hither and thither in a large area. Some of the settlement have a mixed population in which other caste and community people also live with the Chenchus, while the other are entirely inhabited by the Chenchus.

The Chenchu families have been classified according to their size.

TABLE 4.1
FAMILY SIZE

District	*No. of villages*	*Small (1-3)*	*Medium (4-6)*	*Large (7-9)*	*Very large (10 or more)*	*Total*
Mahbubnagar	6	42	47	12	1	102
Kurnool	5	88	70	18	1	177
Prakasam	4	43	63	21	6	133
Total	15	173	180	51	8	412

Source: Bhowmick, P.K., 1992, The Chenchus of the Forest and Plateau, Calcutta, ISRAA, p. 48.

Above Table thus shows that most of the Chenchu families are either small or medium. Bhowmick (1992) also shows that the incidence of divorce without remarriage is practically unknown in the Chenchu society. He has also shown that about 39.2% male and 25.7% female Chenchus are literates in his survey of population. The percentage of literacy is high in the villages where the Ashram Schools are located. After the establishment of Ashram schools in the villages the number of literate persons has increased. However, the 1981 census shows that percent Chenchus literates. A permanent gudém or village of Chenchus appears to be a cluster of colonial or oblong type of huts located at a distance of 50 to 100 yards from one another woven with bamboo splints to form a wattle wall. Its floor is made out of beaten earth slightly elevated from the ground. There is a central pole from which slanting bamboo poles, i.e. rafters are projected towards the pole placed in a circle. The height of these side poles varies from 4 to 5 ft. The diameter of the huts vary from 8 to 15 ft. These poles are tightly tied. The rafters are almost uneven having branches to sustain grassthatching. A communicating door is provided. The door is generally 3 ft. wide, rarely having wooden frame. The entire structure is such that everything can be packed in it and shifted to any convenient place.

The material equipment of the Chenchus are very simple. They include cooking and eating vessels, agricultural implements, hunting accessories like bow and arrow, bamboo mats, bamboo cots etc.

In the Kurnool District Manual (1886) the dress of the Chenchus has been described as follows.

> "The men are nearly in a state of nudity having only a piece of cloth around their loin. The woman dresses herself more decently that man"

Thurston wrote on the dress of the Chenchus as under:

> "Some Chenchus bear on the head a cap of max-cloth, deer or hare ear of bushy tail-and of the large Indian sorrel is attached by way of ornament to the string with which the hair of the head is tied into a bunch behind"

Now-a-days, a male dress consists simply of a strip of cloth called 'gachi' which is passed between the legs to cover the nudity and the end of the cloth are secured by passing them over a most thread. But many have learnt to wear a shirt along with the loincloth; several men have however been putting on an upper-cloth during the cold season. It is also used for covering themselves at night in the absence of drepati (thick body cover). The younger generations are now using shirts and pants may unmarried and married women wear sarees and bodices. The school going children are provided with a set of school dress, viz. snickers and shirts for boys and parikini and jacket for girls. Some Chenchu boys wear collared banians, while married women wear sarees or parinis (a short of skirt). The Chenchus do not care much about keeping their hair clean and combed. The types of wooden combs, locally known as durrena and eorpene, are used for combing the hair.

Men do not wear any ornaments except small rings made of brass, white metal or silver which are worn in the helix and lobes of the ears. Some men wear spirit rings round the fingers which are supposed to act as telisman to prevent swelling from bee-stingings, which they often have while gathering honey-combs. They also wear a waist-string which will protect them from spirits and evil effects of black-magic. The women invariably have a few chains of colour-beads hanging round their neck. The women, who can afford, have started to wear Konkipulla made of silver in the helix of the ear. A silver chain golusu is also tied to correct the ear ring to the rear-knot of hair. Wearing of cheap type of ear-rings made of brass and studded with white stones called mukkari on the lower part of the ear is generally seen among the Chenchu women. The neck-ornaments consist of only a chain of beads. They also use tawdry necklaces of cheap composite metals. Most married women have glass bangles around their wrist. Aluminium wristbands called Kadiyalu are worn mainly by old women. Married women wear toe-rings (mattlely) of aluminium on the second toe of each boot. 'Tail' i.e. marriage locket and a string of black beads are the symbols of married status of the women. Some Chenchu women bear tatoo-mark.

II

The Chenchus were traditionally dependent upon forests for timber and non-timber forest products. Now-a-days with the expansion of the forest department activities their food gathering economy is being supplemented with wage-earning as forest labour. The forest provides them food for about six months in a year through hunting, fishing, collection of major forest products and the like. For the remaining six months in a calendar year they are required to be engaged in other activities as forest labour and some agriculture if available. Minor forest products are collected both for their own consumption and also marketing purposes. Sale of minor forest products provide nearly half of the income of a Chenchu family. They collect Mohua (Basic latfolia) for their own consumption as food and alcoholic beverages. Tamarind is collected for household consumption and or marketing. They also collect a good number of edible rocks, tubers, leaves, fruits, etc., mainly for their individual consumption. Non-edible forest products collected by the Chenchus include soap-nuts, cashew-nuts, gall-nuts, beedi leaves, bicus leaves etc. Gum and honey collection as well as bamboo cultivation are their important forest-based vocations.

Fishing is one of the season's food-gathering activities which help them augment their family income. They collect fish by poisoning water, using fishing basket locally called Kodruma, bow and arrow, line and rod (galem) etc.

Agriculture is also an important vocation of the Chenchus living by the side of the plains people. Family based land holding pattern is given in table 4.2.

TABLE 4.2
FAMILY WISE LAND HOLDINGS

Land holding in acre	*No. of families*	*Percentage*
Landless	38	29. 95
Below 3 acres	9	6.39
3 to 6 acres	75	53.19
7 to 10 acres	15	10.64
11 to 14 acres	4	2.82
15 and above acres	-	-
Total	141	100.00

Source: Bhowmick, P.K. 1992. The Chenchus.

According to table 4.2 about 73 per cent of the total banches own land, the majority being within 3 to 6 acres (53.19 per cent).

The important crops raised are only dry crops namely black millet (arika), Italin millet (Korra), horse gram (Ulava) redgram (Kandi), Castor (amudam), fowar (fonna) etc.

The Chenchus rear animals like goat, sheep, cow, bullock, etc. They are also experts in weaving bamboo mts, wattle baskets etc. Some Chenchus are also employed in Government services on a salary basis. There is evidence about their employment as watchman, attendants in school, cooks in hostels, ayahs in medical centres, headmen in villages etc., but their number can be counted on finger.

Kurnool Manual (1886) records their food habits as follows:

> "They eat Cholan, Ragi and Millet which they get sometimes by stealing the ryot's crops, sometimes by bartering the jungle produce and sometimes by purchasing the grains with money obtained from the sale of forest produce. They also eat a species of wild tuber called Chenchugoddi and the flesh of all animals killed in chase, except tiger, cheetah and wolf. They do not boil the meat but heat it over time and eat".

They cereal-based food habits induced by the hostels attached to the schools in Chenchu-inhabited areas, regular flow of liquid money income through wage earnings, payment of part of the wages in grains and the availability of grain at a reasonable price in cooperative stores might have generally changed their diet to rice-based one. However, rice-eating by the Chenchus is still given less importance than other grain, like millet, jowar and maize. The however continue to be gatherers of jungle tubers, roots, leaves and fruits to supplement their food. Vegetables like tomatoes, angle grams, brinjles, gourds, beans, chillies etc. are grammer the backyard and consumed after cooking. In addition to it, they also consume wild vegetables like drumsticks, wild beams, ustakayahu modapikkalu etc. as are available in the forest. During lean months they subsist on Mohua flowers which are preserved in big pots. They eat the flesh of wild animals and birds like rabbits peacocks, jungle fowls, doves, jungle-sheep, parrots, patridges, squirrel, wild beer, langoor etc. Beef-eating is tabbo with the Chenchus. They catch a variety of fishes for their household consumption. Chintamudda prepared from the dressed tamarind mixed with tamarind ashes is their favourite item of food. They are vary fond of drinking and smoking Mohua spirit and a kind of alcoholic drinks made from jaggery and bark of acacid tree are their favourite drinks. Habit of smoking is also quite common both among men and women. They smoke bidis and cigars made from country tobacco purchased at the local cooperative stores chewing of arece nuts, betel leaves and tobacco are also quite common among the Chenchus.

III

The Chenchus are an endogamous group with exogenous Kulan as well as gotra, i.e. clan. The names of the clans are Marrepalle, Mandla, Eravala, Nimmala, Chicurea, etc. In this regard it has been stated that the census of India, 1961 (1966:8) depicts about 26 clans among the Chenchus while Haimendarf (1943:89) tried to show clans affiliations with particular tracts of land of Nallamalae. On the other hand certain branches in the bygone days seemed to have been associated with particular activities or incidents or objects and a related clan-name was attached to the families of the descendants of those original families. In the following are listed the names of some of the clans and their totems.

On the basis of marriage alliance a class can be divided into the following categories. (i) some classes are brothers class which are believed to be related to one another; consequently, marriage should not take place between these classes. Each class has its brother class. (ii) Some classes are eligible for marriage alliances, if they are in the classificatory kinship relation like mother's brother's children, father's sister's children or sister's daughter. (iii) Some classes are considered neutral persons of these classes can choose their partners from any other classes.

During marriage the class members exhibit more cooperation in making it a success. Great economic cooperation is expected between the members of the same class.

Family is the basic social unit among the Chenchus. Most common type of families prevalent among the Chenchus include parents and unmarried children only. But it is followed by another kind of simple family where old and widowed parent or father-in-law or mother-in-law may stay with; a married son or daughter with or without their children. Joint or extended family which encompasses both vertically extended family in which married sons or daughters live with their parents and horizontally extended family in which married brothers, old parents and unmarried brothers or sisters live together co-jointly are next in frequently of occurrence. Polygynous family where more than one wives live together with their respective children, as well as a kind of simple family where a divorced women or a widow is married to a widower or bachelor with the dependent children of the previous union are not altogether unknown in the chenchus society.

TABLE 4.3
CLAN AND ASSOCIATED TOTEMS

Sl. No.	*Class*	*Associated totemic objects*
1.	Arthi	Banana
2.	Nimmala	Lemon tree
3.	Kudumula	Round or oval-shaped rice bowls preparation cooked on steam
4.	Uttaluri	Squirrel
5.	Tokala	Tail
6.	Nallapotula	Black he-goat
7.	Bojja	Stomach
8.	Gazzala	Jingling bells
9.	Dasari	A kind of forest tree
10.	Pullicherla	Tiger
11.	Bhumani/Bhoomani	Forest pumpkin
12.	Indla	House
13.	Garaboina	Gara tree (A kind of forest tree)
14.	Jalli	Jallalu, a kind of fish
15.	Avula	Cow
16.	katraju	A person
17.	Chigurlla	Tender leaves
18.	Gulla	Body foils
19.	Mandla	Leaves of a kind of forest tree

Source: Bhowmick, P.K. 1992, The Chenchus.

The Chenchu society is both patriarchal and patrilined. Generally they prefer marriage within the village. In these cases, a wife need not go to another village as the husband's residence is in the same village. However, they generally establish a separate family after marriage or sometimes after having a child. Poverty, acute space problem in the midst of their subsistence in single room hut and easy availability of raw materials in construction of huts are some of the causes for the establishment of separate huts just after marriage or after having a child.

In Chenchu family the authority of the father is supreme. He manages the family affairs. An affectionate bond exists between the husband and the wife. The wife participates in the economic activities of her family. She helps her husband in hunting and collection of minor forest resources. But she never collects honey herself. A strong affectionate bond exists between brothers and sisters. Grand-father, grand-mother and other elderly persons in the family are shown due respect by the younger generations. Grand-parents and grand-children relationship between them. The grown-up girls have not restriction in their movement. They are expected to acquire proficiency in the domestic affairs. They are also engaged in cattle or goat-rearing. Many boys and girls have premarital sex experience. Brothers never believe each other. The old and infirm parents usually live with on of their sons, or married daughters in the absence of sons.

Monogomy is the most prevalent form of marriage among them. Polygamy is also practised in rare occasions. Marriage by negotiation is locally known as 'Kudurchu Kinna Pelli (arranged marriage) when a boy attains the marriageable age. The boy's parents search for a suitable bride for him. After spotting a girl the boy's parents approach the girl's parents. Ragu (king), Pradhani (Minister), Kolagadu (Measurer) play an important role in the betrothal ceremony. After a weeks time the bride's parents go to the groom's house and fix up the date for marriage. Marriage must be performed within the stipulated period agreed upon at the time of the betrothal ceremony.

Cross-cousin marriage among the Chenchu is the most preferred alliance. Generally maternal cross-cousin (mother's brother's son) or paternal cross-cousin (father's brother's son) or maternal uncle (mother's brother) is given first preference in the matter of selection of the bridegroom.

Marriage by elopement in socially accepted among the Chenchus. This is reported to either by young Chenchus to circumvent opposition of their parents of to elope with an already married woman or man. However, payment of compensation in lieu of bride price to the father of the eloped girl by the men who enticed her is an a priori correlation for affording social recognition to the wedlock of her own choice.

Love marriage or marriage by mutual consent is distinguished from marriage by elopement by the absence of elopement by the lovers because it does not violate the existing marriage rule. Further, both of them announce their intention to marry and seek the permission of their respective parents, besides requesting them to perform their marriage as per custom. Generally, in such cases class exogamy is usually elders condone the parties by levying a little fine in cash which is used for purchasing liquor. Leviratc marriage or marrying one's own elder brother's widow seems to have been practised until very recently. But now-a-days it is on the wane because of the influence of the neighbouring people who equate their elder brother's wife with their mother.

Divorce means the cancellation of marriage contract. Divorce is initiated either by the husband or by the wife. No particular ceremony is associated with it. When a wife wants to be separated from her husband she goes to her paternal house or elopes with a man of her choice and never comes back to her husband's house. The aggrieved husband reports the matter to elders. When an women descrits her husband and stays with her parents, the elders assemble at the house of the woman's parents, along with the deserted husband. They collect the opinions of both the wife and the husband. Village elders are served liquor by the deserted husband. Parents are asked to repay the marriage expenses and bride price to their deserted son-in-law. After payment of these expenses by the woman's parents, the marriage is deemed to have been dissolved. There are several reasons such as sexual incompetency, drunkenness, ill-treatment, illegal sexual intimacy, barrenness, mutual distrust due to marital infidelity and so on for seeking divorce.

The Chenchu kinship terminology is mainly of a classificatory type. They also use two denotative terms like magadu or permity and pendlamu or bharya which are used to denote husband and wife respectively. Their kinship organisation fit into the Dakota type of kinship organisation of Murdock. This shows that their social system fundament changes from the past owing to the weakness of bilateral kindhip system and emergence of patridineal organisation.

IV

Stoppage of mensuration is taken as the first sign of pregnancy. Two or three months after the stoppage of mensuration the Chenchu women report it to an elderly female member of the family. Generally no special ceremonies are performed before the child birth. However, in some cases Nelluposukunnadi (one who has taken bath i.e. conceived) is observed before child birth. An auspicious day is fixed by the village headman. The pregnant woman stands in front of some one who applies turmeric paste on her forehead and pours water on her head. Sweets are then presented to her and she puts on a new saree after bath. The Chenchus have a strong belief that pregnancy lasts for nine months in case of a male child and ten months in the case of a female child. During pregnancy, the woman are neither allowed to go the burial ground nor to see or touch a corpse. Moreover, she should not attend on a girl in poverty. Even she does not take food from the house of the dead. Her husband during this period is not allowed to perform burial services of any kind and refrain themselves from putting vernulion mark on her forehead. Violation of a taboo is believed to cause suffering and injury to the foetus and might result in abortion. Delivery takes place wither in the pregnant women's mother's hut or in her husband's hut. At the time of delivery, a mid-wife from the Chenchu community, locally called Mantrasani, is asked to attend on the pregnant woman as mid-wife. In case of a difficult delivery they seek the help of an medicine men who also belongs to the Chenchu community. There is a belief among the Chenchus that difficult delivery is caused by the wrath of some angry deity. After his arrival the medicineman catches hold of her hands and makes a sort of performance to ascertain whether the woman is possessed by an evil spirit or not, and finally identifies the name of the deity responsible for the difficult labour. After identifying the deity, her husband is asked to perform worship of that deity for affording easy delivery to his wife. The husband also takes a vow to perform worship of that deity if his wife delivers the child without difficulty. The husband fulfils the vow after the delivery of the child. There is also another practice for affording easy delivery. All the men, women and children stand in front of the expectant mother's house near to the well. The person who stands nearest to the well collects some water in (Chembu, a small water vessel) from the well and the Chembu containing water is passed from one to another in the line. Finally, the person who stands near the woman in labour hands over the vessel to her. The water becomes sacred by the touch of some sacred people who stand in the line. Drinking of this sacred water by the woman in labour may ensure easy delivery. Delivery, i.e. theerdhamaduta literally incoming taking the ball, is performed by the mid-wife or an elderly woman who cuts the umbilical chord by an edged arrow or sickle (Kodevali) or knife. After birth the waste matter, i.e. parupu is put with some ashes in a pot and the husband with the help of the mid-wife or an elderly relatives buries the same by the side of the hut. The pollution period continues for 5 to 10 days. During this period the mother is not allowed to move about in the place or touch anything or anybody excepting her assistant and the new-born baby. Food is served to her in a leaf or separate plate. Food taboo of the lactating mother includes chicken, gourd, egg, meat of rabbit etc. After the stoppage of blood, the mother takes a purificatory bath. She is applied with turmeric on that day. Not much importance is given to naming a child. The child may be named at any time after the ceremonial bath or purification. A child is even give a name 2 to 3 years after his/her birth.

Tonsure or hair-cutting ceremony is an important ritual. An auspicious day is fixed according to the convenience of the parents. The ceremony may sometimes take place near the shrine of the deity. Vow is taken previously to offer hair of the child to the deity. The maternal uncle first cuts the three tufts of hair and the remaining part is cut by the barber. For the service rendered, the maternal uncle often demand some presentation from the child's father.

The first rice-eating ceremony is generally observed when a child begins to sit up i.e., when he becomes 8 months old. The child is given boiled rice and gravy. The child's mother washes rice and cooks. Sometimes milk and sugar are added to prepare it in the form of porridge. The father gives the first morsel of this food in case of a male child and the mother does so in case of female child. This practice is known as Annam Pettua of giving food.

The first menstruation commences between the age of 12-15 years. The local term for attaining puberty is Samarthadindi or Rajaswarlu or Peddamanishi Ayyindi. On attaining puberty girls tell about this to their mothers. Her parents take her immediately to her house and send a word to blood-relatives only. The girl is then smeared with turmeric paste on her face, legs, and hands. Her hair is loosened by the mother and parents bread necklaces. Vermillion mark is applied on the forehead. Then she sits on a mat before any rite is performed. Blood relatives and women belonging to the same class are invited to attend puberty rites. Pregnant women are however not allowed to attend the ceremony. One corner of the house is cleaned and smeared with cowdung paste. The girl is directed to sit on a mat which is spread on this place. Invited persons carry some gift articles like turmeric powder, vermillion, coconut, jaggery, edible articles etc. while attending the ceremony. All the hands for receiving gifts, and other items are given to her mother. The girl eats coconut, jaggery etc. when she feels hungry during the pollution period. Some of the blood-relations present new cloths too. Some of the blood- relations present new cloths too. Sometimes a plate containing betel leaves, vermillion and turmeric powder is kept by the side of the girl and then all the invited women go to her, take betek leaves and smear themselves with turmeric powder and vermillion mark on their foreheads. All the invitees return to their respective houses after being served with some liquor. The pollution period during first menstruation is strictly observed and it varies from 5 to 10 days. During the pollution period the girl is not allowed to cook or to touch any household articles and she sits on the mat only. The girl is always assisted by her mother or another elderly woman during this period. She is never left alone. The girl takes food and water separately in a separate plate and Chembu (small water vessel). Broomstick, knife, sickle, iron rod etc. are kept near the girl in puberty to protect her from influence. They also put some mark with piece of coal on the left leg of the girl. During the pollution period children and men are not allowed to go near the girl. A ceremonial full bath early in the morning brings the pollution period to a close. On that day, the girl goes to the nearby well or hill stream, accompanied by her mother or some other elderly women and takes a head bath. In some cases they take bath near the house. After taking the ceremonial bath, the girl wears a new cloth or a washed fresh cloth. Her hair is neatly combed by her mother. If they are economically well-off, they invite women folks of the village and entertain them in a feast. The mat used by the girl during the pollution period is thrown away. The mat used by the girl during the pollution period is thrown away. The earthen vessels used by her are broken at a place at bit away from her residence. The aluminium vessels are heated and are kept aside and are used for a similar ritual in future.

There are two main ways of getting mates amongst the Chenchus. One is Palli, i.e., marriage by negotiation and other by mutual consent or love, locally known as Magi. Class exogamy is strictly observed and crets cousin marriage is preferred in both the ways of acquiring mates. It has already mates. It has already been stated that marriage negotiation, betrothal and marriage preparation takes place before the marriage ceremony.

On the marriage day the groom's party starts for the bride's house sometimes accompanied by musicians, local band party or orchestra party. The party is generally received by the parents of the bride at the outskirts of the village. Just after arrival at the bride's house, the bride price is paid in cash as settled earlier. Newly-purchased clothes, ornaments etc. are ceremonially presented to the bride. After the presentation ceremony is over, an entertainment with vegetarian meal is served to the party. Next, a ceremonial bath is arranged in which both the bride and the groom are to take the bath. They then take the new clothes and prepared themselves for the actual ceremony. The bridegroom wears a new cloth skirt and a gochi, a headgear and a shoulder-wear. Then they are allowed to sit beneath the pandal. Dasari or

Ullaluri or Madle class acts as priest to solemnize the marriage ceremony. Betel leaves and betel nuts are placed on the ground in the name of some ancestral spirits imploring their blessings during marriage. Then the priest places the hand of the bride on the hand of her maternal uncle who ultimately places it on the hand of the bridegroom. Then the ceremonial tying of the corner of the saree with the shoulder-wear of the groom is performed. This is called a bridal knot. Next talibottu (marriage locket) is tied by the maternal uncle around the neck of the bride. Sometimes this ceremony is performed by Kolagadu (the gotra elder), who gives a set of neatly-folded betel leaves and nuts to the hands of the bride to keep it in her mouth. Then the bridegroom is asked to bits off the protruded and the folded betel leaf held in the mouth of the bride. As habites, the whole assembly claps innovation and approval. The bride and bridegroom are directed to pour talambradu (rice mixed with turmeric) on each other's head. The elders attending the ceremony sprinkle a kshintalu on the newly married couple. Then everybody including the bride and the bridegroom prays to God for a happy and prosperous union. Then a traditional dance is performed in accompaniment with the beating of drums (tappeta) throughout the night. Another ceremony takes place when the groom's sister ceremonially blockades the door and demands a little presentation from her elder brother. When some presentation in cash given to her, she allows them to enter into the house. The couple stays in the bride's place for three days. On the third day, they start along with the respective parents for the groom's house. After marriage the bride and the bridegroom are left to themselves. During this time some presents either in cash or kind, are given to the couple. Then a ceremonial feast is extended to the guests and kinsmen present.

Death is considered to be natural after old age and the Chenchus think Swami, i.e., Ged. Disposal of the deadbody is associated with performance of elaborate rituals. Cremation and burial are two methods of disposing of the deadbody. The custom of burning the deadbody seems to be a recent introduction borrowed from the neighbouring Telegu peasantry. Now-a-days, comparatively wealthy persons practice cremation. Just after the death, the news of the same is conveyed to the class-members in the village and to the blood relations. Then a funeral party assembled at the house of the deceased. They bring the deadbody outside. It is washed by the members of the deadbody's class since others are forbidden to touch the deadbody. After death, the deadbody is decorated with the symbols of a vaishnavite bearing three vertical marks (naman) with lime-powder and vermillion on its chest, forehead, middle of the legs and hands, besides his palms. Coconut oil is applied to his head and the hair is neatly combed. They put some incense (Sambrani) on the deadbody. In the meantime a bier is made with a long bamboo pieces having horizontal poles lined to it with strings to which the deadbody is tied by means of a cloth which is supplied by its parental uncle. Class members carry the bier on the shoulders. Any class members of the dead irrespective of age and sex excepting widow of the deceased and pregnant woman accompany the deadbody. The funeral party follows the corpse by sprinkling some flowers, betel leaves and blackgram on the deadbody which is kept on the ground at a place called dimpudu kallam or resting place. All of them remove the piece of cloth covering the face of the deadbody and look into its face for a couple of minutes. The deadbody is once again tied to the pole and carried to the burial ground. Along with the deadbody articles like jaggery, flower and bingalgrm are carried to the funeral ground. After reaching the burial ground, the deadbody is kept on the ground. The class members start digging a pit suitable to the size of the deadbody. Sandalwood leaves are then spread out at the bottom. Then the red thread and gochi (loin cloth) are removed from the deadbody. The red thread is then tied to the nearby tree. The corpse is then laid in a pit, facing upward and the head directing the north. The deadbody is buried naked; after buring the deadbody the class members covered the pit with earth. The surface of the grave then levelled neatly. All the ken are served with liquor and the members of the funeral party go to the well located in the village without looking back and wash their face, hands and legs. Vermillion marks are also applied on their foreheads. The articles which are carried along with the team to the funeral ground are distributed to the participants. All of them then wash their hands and legs with water on a spot where the deadbody was bathed last. Then an earthen lamp is lighted on a spot where the person died. All the participants one by one go to the spot and fold their hands before the lamps and go to their respective houses. In the evening the funeral party again assembles in front of the house of the deceased. A fowl is sacrificed at the spot where the person died and rice and fowl curry is cooked. The cooked food is offered to the soul of the deceased person in front of the earthen lamp kept at a spot where the person had breathed his last. All the persons assembled them bow their heads in reverence with folded hands, after which the offering is distributed to them. All of them then are served with liquor. The earthen lamp is then removed from that place and some ash is kept in a circular form of Achembu (a small water vessel) of water on the ash and three balls of rice by its side. Nobody remains in the hut for that night. It is believed that the deceased person comes during the night in the form of a child or some animals to eat the offering and drink water and hence footprints of child or animal are found on the ash. Next morning the remaining water and offered foods are thrown away. During noon a special priest, locally known as Sathandu or Samulu or Ayyagaru, comes for performing rituals on the third day after the death of a person. The priest carries three figures of the deity of Perumelle Swami with him. He enters the hut and draws three concentric circles at the spot where the person died, one with rice flour (inner circle) one with turmeric powder (middle circle) and third with vermillion (outer circle). He also keeps sun-dried rice on the circles and betel leaves around the counter circle. He paces the three figures of Perumalle Swami in standing position on the centre of the rice. He keeps some jaggery in dried coconut piece and asks a relative of the deceased to keep some dakshina (gift in cash) on it. A goat is sacrificed on that spot in the name of god. Then the priest along with some close kins and clan members of the deceased go to the burial ground and keep pulses, jaggery, borogulu (fried rice) two bottles of liquor and a pot of water on the ground near the place where the person is fried. They keep some stone near well-mud on the grave. A stick is placed vertically at the centre of the graveyard by the priest. He utters some incantation after which the good items carried by them are eaten. All of them including the priest are served with liquor. All of them come to the house of the deceased without turning back, wash their hands and legs and put vermillion mark on their forehead. During night the priest sits on the ground in front of the hut with some pankan (jaggery mixed with water) in his hand and with a leaf in it. All the persons one by one go to the place, bow down, touch his feet with one hand keep the other on his mouth. The priest then puts vermillion mark on their forehead. He then gives some panakam to each and every one by addressing the soul of the deceased person that is giving theeradham (sacred water) of the deceased to so and so person. After wards, members of the obsequies party, including the priest, to the grave yard carrying with them cooked meat curry, payasam (rice cooked with milk and jaggery) and other food items liked by the deceased. They also bring two pots of water in newly purchased earthen pots. All the articles are called talapu. The priest first sprinkles panakam on the grave. The funeral party starts making perambulations thrice around the grave and sit down around it. The priest prepares the mixtures of llapy. Then he removes the stick placed at the centre of the grave and places three balls of mixture at that place. The priest also receives dakshina (gift in cash). Talapu is then distributed among the participants including the priest. The small hole modely erecting the stick previously is covered and spread with mud and water. A tulsi plant is planted at that place. A small pit is dug beside the grave towards the beet of the deadbody and water is poured in it. All the participants wash their hands in it after taking prasadam (the consecrated food offer to the deceased prepared by the priest). Then a fire is lit in front of the grave to protect it from being disturbed by wild animals. The party comes back to the deadman's house. The priest enters the hut and sits down at a place where rice and figures of God Perumalle Swami are kept in the morning. The priest lights a flame by means of a wooden stick, one end of which is covered with caster oil-soaked cotton and light is lit on that cotton. The lighted torch is shown to the people and then is kept beside the figure of Perumallae Swami. All the participants and the priest are offered meals along with some liquor. Some ash water and three balls of rice are kept at the spot as it is done on the first day.

Paddadinam is another ceremony performed on the ninth

day after death. The priest enters the hut and sits down at a place where the person died. He again makes three concentric circles and rice is kept on it. He places the figure of Parumalle Swami at the centre and betel leaves around the outer circle. A fowl is sacrificed at that spot and they prepare fowl curry, payasam, fried rice and pan cakes. In the meantime the obsequies party assembles at the house. The widow is directed to take full bath. Then she wears a white saree without any border and a white jacket. She is also applied with turmeric paste on her face, hand and feet and vermillion mark on her forehead. A little coconut jaggery, betel nut, betel leaves and rice are tied in a cloth. It is known as odibala. It is tied around her waist. She goes to the funeral ground accompanied with the claps of the funeral party members. She keeps odibala besides the grave towards the head of the deceased person. All of them go to the nearby stream. The widow in the stream. Then her bangles are broken by the priest who removes her matterly (toe ring) tali (marriage locket) and vermillion mark from her forehead. He covers her face with the end of the saree. All of them then return to the house of deceased person. The widow is kept outside the hut. An earthen lamp is lit on a spot where the person died. All the clan members one by one go to the widow, remove the cloth covering her face and then towards the lamp. A feast is also thrown to all the participants to that day. The priest then sits down the hut with a glass of goat milk in which a tulsi leaf is placed. The priest pours the milk with the leaf into 'the mouth of all the clan members. He also sprinkle milk on the shoulders of all persons who carried the corpse. The priest also puts vermillion mark on the forehead of all the participants of the ceremony. Then the priest takes some cow panchakam (urine of the cow) in chembu (small water vessel) and sprinkle it on each they and every one in the hut with a tulsi leaf. Thus all clan members become free from pollution. Again, in the night some ash is kept where the person died. A mug of water and three balls of rice are also kept on it. The souls of the dead is believed to come for the last time in the form of a child or an animal to eat the offerings and the foot-prints are expected to be imprinted on the ash. Next morning these offerings are thrown away. The hut is then cleared and smeared with cowdung paste.

V

The Council of Chenchus tribal elders is locally called Nasab (or Kula Panchayat). It is headed by the headman of the village. Nasab comprises 4 to 6 members who are called peddamenusulu (elderly persons) representing all the clans of the village. This kule panchayat claims authority over the village in which it is organised. It is an independent and autonomous organisation. The members of the village council try to settle disputes originating within the village and normalise the behaviour of the covillagers. But in case of disputes of the serious nature, assistance is secured from the neighbouring village council or from another tribal elder of the neighbouring village, who has popularity for settling the disputes tactfully. The Nasab is headed by an elderly person generally from the numerically dominant clan of the village who also mostly happens to be the original settlers. Succession to this office is usually hereditary. The head of the Council is known among them as Raju (stems from the root ward raja i.e. king). He usually presides over the assembly meant for the purpose of village or community discipline. Next to Raju is Pardhani (minister). Another official who assists the Raju, i.e. head of village organisation, is known as Kolagadu (whip, attender and servant). His main duty is to run the command to the villagers and to convene the meeting intimating time and place to all concerned. The Raju is usually recruited from the dominant clan like Bhumani, while Pradhani and Kolagadu are usually recruited from the Kudumale and Utlaturi clan respectively. But deviation from the rule is also seen. Usually the dominant clan or early settlers claim such spots in respect of village political organisation. Besides settling disputes the headman also plays an important role in the socio-religious and economic activities of the village on the occasions of communal rituals to collect subscriptions from the villagers and purchase the required articles for performing the worship from the local market. He takes the entire responsibility of the worship. During the fixation of any marriage he also acts as a mediator and stands witness to the marriage. If an outsider first comes to the village, it is the headman who is contacted first. He also approaches the officials on behalf of the fellowmen for their development.

The members of the tribal council are called Paddamanusulu.

There are people who are economically well-off or vociferous, and here those who have convincing capacity, education, intelligence and dynamism are selected as Paddamanusulu by the villagers. This post is not hereditary. They always try to solve various village as well as tribal problems. The numbers of tribal elders in each village ranges from 4-6 and their main function is to assist the village headman in arriving at a decision for settling the disputes.

The local panchayat deals with different cases like elopement, quarrels due to suspicion and mutual distrust, divorce, violation of tribe endogamy, petty thefts and other minor disputes. Justice is dispensed according to the traditional tribal norms applied in the context of different situations. The local Panchayat is empowered to impose a fine orders punitive feasts or excemmunicate an offender for serious violation of social customs like tribe endogamy, incestuous, sexual relations, etc. Dipping the hand into boiling water, gripping the red-hot crowbar, walking on red-hot charcoal touching a red-hot wire with the tongue etc. are some of the methods through which guilt or innocence of an accused person is proved.

The Panchayat Raj system has been introduced by the Government to ensure people's participation in the development process through elected leaders armed with some power. But it has little impact on the life of the Chenchus owing to their lack of enlightened leadership, persisting hold of traditional norm etc. However, for major crimes and murder they report to the Police.

VI

Magic forms part of religion as it involves commissioning the services of supernatural powers. By following some magical practices, certain desired effects are expected by the individual or by the community. The Chenchus perform magical rites only through divination. The Chenchu magic is broadly divided into two categories, viz. white magic or protective magic and black magic or destructive magic. The Chenchus use white magic for curing the eseases and preventing their recurrence. The person who knows the art of white magic is locally called Goddecheppuvaru. These person diagnose the causes of the disease in a state of spirit-possession and suggest remedial measures.

These magical practices accompany incantation, using talisman special prohibition etc. They are the healers and use their art only for bringing good for the people. The Chenchus have their own method of treatment with medicinal plants for various kins of diseases like pain of women at the time menstruation, skin diseases, paralysis, cough etc. Medicinal herbs are also used to avoid pregnancy, to make a person potent and also during snake bites. Even fever is believed to be caused by the malevolent influence of some evil spirits or due to the wrath of some deity. Sorcerer by divination find out the deity that causes the disease and also the method of appeasing it.

There are also snake-chermers among the Chenchus who go to the jungles and catch various types of snakes. They also cure persons suffering from snake bite. The object of black magic or destructive magic is criminal or antisocial and it involves commissioning of services of supernatural powers for wicked ends. Any person can perform black magic by praying and uttering some in contation to some deity. The deities like Rakle veeradu, Onti veerodu, Peddamma Veerabhauhrudu, Bhyhavaswami and Mysamme are prayed by them for casing harm to the enemy.

The Chenchus have some superstitious beliefs and are very particular about omens and portents. They also have specific interpretation of the consequences of dreams. The appearance of particular objects or individuals etc. in dreams are expected to cause particular results. Day-time dreams are not considered significant. The effect of the evil eye is believed to cause evil effects like ill health, impeded growth and loss of prosperity of persons on which the glance is cast.

Definits temple or sacred spot is conspicuously absent though the same spot is used several years for warships. Only undressed pieces of stones are generally considered as the resting place of certain deities where propitiation is made. Some of the Chenchus keep the figures of some deities; a few have silver figures representing the deities. The connsorts of Shaivite and Vaishnavite deities are believed to be Chenchu girls; even their popular seven malignant sister deities seem to have been adopted from the Bangara Tribe. The Chenchus offer sacrifice of various type which they can procure. A large number of goats and fowls are offered as sacrifice. Village or community level worship takes place once in every year. For community or village worship, a convenient day is fixed by the headman of the village in consultation with the village elders. Collection of subscription purchase of various materials, appointment of temporary priest for the performance of the ceremony are the phases of the celebration. Food is cooked and eaten by the villagers along with the constumption of liquor. Deities like Lord Veerbhandra (son of Lord Shiva), nandisware (famous bull of lord Shiva), Sri Rama (Lord Rama of the Ramayana as Avatara), Nagamayya (the Cobra deity) etc. are worshipped without any animal sacrifice while key offer animal sacrifice to Tirumalaswami and Lingamayya sundried rice, turmeric, vermillion, incense-stick etc. constitute the items of worship. At the time of animal sacrifice (goat or fowl) they keep some apayasam (porridge prepared with milk and coarse sugar) in front of the deity over a flat stone. There is no systematic incactation used at the time of offering sacrifice or other foodstuff to the deitities in connection with their proptiation. The festival generally ends up in a civilian fashion and merry-making in the accompaniment of dance. Goddess Polerra is connected with epidemic diseases like cholera, small pox etc. They believe that if proper prayer, worship and sacrifice are made she becomes pleased and bevolent. She is malevolent in nature and wants blood sacrifice of goat or fowl. She is worshipped once in a year on a communal basis. She is also worshipped at the time of epidemics.

Ankalamma is an important goddess. She is symbolised by a stone slab under a tree and worshipped by individuals and families and she protects them from diseases. She is often represented by a stone slab. Some Chenchus also keep the figure of this deity in their house. It is generally worshipped on a family level. Vermillion and turmeric powder are applied to the deity and to the coconut also. Payasam prepared by rice, milk and jaggery and coconut are offered to the deity. Fowl is also sacrificed.

Goddess Maisamma is very powerful; she is also referred as Shakti. She is represented by a stone slab kept under a tree and worshipped for individual benefits. She is also worshipped for wreaking vengeance on the enemies. She is often worshipped in the houses as a household deity.

Lanchchamma is a village deity connected with land. Persons with landed property only worship her after harvest. Till the worship is over, no grain from the land is brought home from the field. After harvesting the crop, some area is cleaned in the land with cowdung paste. One stone slab is placed on this spot representing the deity. The Chenchus have adopted this worship from the caste farmer's.

The word Darbian is possibly derived from the name of a place called Darbians. The deity is symbolised by a stone slab. At the time of worship they offer animals like goat and fowl as sacrifice. They pray to the god for their general welfare.

Peddamma is a powerful goddess located outside the village under a tree and is represented by a stone figure. She is believed to take the form of a tigress, and she protects their domesticated animals from the tigers. She is individually worshipped with goat sacrifice.

The deity Gurrappa is very popular among the Chenchus. He has no permanent shrine. Animal sacrifice is not essential. He accepts vegetarian offerings also.

The deity Bhyrava Swamy has shrines in the interior forest. He is worshipped for safeguarding the cattle from the tiger menace, as he is considered to be a forest God.

The Chenchus also worship deities like Mutyalamma, connected with diseases. Nandulu veeranna is worshipped for individual protection; Bottimidi, a forest god represented by a stone slab, chintala veeramma, is representation in the shrine with nose, eyes, moustache and teeth made with vermillion, is also worshipped by them.

Lord Venkateswarlu of Tirupati is the most revered Hindu God, who is also incorporated in the Chenchu pantheon in the name of Venkateswarlu. The Chenchus also keep photos of Lord Venkateswarlu in their houses. He is worshipped for individual protection and benefit. He is also worshipped on the occasion of marriage.

The deity Hanumanthudu is another name of Lord Mallikarjuna and Bourammiah and his consort Bhramaramba. These Gods and Goddesses are the presiding deities of the temple at Srisailam. The Chenchus offer vegetarian dishes to the deities.

The local legend and the Chenchus long standing service right in this temple amply shows that the deity is originally a Chenchu God.

Narasimha Swami has a temple at Ahobilam, a Vaishnava Centre. Hence, he is called Ahobilan Narasimha Swami. The Chenchus worship him through out the year with vegetarian offering. The mythical nexus between Chenchu girl, Lord Vishnu and Narasimha can be treated in their legends.

Ugadi is a festival connected with the worship of household deities in Chaita Sudha Payan during the month of March-April with animal sacrifice, coconut and payasam offering. Dasara, a two-day festival is celebrated in Asviyja Sudha Podyama in September-October just outside the house. Kanakadurga and Lingamayya are worshipped with animal sacrifice during Ayyadhala puja (9th day) and Vijayadasami (10th day).

Household deities are worshipped during Sankranti festival. This two-to-three days long festival takes place in Pushyam during mid-January. During this festival coconut, jaggery and paysam are offered to the household deities. Animal is also sacrificed on the 3rd day. A two-days long Deepavali is celebrated in Asviyuga Bahula Amavasya in the month of October-November with payasam and coconut offering. Household deities are worshipped during Deepavali. Nagulachavite festival is marked with worship of nagendra with offering of millet at the mound milk. It is a three day-long festival which take place in kartika suddha Chavithi in October-November. Shivaratri is celebrated either at Srisailam or in the village to worship lord Shiva in stone slab with the offering of coconut and fruits. It is a day-long festival celebrated on Magha Bahula Chatrudashi in February. The ancestors are worshipped in Pitharla Amavasya. The festival is a day-long celebration performed in Bhadrapada Bahula Amavasya during September-October. Animal sacrifice is made during this festival. Kamuni Punnami is celebrated during February-March with the propitiation of Manmodha in the respective houses with offerings of jaggery and Pangal (rice cooked with jaggery). Vinayaka chavithi is the festival when stone slab representation of Lord Vinayaka is worshipped in the respective houses. The festival takes places during Bhadrapodasudde chavite in August-September. This day-long celebration is performed with offering of Kufmuly (cooked jaggery and flour balls) to Lord Vinayaka. Srivama Navami is also enthusiastically observed by the Chenchus with worship of Lord Rama in the drawing of Rama. It takes place at the shrine of Rama in Navami in April. Lord Rama is worshipped with offerings coconut and payasam during this festival.

Five

Tribal Development

Programme and Strategy in Historical Prospective

The tribes are generally considered as early settlers or autochthones. There is no particular definition which is universally accepted. Nevertheless, certain characteristics have been put forward as criteria for determining a tribal community. These are endogamous organisations with a simple social structure and self-contained economy. There is minimal contact with the other groups. They live in seclusion, are governed by their own social norms and largely manage their own affairs. This is the ideal type for a tribal community. However, the situation has been undergoing such fast change that today it would be difficult to satisfy all these criteria for a number of communities, termed as Scheduled Tribes.

It may not be necessary to go into the history of recognition of the aboriginal tribes, yet it will be useful to clear the concept. It was in the early reports of some British travellers, and latter in the Census reports that certain communities were termed as aborigines. Before the advent of the British India, substantial areas were ruled exclusively by the tribals themselves. The areas predominantly inhabited by the aboriginal communities in regions under direct administration of the British were excluded from the normal administration of that time. On the eve of Independence it was decided that the communities which were hitherto recognised as aborigines should be put in a separate Schedule. "Excluded" and "Partially excluded" areas were enlisted in two schedules. It is the communities included in the Schedules to the Presidential Order of 1950, as amended from time to time, which are today known as Scheduled Tribes and these groups of people were considered as 'weaker section' as they were found lagging behind for the 'stronger section' of the country and their problems were given more attention for solution than before. Article 342 of the Constitution of India has empowered the President to declare a group of groups or communities as scheduled by public notification and on the basis of this the scheduled tribes or castes can have the privilege of benefit out of the provisions made in the Constitution.

The main concern for tribal development appears to be oriented towards bridging the gap between the tribals and the non-tribals, so that the former can become partners in the new productive processes and development programmes, through their active participation and involvement. In fact, growth with social justice has been the guiding principle of the Indian Government. In pursuance of this policy special emphasis was laid upon uplifting the backward and underdeveloped communities so as to bring them on a par with the rest of the country's population. Development of tribal population received special attention as their problems were different from those of other backward communities. In this chapter, the devilment measures taken up for the tribals prior to independence and also after independence have been discussed.

Tribal Development before Independence

In pre-independence days, the study of the social and economic conditions of the tribal people were difficult, for the areas inhabited by them were inaccessible, and it was difficult to establish contacts with them. However, a few Government officers, anthropologist, welfare workers and missionary workers who maintained constant touch with them have left valuable accounts which depict the conditions under which they used to live.

The tribal people, living in remote hill regions and forest areas for many centuries, led a life of their own, generally uninfluenced by the main currents of development outside. It was only after the entry of the missionaries into these areas that the officers of the Administration started paying some attention to them. But this contact of the officers with the tribal people was only superficial and it prompted them to come to an equally superficial, conclusion, the first and foremost of which was the need they felt to isolate these people from the rest of their countrymen and to separate the entire Tribal Areas (Scheduled

Districts Act of 1874) from the purview of the normal administration - a rather harmful move against the tribal groups.

J.H. Hutton, a distinguished member of the I.C.S., who made an in-depth study of the problems of the tribal people wrote on the effects of British rule over them (quoted from Dhebar Commission Report, 1961) as follows:

'Far from being of immediate benefit to the primitive trials, the establishment of British rule in India did most of them much more harm than good.... It may be said that the early days of British Administration did very great detriment to the economic position of tribals through ignorance and neglect of their rights and customs...many changes have been caused incidentally by the penetration of the tribal country' the opening up of communications, the protection of forests and the establishment of schools, to say nothing of the openings given in this way to Christian missions. Many results of these changes have caused acute discomfort to the tribes'.

Commenting on this, G. S. Ghurye (1959) says "The acuteness of discomfort was very often so great that it led to apathy, indifference, moral deterioration and even a decline in population". The British policy of isolating the tribes resulted in exploitation. The zamindars, landlords, money-lenders and contractors exploited the tribals to the maximum. Their contact with non-tribals was none too happy for the tribals. This policy of isolating the tribals led to their misery as it openly threw them to the fury of exploitation by zamindars, money-lenders and local designing chiefs. The policy of conservation of forests resulted in curbing the age-old rights and practices of the tribals, i.e., stoppage of shifting cultivation, hunting-gathering facilities in forests etc. The intrusion of forests contractors not only led to a greater exploitation of forests but also emaciated the tribals living therein. The entry of merchants and money-lenders further impoverished the tribals who were already facing many difficulties which as the vagaries of nature, denudation of hills and forests, loss of soil fertility etc. Under these conditions, the policy of non-interference of the British with regard to the tribal areas helped only perpetuate the socio-cultural hiatus between the tribals and the non-tribals, besides exposing them to the nefarious practices of the merchants, money-lenders and usurers. Due to unbearable exploitation conditions, a series of rebellions and tribal unrest took place before independence viz. Kol insurrection (1832), the Santal rebellion (1955), the Sardari agitation (1887) and the Birsa movement (1959). During that time the most important administrative reform was the promulgation of Regulation XIII of 1933. These reforms and administrative steps which remained only on paper were followed by the settlement and survey operations in Ranchi District. There was at that time the Agency Tracts Interest and land Transfer Act of 1917 of the Madras Presidency. According to the provisions of this Act the rate of interest of an debt of liability against a member of Schedule Tribe shall be below 24 per cent per annum. Another important Act was the Andhra Agency Debt Bondage Abolition Regulation of 1940 of the Madras presidency; under Regulation III of the Act the system of debt bondage in tribal areas was abolish and the violaters were made liable for punishment.

Though the spirit of these regulatory measures was to realize socio-economic uplift of the tribals, the British policy towards them was to maintain a policy of isolation i.e., not to interfere much and to maintain a status quo. As a result, the tribals had to remain at the mercy of the official henchmen who were supported by the British administration.

After independence, the successive Five Year Plans have been implemented and the task of development to these a tribal people has been given due importance. Plan provisions for the welfare of the tribals were made, either directly by the Central Government who sanctioned the funds by the State Government who also spent money for their amelioration. The schemes were divided into four broad categories, namely (1) Education, (2) Economic Uplift, (3) Health/Housing and other similar schemes and (4) Removal of social disabilities.

In planning for the development of tribals and tribal areas the ethnic diversity of tribal people who constitute 7.68% (1991 Census) of the total population has to be kept in view. Unlike the Scheduled Castes, they are mostly concentrated in certain areas and belong to diverse socio-economic levels of tribal societies. In this context Elwin (1954) initially suggested creation of a 'National Part' by completely isolating them from the rest of the population of India. But later he shifted from this view. On the contrary, Ghurye (1963) emphasised a total assimilation of the tribals into the mainstream. Some other (Nehru: 1960) suggested to keep them between the two extreme positions. In this connection, five clauses, popularly known as 'Panch Sheel', were advanced as guidelines for promoting the interest of the tribals. They are: (1) We should avoid imposing anything on the tribals, (2) Tribal rights on land and forest should respected, (3) We should try to train and build a team of their own people, (4) We should not overwhelm the with a multiplicity of schemes; and (5) We should judge results not by statistics but by the quality of human character evolved.

Tribal Development in Post Independence India

The First Five year Plan (1951-56) projected efforts to provide for the welfare of the Scheduled Tribes and Tribal areas through a special sector of development, viz., welfare of the Backward classes. The programmes under this sector were meant to supplement the general development efforts for the Backward classes including tribal population. The programme for providing direct benefits to the Scheduled Tribes and Scheduled Castes were drawn p under the State and Central Sector for the economic, educational and social progress of these communities. The First Five Year Plan for India was to spend to the tune of Rs. 2,356 crores, out of which a lump sum provision of Rs. 3.39 crores was made for the Schemes for the Backward classes. Against this plan provision, an expenditure of Rs. 25.98 crores was incurred by the State Governments on the Backward Classes. This included an expenditure of Rs. 17.36 crores of the welfare of the Scheduled Tribes. The Report of the Scheduled Areas and Scheduled Tribes Commissioner (1960-61) shows that of the sixteen sectors identified for allocation of the amount, education, communication, agriculture and medical and public health were given special attention for development.

This was a beginning which can justifiably be regarded as fairly good, keeping in view the intensity of the problems.

The Second Five Year Plan (1956-61) was initiated with a significant change in the approach to the schemes of development.

The expenditures on economic uplift was raised fro Rs. 4.32 crores in the First Plan to Rs. 16.86 crores in the Second Plan, indicating a arise of 29 per cent Similarly, the budgetary provisions for education and communication were increased from Rs. 4.07 crores in the First Plan to Rs. 8.82 crores and Rs. 8.79 crores respectively in the Second plan. The rise in the actual expenditure on education and communication was 75 and 100 per cent, respectively. Attempts for integrated development of the tribal population were made in the Second Five Year Plan by establishing Special Multipurpose Tribal (SMPT) Blocks were set up in the scheduled areas ad the programme of each block was given an a additional thrust by siphoning a special allocation of Rs. 15 lakhs for five years This allocation was obtained from the Government of India (Home Ministry) in addition to Rs. 12 lakhs available to the usual community Development Blocks.

To assess the performance of these Multipurpose Projects and suggest further measures for plugging the loopholes in the future programme formulation and implementation, for evolving a more realistic approach India appointed a Committee in 1959 with Verrier Elwin, the well-known anthropologist and the then adviser on the NEFA, as Chairman.

After a careful and extensive study of all the 43 Multipurpose Projects, the Elwin Committee (1960) made in following observations:

1. While agreeing that the situation is very fluid, the committee opined that the other picture is changing very rapidly....... and the development schemes which started very slowly have now achieved a new tempo, which by the end of the Second Five Year Plan period, will result in very different pattern of expenditure and achievement.
2. The coverage of the Project which was fixed at 25,000 population and an area of 200 sq. miles, with a per capita outlay of Rs. 108.00, was exceeded by some States be carrying out projects with more than double the area and population and this resulted in thinning development efforts and ineffective programme implementation due to unwieldiness of the project coverage.
3. In many of the projects, the non-tribals were quite sizable

in number, sometimes exceeding the tribals population, and the consequent dilution of development efforts as some of the non-specific programmes like education, health and communication etc. were serving better the interest of non-tribals.

4. The location of a project should not be in terms of the primitiveness of the tribes inhabiting that area, but with reference to the level of development of infrastructural facilities, social services, economic needs etc. of the areas of the tribal concentration.
5. Because of the schematic budget and the non-use of powers vested in the State Government to transfer founds from one head to another with the same project, adapting the programmes to urgent tribal needs could not be achieved.
6. Expenditure was not in tune with programme priorities.
7. The programme was not given the much needed tribal basis.
8. The Multipurpose projects could not generate the necessary employment opportunities for tribals.
9. The heavy outlays earmarked resulted in instilling a sense of hurry among the officials to spend the money (within the Five Year Plan Period).
10. Multitude of Programmes and the various fronts in which they are proposed to be tackled resulted in confusion for the P.E.O. and the staff and they tended to go round in circles trying to make up their minds what to do first.

After carefully studying the whole situation, the Elwin Committee made the following recommendations:

1. As Rs. 27 lakhs is too big an amount to be usefully spent with a five year period, the Home Ministry's contribution may be reduced from Rs. 15 lakhs to Rs. 10 lakhs, while retaining the normal contribution of Rs.12 lakhs from C.D. Ministry.
2. The new tribal Blocks should cover a area of 200 sq. miles with an overall population of 25,000 and extend not only over scheduled areas, but also non-scheduled areas if the tribal component is around 55 per cent of the total population.

3. To avoid the drawbacks of the schematic budget and introduce the much-needed flexibility, there should be a regular schematic budget for the tribal Blocks in future, but the allocation can be divided into three sections as given below:
   (a) Schemes for economic development 60per cent
   (b) Communication 25per cent
   (c) Social services 15per cent
4. The Committee felt that while giving high priority to agriculture and allied sectors like irrigation, land reclamation and soil conservation with an allocation of not less than Rs.10 lakhs under these heads, the allocation under education should also be raised as it has been very meagre so far.
5. The Committee also made certain suggestions for further action in evolving schemes, sanctioning funds, appointing the Block Staff and training them etc.

The recommendations of the Elwin Committee were accepted by the Government of India. Notable among them were that the tribal component of the new tribal locks should be not less then 60 per cent and Bloc Development Officers instead of PEOs should be appointed as heads of the Block Extension Teams.

After Elwin Committee, Dhebvar Commission (1960-61 was appointed to study the whole gamut of tribal development. The Dhebar Commission recommendations went a long way to strengthen the protective shield and giving the Panchayati Raj a tribal bias, besides taking a comprehensive and integrated view of tribal development. The Commission's recommendations on planning and development were more specific for solving the problems of land, alienation, indebtedness, promotion of education, protecting tribal interest in forest and sectorial development. The Dhebar Commission also recommended the establishment of Tribal Cultural Research and raining Institute in states for official and no-official development functionaries and workers taking part in research studies, so that their results can be used as feed-back in planning and administration.

On the basis of the above observations the programme of S.M.P.T. Block were modified during the Third Five Year Plan (1961-69) and the Plan Holidays. A total of 415 Tribal Development

Blocks were set up. The schematic pattern of the earlier S.M.P.T. Blocks was given a go-by, though the main emphasis of the programme continued to be on economic development. In the Third Plan, the priorities were in the order of economic uplift, education, health, housing and communication.

A review of the Tribal Development Programme was taken up by a study team set up by the Planning Commission under the Chairmanship of Shilu Ao in 1969. The team made a review of the measures undertaken for tribal development during the course of the first three Five Year Plans. It was noted that during the First Plan the main scheme undertaken related to education and economic development, improvement of reads and communication and provision of medical and public health facilities. The main observation of this team regarding the Tribal Development Blocks was that although the achievement under the programme had helped being about psychological change in the outlook of the tribal some of the main drawbacks pointed out by the Shilu Ao team were as follows:

1. The Tribal Development locks failed to get many significant support from the general development programme including the C.D. programme.
2. The schemes formulated for these Blocks were not adapted to the felt needs of the specific areas.
3. The benefits had mostly accrued to the ore advanced among the tribals.
4. The T.D. Block was too small a geographical entity for coordinated planning. Programme like education at the Secondary and Higher levels, soil conservation and other programmes relating to infrastructural development had cut across the Block, the District or even the State boundaries and could not be financed out of the meagre allocation for the Tribal Development Blocks.

The team suggested that the programme for the tribal development should be based on an 'area approach' and be financed to of the general plan in suitable cased.

In the background of the pronouncements of the two study teams of 1959 and 1969 and the Scheduled Castes and Scheduled Tribes Commission of 1961 the Fourth Five Year Plan (1969-74) as many as 43 per cent of the tribal population was covered in 504

T.D. Blocks. For further intensification of the programmes, supplementary allocations were made by the Central Government, as in the past, and the life of each block was extended for another five years. In this period several programmes were taken up for small farmers, marginal farmers as also crash programmes of employment and rural employment schemes. With the emphasis on the conditions of the rural poor, some of the backward tribal areas received greater attention. Individual family programmes were introduced and a new programme of Tribal Development Agencies was taken up by the ministry of Agriculture which has a variant of the small farmers programmes.

Having been seized with the weaknesses in the policies and programmes of tribal development in following up to the end of the Fourth Five Year Plan (a) the programmes got atrophied financially and consequently physically since it become a sectorial programme for execution of certain schemes with the limited resources of the backward classes welfare sector; (b) there was failure to comprehends the distinctive characteristics of the tribal areas and scheduled tribes; (c) the policies and programmes as well as the administrative machinery were hardly moulded to their needs. These were kept in view while formulating the policy, approach and strategy for the Fifth Five Year Plan (1974-80). The problem of tribal development basically pertained to the development of the following categories:

(a) Areas of tribal concentration
(b) Dispersed trials and
(c) Primitive tribal communities.

While evolving the strategy of the Fifth Plan it, was felt that attention had to be focused on the specific problem of each identifiable group and area. The situation in regions of tribal concentration and in the areas of dispersed tribal population would be quite distinct and would require different approaches. In the regions of tribal concentration, the area development approach had to be introduced, keeping in view the problems of the tribal people. In the case of dispersed tribal population, family approach would have to be adopted. In the case of primitive tribal communities, special group-oriented programmes would have to formulated for them.

The basic approach towards tribal development adopted in the Fifth Plan .was to identify larger areas of trial concentration which included the scheduled Areas, contiguous T.D. Blocks and other blocks/areas having 50% tribal concentration. All such blocks/areas in a State were to be brought under a separate sub-plan under the overall State plan.

For the preparation of the Tribal sub-plan, the Planning Commission issued a set of guidelines to the States. The guidelines spelt out the long-term objectives of the tribal sub-plan as: (1) narrowing down the gap between the levels of development of the tribals and other areas and (2) improving their quality of life. Among the immediate objective were: (1) elimination of exploitation of all forms; (2) speeding up the processes for social and economic development; (3) building up inner strength of the people and (4) improving their organisational capabilities. The guidelines also stated that the sub-plan area in each State should comprise a number of viable project. For each such Integrated Tribal Development project (LTD), an integrated area development plan, focusing attention on the specific problems of the areas and tribal people, was to be formulated. The sub-plan areas in each State thus composed a number or viable projects.

During the Sixth Five Year Plan period (1980-85) the major objective is to wage an all-out war against poverty and mobilise all the country's latent energy for the creation of more dynamic and equitable society. The programmes formulated for the Scheduled Tribes can no longer be kept confined to mere education incentives, grants and subsidies for economic activities, housing drinking water, wells etc. Comprehensive development plans are required to be formulated keeping in view the special problem and needs of each of these tribal communities. Further, these programmes have to be integrated with other general programme in the context of the overall development strategy of the plan.

For the Scheduled Tribes, the present sub-plan approach which operates through T.D.P. will be continued. The tribal identity and the tribal way of life will be preserved in a manner consistent with their operation for development.

The main thrust of the policy for tribal development during the Sixth Plan is four-fold, viz. (a) integration of services at the delivery point to the beneficiary with a view to developing a sense of self-reliance in them, (b) development of services from the bottom upwards instead of the top downwards, (c) development of skills to diversify the, occupation and (d) introduction of latest technology based on local materials and local skills. A simple subsidy-based approach, however, has perpetuated dependence and curbed initiative.

The main programme is for the generation of augmentation of the purchasing power through schemes like National Rural Development Programme, the Integrated Rural Development Programme, Agricultural Programmes, Animal Husbandry, pisciculture, Sericulture etc. In addition, the basic needs of these communities would be met from the minimum need-based programme. All these programmes should be integrated.

The socio-economic development of the Scheduled Tribes was accepted as a general goal to be achieved through the implementation of sectoral programme. No special appreciation was made, in the formulation of the scheme, of the needs of these communities who had their own social and cultural milieu distinct from the rest of the population. A detailed and comprehensive review of the tribal problem was taken on the eve of the Fifth Five year Plan period when the concept of the Tribal sub-plan strategy was evolved. This strategy, followed since then, has been implemented with refinements during the successive plan periods.

The objective of the strategy in all these years remained two-fold:

(1) Socio-economic development of the Scheduled Tribes and
(2) Protection of tribals against exploitation.

For the implementation of the strategy, the Integrated Tribal Development Projects (ITDPs) were conceived during the, Fifth Plan and these have been continued since then. During the Sixth plan, the Modified Area Development Approach (MADA) was adopted to cover smaller areas of tribal concentration having 10,000 population and of which 50 per cent or more were tribals. During the Seventh Five Year Plan (1985-90), the Tribal Sub-plan strategy was extended to all the tribals in the country including the dispersed tribals for the beneficiary-oriented programmes.

The strategy which has been adopted from the Fifth Year Plan onwards has yielded results and has proved beneficial to the development of the tribals and the tribal areas., The strategy has generally helped in focusing the attention of the planners and implementers on the special needs of the tribal society and tribal areas an on adopting a more integrated approach for their development: As a result of this there has been sudden increase in investment in tribal areas. During the Fifth Plan, Rs. 1102 crores were invested under the Tribal Sub-plan, which went up to about Rs. 5,000 crores during the Sixth Plan. In the Seventh Plan, the investments under the Tribal Sub-plan from State plan are expected to be of the order of nearly Rs. 7,000 crores. During the first four years of seventh Plan, the flow from the State Plan has been of the order of Rs. 5270 crores. In addition another Rs. 6415 cores have been given to the States and the Union Territories as special central assistance by the Government of India. There will also be investments under the strategy from the centrally sponsored schemes of different Departments/Ministries of Govt. of India and institutional finance. Though the exact quantum of these flows are not know these are expected top be sizable.

After the adoption of the TSP strategy, the Central and States Governments have enacted protective laws to check exploitation of tribals by non-tribals, especially by money-lenders and private traders. These include land lows to non-tribals laws regulating money-lending in tribal area as and laws for acquiring monopoly rights in the collection and marketing of the tribal produce. The group felt that the implementation of these laws has helped to an extent in prevention of the version of the economic base, which is land for the tribals. The laws/regulations regulating interest to be charged by money-lenders from the tribals for the loans given to them have been enforced in the tribal areas, although their implementation has been a subject matter of debate. The marketing of the tribal produce was another area where they were generally exploited. After the adoption of TSP strategy, States set up Tribal Development Cooperative Corporations/Minor Forest Produce Cooperative Federations to ensure remunerative prices to tribals for their produce. The States also nationalised the collection and trading of certain items for this purpose..

There has been no change in the strategy during the Seventh

Five Year Plan The efforts have all along been to consolidate the gains under the strategy and to orient them to the target groups viz. the Scheduled Tribes. For this purpose, guidelines were issued during the Seventh Five Year Plan laying down principles which should be adopted for quantification of funds under the capital intensive projects. Instructions were issued to the State Governments to utilise special Central Assistance for the family oriented schemes and for this purpose a set of illustrative schemes was also sent to them to serve as a model. ITTDPs and MADAs covered only 75 per cent of the total tribal population in the country.; To cover the remaining 25 per cent a cluster approach was advocated to the States to be adopted during the Seventh Five Year Plan. The strategy was further refined by a decision to cover all the tribals in the country, including the dispersed tribals and the Central Government decided to allow special Central Assistance for giving assistance to the dispersed tribal groups for beneficiary oriented schemes.

Though the TSP strategy has yielded results, these are not commensurate with the expectations and the investments made so far. First, it has been observed that regarding adoption of the TSP strategy the States have been adopting different methodologies. Secondly, in several States, the ITSP approach is interpreted as an area approach and, therefore, a very heavy emphasis is laid on infrastructure development without corresponding emphasis on the development of the Scheduled Tribes. The Working Groups made an analysis of the investments during the first four years under the Tribal sub-plan for the country as a whole. It emerged that nearly 37% of the total outlay under the Tribal sub-plan from the State plan during 1985-86 to 1988-89, was for infrastructure development. The Group also felt that in the sectoral fragmentation of the Tribal sub-plan, the scheme under which quantifications are made do not reflect the felt needs of the tribals and, therefore, these do not create the desired impact.

Tribal Sub-plan in the Eight Five Year Plan

Since the TSP strategy must be continued in the Eighth Five Year Plan (1990-95) too, there is a need to make it more result-oriented and purposeful so that not only an adequate flow of funds is ensured, but the benefit of the investments under Tribal sub-plan will actually go towards improving the socio-economic conditions of the scheduled Tribes. The fist area which will have to be tackle is relating to the quantification of funds up further by decentralised planning, which will envisage the preparation of ITDP-wise plans and adoption of suitable administrative structure at the ITDP level.

On the quantification of funds, the working group expressed the view that even though the Tribal sub-plan is a plan within the State plan and each department has responsibility for providing funds for development of the Scheduled Tribes, the present approach on quantification of funds by sectoral department required a new direction. Against the existing practice under which each department is obsessed with showing quantification under the schemes irrespective of weather these schemes have any relevance to the tribals or not, it would be to earmark separately a portion of outlay from the State Plan and place it with the Tribal Development Department of the States, which may intern allocate it to the sectoral departments looking after the plans/schemes prepared by them for the development of the Scheduled Tribes. In such an arrangement, the Tribal Development Department will be able to decide priorities of the schemes to be implemented in the tribal areas and will also be in a position to related them to their felt needs.

The working Group felt that the present planning process, which is a top-to-bottom exorcism, will also be required to be reversed. Planning shall have to be decentralised with ITDP as the basis and the ITDP-wise plans shall have to be prepared. The decentralised planning can make a success only if there is a corresponding devolution of resources. This can be possible only when the Tribal Development Department allocates funds from common pol placed at its disposal under the State plan,. The decentralised planning with corresponding devolution of funds at the ITDPs level will require strengthening of the existing administrative structure to give the project officer/administrator a much wider role. The quality of the existing administrative machinery will require improvement and the administrative structure shall have to be made simpler, more efficient and more responsive to the tribal people. Unless systems are created, which are capable of giving protection to the tribal people, the economic development programme may not succeed. Indebtedness in tribal areas cannot be tackled through legislation alone. The LAMPS shall have to be strengthened and developed as alternative credit agencies. In fact, the LAMPS should perform a three-fold functions viz. (a) collection of Minor Forest Produce (b) distribution of credit, including consumption finance, and (c) supply of essential commodities by acting as PDFS outlet. There are 74 primitive tribal groups identified in the country in TSP States/UTs. SCA is given by the Government of India for their development since 1975-76 Rs. 22.93 crores had been given to the States for the development of the primitive tribal groups by the end of the Sixth Plan. During the First four years of the Seventh Plan, another Rs. 21 crores have been given by the Government of India as SCA to States for these groups.

Till February, 1987, the TSP strategy was applicable to the identified project areas, MADAs and clusters. But now the strategy applied to all the tribals in the country including the dispersed tribals, for they constitute nearly 25 per cent of the total tribal population.

Six

Welfare Programmes P.T.Gs (Primitive Tribal Groups)

I

In the previous chapter, an attempt was made to discuss tribal development programmes and strategies in general in a historical perspective. In the present chapter, an attempt has been made to discuss the various welfare programmes introduced by the government agencies and various voluntary organisations for the uplift of the tribal communities, namely the Totos, the Lodhas and the Chenchus, considered to be the Primitive Tribal Group. From the earlier ethnographic descriptions about these three primitive tribal groups we are able to understand their ethnographic backgrounds along with the various socioeconomic problems and constraints which sometimes stand in the way of their transformation. To arrest the various socio-economic problems from time to time during the planned era, various development programmes have been introduced for their overall development and transformation. The details of welfare work for these tribal communities will be discussed critically with a view to understand the process of their transformation.

II

Welfare Programmes for the Totos

The Totos are a group of people who live in unhealthy, infertile hill slopes having hardly any interaction with outside. But certain factors arose when they were pushed into the narrower environment as the outsiders encroached upon their privileges. Besides ill health and sickness, unclean habits have put them in a more precarious condition which threatened them all the while. Naturally, education, modern health and hygienic measures are the needs of the hour for them, just to make them shake off their old habits. It has been reiterated that the tribal groups in general, and the Primitive Tribal Groups in particular, have a long association with poverty and hunger and, as such, they with their crude technology utilise the ecological and environmental resources in their circumstantial exigencies; but these are not sufficient enough to reflect a state of sound economy. Naturally, welfare or development schemes meant for these tribal groups through constitutional support requires a full analysis of the cultural background to find out the various forces operating in them. It is true that in many cases the result of development might be confined to a smaller section of the group due to uneven percolation of development efforts. In this context, Dube (1988:46) says:

> Economic development is need-oriented, endogamous, self-reliant, ecologically sound and based on structural transformation. It is aimed at those who have been deprived and exploited. It recognises the importance of equality, freedom of expression, conviviality and creativity. No universal model is to be imposed.

We have to consider carefully the various projects and schemes sanctioned by the respective District Advisory Committee or other appropriate committee who are being entrusted to design and to implement these for the Primitive Tribal Groups in West Bengal where these people have genuinely different cultural and sometimes ecological background. We all know that the development programmes are time-bound to achieve the desired future, considering the felt-needs of the people, and to equate them with the proportionately stronger brethren of the society. We can easily visualise the condition of the people as they are close to hunger and property. Their impoverished condition leaves them with the imprint of less productivity and ill health. Insignificant literacy among them makes them unable to understand the situation in the proper perspective in and around, and it becomes a continuous pull force towards backwardness that already prevails, and creates disillusionment about others as also narrow down their world-view. This also leads to a position of inescapable maladjustment by occasionally surfacing many violent incident. In this connection, it can be said that the District Advisory Committee generally provides some items of welfare for these groups of people, considering their pressing needs.

TABLE 6.1

NUMBER OF PROJECTS/SCHEMES UNDERTAKEN FOR THE TOTOS

Sl. No.	*Project sanctioned during 1981-1989*	*Allotted*	*Not allotted*
1.	Community Agriculture		-
2.	Soil Conservation		-
3.	Irrigation		-
4.	5 H.P. Pumpset	-	
5.	Agricultural implement	-	
6.	Excavation of tanks	-	
7.	Minikit	-	
8.	Supply of Bullock		
9.	Dairy or Milch cow scheme	-	
10.	Piggery	-	
11.	Sheep	-	
12.	Goatery	-	
13.	Poultry	-	-
14.	Fruit bearing plants	-	
15.	Babulgrass		-
16.	Rope Making	-	
17.	Preparation of leafplates	-	
18.	Cultivation of Mat-stick and Mat-making	-	
19.	Trolly	-	
20.	Club house	-	

Table 6.1 reflects the number of projects initiated for the Totos from 1980-81 to 1989-90. These are the continuous schemes and projects which have been sanctioned for these groups of people by the appropriate authorities with an idea to improve their economic condition which, in turn, will bring other changes for the overall betterment of these tribes.

Regarding the nature of impact of the schemes and projects the following observation has been made by the researcher during the course of investigation.

1. Community Agricultural Scheme

Community agriculture scheme meant for the Totos of Jalpaiguri and for this purpose a sum of Rs.1,73,440 has been sanctioned during 1986-97, but the full amount is yet to be spent; or for Rs. 1,65,803 only has been spent.

2. Soil Conservation

During the year 1988-89, a scheme for this purpose amounting to a sum of Rs. 1,50,000 was sanctioned for the Totos. During the course of survey it has been observed that the scheme was expected to start, but no effective step was taken in the direction.

3. Irriga'ional Facilities

Towards this facilities a sum of Rs.4,17,500 has been allotted for the Totos.

TABLE 6.2
IRRIGATION SCHEMES FOR THE TOTOS

Sl. No.	*Scheme*	*Year*	*Amount sanctio-ned (Rs.)*	*Target*	*Present status*
1.	Pujagaon Irrigation	1985-86	25,000	1 (for 12 families)	Not functioning
2.	Pujagaon Irrigation	1985-86	25,000	1 (for 10 families)	Not functioning
3.	Pujagaon Irrigation	1985-86	50,000	1 (for 30 families)	Not functioning
4.	Protection of Pujagaon Irrigation	1988-89	17,500	1 (for 30 families)	Functioning
5.	Banjokhola Irrigation	1985-86	25,000	1	Functioning
6.	Irrigation Scheme New Inspection Bunglow	1985-86	25,000	1 (for l4 families)	Functioning
7.	Irrigation Scheme at Totopara	1986-87	1,00,000	1	Failure
8.	Irrigation Scheme at Daljho	1987-88	50,000	1 (for 20 families)	Functioning
9.	Extension of Irrigation Scheme Bonjokhola	1987-88	50,000	1 (for 30 families)	Failure

In Totopara, an ambitious plan was chalked out extending irrigational facilities and this was to have covered the entire village. River water was to be stored for being used in agriculture. Actually, 4 minor schemes are found to be operating and the others are yet to be completed. Again, about 6 such minor projects proved to be failure.

4. Poultry

Poultry birds were supplied to the Totos. In the year 1986-87 and 1987-88, a sum of Rs. 28,925/- was allotted to the Totos. During the course of survey it was found that nothing whatsoever was in existence.

5. Fruit-bearing Plants and Social Forestry

This scheme is successful among the Totos where a beautiful nature encouraged them to, embark upon such an endeavour in their blissful surroundings. Trees, especially arecanuts, were given to them and those are yielding bumper fruits to the Totos.

6. Education

The literacy rate of the Totos was 9.05 in 1989. It changed however due to certain amount of sincere endeavour taken by the voluntary organisations, like Bharat Mahajati Mondoli and the Lutheram World Service initially and, later on by the Tribal Welfare Department. A report (Dhali:1987) reflected that out of 539 persons (227 male and 265 female) only 44 males and 3 females are considered to be literate, calculating 8.17 per cent as literacy. The Christian missionaries up to 1968 encouraged only 7 toto students to be regularly present in school. Later, this number rose to 26 in 1969. The situation began to change for the better again in 1979 when the number increased to 61, Residential quarters were built in Totopara and this enabled the teachers to take interest in the matter of spread of education among the Totos and ultimately this interaction has had a definite impact on the life-style of the said tribe. A few students went out of their narrow environs and at least one passed the Madhyamik Examination. The said missionary organisation also started a Junior High School in 1979. The same report (Dhali) shows that 15 boys and 2 girls were reading in different Secondary classes outside the villages, especially in madarihat and Cooch Bihar. The Junior High School is named Dhanapati Toto Memorial School (1979). The State Government Education Department took over its management in 1982. No

Ashram facilities have been extended for the students of the Junior High School.

Again, in six wards, six adult education centres have been started. Out of these, only 4 centres are running at present, but the attendance of the students in these centres is very irregular. The teacher of the Adult Education Centres are paid Rs.100 per month by the Government Education (Social) Department, West Bengal. In 1982, a Rural Literary Centre was organised at which the people of the locality interact with others. Two Toto boys have been assigned the charge of looking after the literacy work. Here, infrastructures are there, but the lack of initiative on the part of the members is a great malaise which will be apparent even to a casual onlooker. The Ashram Hostel for the Totos has 30 seats, but at, the time of inspection there was only a record of 24, but actually all those were not present. This is meant for the bcy only. There is no Special Superintendent; the Headmaster of the School acts as the Superintendent of the Hostel. He frankly admitted that the amount sanctioned by the government (Rs.100 per month) at that time was so meagre that it could not attract anybody for this job. Besides, the release of the grant is extremely tortuous. Naturally, irregularity prevails. The cook and the lady helper generally look after them as they belong to the same community.

7. Health

We have already dwelt on the background information of this group systematically concerning the nature of their physical setting and the way the facilities have been extended to them, not only through the general welfare work but also after these people were categorised as P.T.G. since 1980-81. In spite of these ameliorative scheme and projects for them, we can categorically say that the attempts to provide good drinking water from masonry wells has not been successful.

The Totos living in the hill slopes could not utilise the water as it is beyond their reach. From the very beginning stage of the welfare work among these groups, many attempts were made by which they could get good drinking water. Many kinds of skin diseases developed by these groups of people were the result of their shabby and unclean habits and the stinks of their body attracts even a casual onlooker to these people. Though there are a series of complaints against the contractors, who were responsible for many ills, as per the Government version, in the matter of supplying good water at the Totopara, nothing could be done to set things right. The Lutheran World Service took initiative to open a Heath Centre at Totopara and they tried to attract the people there to make the fullest use of it.

This depends mostly on the nature of health education imparted to the Totos, and develop a habit of cleanliness, provided plenty of water and clothes are there for them to change and a habit of better maintenance of health through clean atmosphere is imbibed. Due to lack of sufficient water supply, some of the Vector-borne diseases prevail, but these people have their own remedial sorcerer, shaman and priest. But the basic difficulties in respect of health and hygiene are to.

1. provide good drinking water;
2. acquaint them with the Primary Health Centres;
3. acquaint them with the health guides who will take initiative;
4. regular survey and report to the nearby Health Centre.

III

Welfare Programmes for the Lodhas

Some measures were taken for the betterment of the tribals after Independence in various ways. Our state is welfare state and many such projects have been taken in hand by the Government and some voluntary organisations with financial assistance from the former. During the various plan periods thrusts were put on different matters, and attempts were made accordingly to implement them. Again, for the evaluation or rather assessment of the nature of changes some commissions were set up on an all India basis and even some proliferations were made at the State level. However, recommendations were made from time to time to supplement the measures in order to remove constraints, if there be any, in the work. It is true that rehabilitation is regarded as a very important phase of development of the weaker sections. As such, a good number of rehabilitation colonies were started initially with Central Government money; and the State

Government also had initiated it with their scientific procedure. However, it requires more scrutiny before implementation of the scheme for the intended purpose. But so far, it has been observed that most of the rehabilitation colonies set up by the tribals were not properly scrutinised before the plan was drafted. It was implemented either by the Voluntary Organisation on behalf of the Govt. or by the district administrative directly.

In the case of the Lodhas, initially some measures were taken by the Home (Police) Department as the Lodhas were considered to be a 'Criminal Tribe' till the revocation of the C.T. Act in 1952. In Kukai village, under the Police Station of Keshiary, one such attempt was made under the guidance of a social worker named P.C. Midya, who took a keen interest in the matter. As such, a Co-operative was formed and some land as well as agricultural implements and bullocks were purchased to make the Lodhas a 'settled people', and to develop among them a 'sense of belonging'. Rehabilitation of these people not only includes housing facilities, but also other subsidiaries, such as, purchase of bullocks, goats, other implements and seeds along with the purchase of land and their reclamation. This indicates that most of the rehabilitation schemes implemented so far were agriculture-based, whether the people intended to be rehabilitated in an area of good agricultural facilities or were basically agriculture-minded or not. The main object of rehabilitation is to provide the beneficiaries a stable economic background, so that by getting much benefits, they might equate themselves with other more progressive communities of the country, gradually narrowing the economic and social distance which so long prevailed amongst them.

After the rehabilitation schemes were implemented for the tribal groups, a few such rehabilitation colonies for the Lodhas were initiated by some Voluntary Organisations. One such colony was initiated at Auligeria in the Police Station of Jhargram (Medinipur) under the stewardship of late Prof. Priyaranjan Sen, who was the Secretary of the Harijan Sevak Sangha, Bengal Branch. They were to have rehabilitated 46 families with an allocation of Rs.1500/- per family. Facilities were extended to all the families to own a cottage, little land, bullocks etc. Of course, due to the patronage of the then Congress Government, Prof. Sen started a Pre-basic School and a Basic (Primary) School. From different sources, he procured money to construct a link road (non-metalled) from the metalled road (Garh Salboni) or the jungle-covered side and ultimately it touched the village Auligeria, newly named at the time as Satigarh or 'the place of peace'. This village was a seat of the criminals.

Secondly, a full-fledged colony was started at Dhokat-Pukuria under the direct supervision of Bharat Sevashram Sangh, Kolkata. Previously, this forest-covered village was selected by the Swamiji's (monks) to be used as a place for resting. But when the Government, i.e., the Tribal Welfare Department approached to take initiative in a constructive work of rehabilitation, the monks readily agreed to part with it. In the same manner, land purchase, construction of huts, purchase of agricultural implements, seeds etc. were arranged as parts of the programme of welfare work. Thus, it was working well as per direction of the Tribal Welfare Department, and the items which were in existence there were also properly utilised. In course of time, an Ashram hostel for the Lodha boys was started, and later a Primary School. Apparently, the scheme looked as a complete success, but no fundamental change in the life style of the Lodhas could be effected by this. During the Lodha-Santal riot in 1968, four Lodhas of the two Rehabilitation Centres, Santigarh and Dholkat, were victimised by some infuriated groups of the other tribal communities, viz. the Santals and the Mahatos, because of the Lodha's persistent involvement in criminal activities.

In the third phase of rehabilitation, a place was selected at Daharpur, under the P.S. of Narayangarh. Initially 31 families, and later 20 more, were settled there. The responsibility of the work was given to a Voluntary Organisation known as Samaj Sevak Sangha, with which some Social Scientists were associated. Considering the political pressure and other difficulties, the said organisation constituted a Rehabilitation Sub-committee in which they included three Government officials, viz. the B.D.O. of the area, the Special Officer, S.C. and S.T. Department of the district Headquarters and one Asstt. Director from the State Level. This facilitated the change in programme or items which were considered to be expensive and repetitive. More money was spent for the purchase of land, almost all the huts were repaired and about eight huts were newly constructed for those who had no shelter at all. A community hut or dormitory for the bachelors and a social worker-cum-Guest House were also constructed allowing for the facilities of weaving, tailoring etc. along with a small library house. Subsequently, a Junior Basic School was started and the first Ashram hostel for the Junior Lodha boys (up to class V standard) was started sometime in 1964, after the All India Conference of the De-notified Tribes was held in Delhi at the Old Parliament House. Late Lal Bahadur Sastri was the President of the Conference; and the then Prime Minister Pt. Jawaharlal Nehru also attended along the congress President U.N. Dhebar. A sizeable number of anthropologists were also present at the meeting from various parts of the country to discuss the ameliorative measures for these backward classes. As per their decision, the State Govts. were directed to implement the schemes discussed and resolved in the conference.

Again, at Bhumij Dhansol (under Binpur P.S. of Jhargram Sub-Division) another Rehabilitation colony was set up. This was a measure taken to rehabilitate the Lodhas, who were then facing a rough weather due to a communal riot between the Lodhas on one side and the Santals and the Mahatos on another. The entire village was set on fire because of the constant acts of thieving and dacoity which angered the Santals so much that they took a unanimous decision to destroy the Lodha hutments and also attempted to assault them. Ultimately, however, the rehabilitation colony was very much attractive and, as such, the Lodha boys were sent to Daharpur Ashram hostel and for that purpose seats of the Ashram were increased by 10, totalling 30.

Again, sometime in 1974, a village named Chhoto Jhauri, under the Police Station of Gopiballavpur, near the border of Orissa (1½ km away), where more than 22 Lodhas (almost all male persons) were arrested on charge of decoity in some villages. Mr. R.K. Gupta, the then I.G. of Police, West Bengal, took the initiative to rehabilitate them through the Institute of Social Research and Applied Anthropology of which he was the President, Wells were dug, a social worker and a constable, well versed in agriculture and kitchen garden, were put at the centre, and ultimately a good relationship developed among the rural people through socialisation and education. Even to-day no crime has been recorded and no participation of the Lodhas was recorded in mass killing of 1979 at Patina.

This was the nature of rehabilitation programme for the Lodhas, the so-called de-notified tribe. Of course, during the period some provisions were made to accommodate the Lodha children through Ashram Hotels at different Lodha-concentrated areas. The State Government, through district officials, took initiative in the rehabilitation work by providing cottage developing roads, digging well, constructing school buildings here and there, wherever possible. But ultimately most of them ended up in a fiasco they either failed or flopped.

Ultimately, the Lodhas were described as Primitive Tribal Group (PTG) not only in West Bengal but also in Orissa due to constant suggestion made by Professor P.K. Bhowmick. He asserted that the Lodhas have a pre-agricultural economy and less literacy, and as such they require special attention. As the Lodhas were considered PTG, the welfare of this group was undertaken by the Ministry of Welfare (TD). At Jhargram a Lodha cell was constituted in which many more persons (majority belonging to Lodha) were recruited. Through them with the approval of the Zilla Parishad various plans and 'projects were initiated. Somewhere these are apparently successful, whereas in many places these are an absolutely failure. The Central Government undertook an evaluation project not only for the Lodhas but also for all the Primitive Tribal Groups (Toto Birhor, Lodha and Kheria) of West Bengal, and the report is ready for publication. These reflected the wastage of Government money as these were implemented through the Panchayats. And the plans were done by the people who have no idea of planning which is required for this type of people. Besides, there is no Monitoring Cell to promote the welfare activities.

Long ago, Prof. Bhowmick organised a few adult education centres in remote areas of Medinipur and also Khadi work in some villages only to bring the Lodhas in touch with the other groups of people. Dirker, Dihipur, Kadamdiha Sankaridanga, Daharpur are some of the villages which had such work centres.

Ultimately, the then School Board of Medinipur sanctioned these centres as one teacher-Special Cadre Primary Schools. These are located in the Lodha-concentrated areas and these enabled the Lodhas to have a school of their own Provision for Ashram Hostel up to Primary level students was added for the development programme of the Lodhas as they belonged to the de-notified community. Initially provision of financial grants were made under the following heads: (now changed)

1. Construction of building Unit for 20 students Rs. 20,000/-
2. Meal Charges Rs. 40 × 12 × 20'per head
3. Misc. hair-cutting, K. oil. soap etc. Rs. 0.84 paise per head
4. Sports and Games (annually) Rs. 100/-
5. Clothing for one year Rs. 40/- per head
6. Medicine for all Rs. 100/-
7. Agricultural training (one year) Rs. 200/-
8. Workers' wages per year (Rs. 50/- × 12) Rs. 600/-
9. Helpers' wages per year (Rs. 30/- × 12) Rs. 360/-
10. Superintendent's pay per month Rs. 100/-

A sum of Rs. 3000/- was sanctioned for the purchase of utensils blankets etc. for the inmates. These were the monetary provisions for the Ashram Hostels which were set up by the Govt. of India and this type of unit was started in 1964 after the conference held at Delhi for the amelioration of the lot of the Lodhas. In addition, some educational facilities were also extended to them from time to time, as and when situation demanded and Govt. funds were available. All these attempts appear to be of an exploratory nature and it so happened that many more correctional or experimental provisions could have been started accelerate the speed by overcoming the snags of all types. But it did not happen so; nor were they evaluated or alternatives sought for by the Government.

The Lodhas were treated as a criminal tribe before the revocation of the Act in 1952. Naturally many more hostile attitudes of the neighbouring public and administrators were hurled at them. Practically, the Lodhas were never encouraged to get schooling in the pre-independent India. No efforts were made to educate them by anybody and at the same time they were made to educate them by anybody and at the same rime they were reluctant to attend any school. But, after independence, some facilities were extended to them. The mentality of the Lodha children was not to have any schooling even if the school is at a stone's throw from their residence. Besides their parents did not like it too. A thorough survey made in this regard indicates that the literacy rate of the Lodhas in two distinctive zones of Jhargram-Narayangarh-Gopiballavpur-Jamboni and Binpur Blocks it is 0.29 per cent; whereas in the other zone which is more associated with the neighbouring caste Hindu people the literacy rate is 2.59 per cent. This very clearly indicates that interaction with the neighbouring groups prompted them to attain a better literacy rate. But a recent survey indicates a 10.96% literacy rate which shows an increase over the rate shown in Bhowmick's study. This is due to certain factors and steps initiated by the Government.

In this connection, the claim of the Government about the total eradication of illiteracy (in 990-91) will add a new dimension to it. It has been stated that some limited voluntary efforts were made at different Lodha-concentrated zones by a few individuals associated with some Voluntary Organisations. They had practically to steer clear of the difficulties for the spread of education. Along with this an Ashram Hostel Scheme was added after 1964 to many voluntary organisations having Basic Schools. After the CPI(M) came to power the Panchayat authorities were made incharge of welfare activities. The Samaj Sevak Sangha had the privilege of doing welfare work and rehabilitation of the Lodha tribe sometime in 1963-64; and gradually it raised grain-gola and multi-purpose Cooperative Society not only for the benefit of the Lodhas alone but also for the other tribal people of the locality. Naturally, the attempt so far made for their welfare created confidence in the mind of the Lodhas and the people of other tribes. The administrators were very much satisfied with the work at 'Bidisa'. Gradually, a- few more Ashram Hostels were sanctioned to some other organisations, though there was some violation of the principles of sanctioning the Hostel to them, in as much as they had no school under the management of their authorities. Again at Bidisa, the Samaj Sevak Sangha had the advantage of a second Ashram Hostel in 1968 when the Lodha-Santal-Mahato riots broke out and a few Lodhas were killed and their villages set on fire. The then District Magistrate, Medinipur brought 20 Lodha children from the riot-torn areas of Jhagram and requested the authorities to accommodate them, and a separate unit was started to cooperate with the administration in such crucial circumstances, As usual, a sum of Rs.20,000/- only was sanctioned for the Second Unit to construct the building. By this time, a good number of. Ashram Hostels were sanctioned at different Lodha concentrated areas as a routine matter. Particulars of Ashram Hostels are given in Table (A-1).

It may be mentioned here in this connection that most of the Ashram Schools were previously attached to a society having their own schools run by the same management, except at Chaksahapur. The authorities failed when a huge sum of money as allotted to them as this organisation wanted to work for the tribal, economic development. This society was registered and two units of Ashram hostel (boys 30 + 30) were allotted to this organisation. Later on, one unit of Girls' Ashram Hostel was stated for which initially a sum of Rs. 1,21,000/- was sanctioned and this money was misused. As a result the scheme had to be left abandoned for a long time. A further sum was released by the I.T.D.P. and T.W. Department for completion of the work. It was materialised through the Panchayat in 1988; and it is now functioning. Five more Ashram Hostels were started at Nayagram after the mass killing of the Lodhas in 1979.

While assessing the Ashram Hostels different pictures emerge. But 'Bidisa' is a model example by itself, for the authorities here are in a position to run the Hostels independently when grants are released later. Regarding the Pukuria Ashram Hostel run by the Bharat sevashram Sangha, Ramkrishna Sarada Vidyapith (Jhargram) looked after by the Ramakrishna Mission and one Kharikamathani Girls' High School was allotted one unit of Girls' Hostel, the authorities perform their work very satisfactorily Another Bidisa-trained Lodha boy is in charge of Krishna Rakshit Chak Ashram Hostel (1980); his personal endeavours and initiatives in this regard are praiseworthy. The post-riot recommendation for the spread of education among the Lodhas at Singdui is almost a flop. Similar is the case of Raiberia Hostel. Nobody was present at the time of inspection. This indicates that nobody really looks after it, so it is almost defunct. During the visit of the survey team, the Hostels under the Samaj Sevak Sangha, Bharat Sevashram Sangha, Ramkrishna Sarda Viyapith and Kharikamathani Girls' School were found on the rails and moving. Krishna Rakshit Chak showed an attendance of 22 students, Badalpur (Sabong) had only 7 out of 20 and Pathardahra 12 (as it was closed for a long time). At the time of a second visit of the team to the campus, the Superin-charge of the Chaksahapur group of hostels (3 units having 100 seats) confessed that very recently the Panchayat received a partly sum as grant, just to keep the pot boiling and hence the forlorn condition. They did not give out the details as per advice of Panchayat. Satsol P.S. reflects a gloomy picture. It is run by the local Panchayat. They have been allotted 30 students, but the figure never goes beyond 14 or 15. Of course, practical difficulties are there and it is what it should be under the circumstances. At the time of visit to Chaksahapur where two units for boys (30 and 30) Hostels were sanctioned only 41 students were found and 27 girls were shown out of the sanctioned quota of 40. Sanction of one unit after another is due to the efforts of Sri Prahlad Bhakta who is an employee of the I.T..D.O. and it was he who managed to get these units sanctioned on the priority of ethnic claim.

Again, to guild up a campus just for keeping the Lodha students in a blissful setting for their psycho-emotional problems a huge sum was allotted by the Central Government but the entire money was diverted to five Secondary Schools in different areas of the Lodha belt recommended (1987) by the Zilla Parishad.

1. Ektal D.M.High School, (Jhargram) for 20 students
2. Baligeria S.C.High School, (Nayagram) for 40 students
3. Gokulpur High school, (Medinipur) for 40 students
4. Santrapur High School, (Keshiary) for 40 students
5. Narayangarh High School, (Narayangarh) for 40 students

An inspecting team met the teaching staff and enquired about the Lodha students reading in these schools. At almost all the Places, the buildings were found under construction (1990) or about to be completed. Ektal School showed a register containing names of the Lodha boys and they expected to make up the lee-way existing till that tie. Baligetia High School had a roll strength of the Lodha students (24), and other students will be accommodated in due course as and when the building is completed. The Gokulpur High School had yet to see their buildings completed and the teacher-in charge claims that they will get Lodha boys here. Similar is also the case with the school at Santrapur under Keshiary P.S. Narayangarh High School has been given one unit of Lodha Hostel of 40 students, but is being used for other purposes and the state of the Hostel at this place is in complete disarray. This is mostly due to the influence of the local political party which got these sanctioned.

Allotments for the spread of education (1988-89), for both the Lodha and the Kheria/Kharia students, in the following schools/places have been earmarked by the ITDP.

1. Ujan High School Pingal for 30 Lodha boys (Primary) — Rs. 1,50,000/-
2. Chaksahapur Debra Unit 4 for 30 girls (91-92) — Rs. 1,50,000/-
3. Dubra High School, Jamboni 30 Lodha boys Primary (90-91) — Rs. 1,50,000/-
4. Sevayatan Jhargram for 30 for boys (90-91) — Rs. 1,50,000/-
5. Ramakrishna Sarada Vidyapith Jhargram 2nd units 30 girls Lodha of all classes (88-89) — Rs. 1,56,000/-
6. Udalchua, Binpur II or 30 Kharia boys (88-89) — Rs. 1.00,000/-
7. Silda Girls High School for 30 Kheria girls Primary level (88-89) — Rs. 1,30,000/-

In this connection, a series of complaints against the Chaksahapur organisation having groups of hostels for the Lodhas, both boys and girls were submitted to all the responsible authorities, including the Sabhadhipati. In consequence, the grant was withheld temporarily and the tragedy of tragedies is that it has been released without a thorough probe on a later date. They have 100 students (boys 60, girls 40), and then another girls unit of 30 students was sanctioned (1991). Their performance is not at all satisfactory and an investigation into the matter is a crying need to investigate how the Hostels are being sanctioned and why the grants are being released. All the time the Panchayat or the organisation in charge of running the hostels has actually no schools under their management and the progress claimed by them is yet to be proved. It is said that Sri Bhakta, an ITDP employee got two schemes for fishery and dairy with large amounts, but the schemes are a complete failure. It is said that while sanction for the first girls Ashram hostel was made, the money was diverted by the organiser to the purchase of a truck for business with a claim to build up asset. The Govt. took action and a fresh grant was released to complete the first girls unit (40) by the Project Office.

Due to the change of Government, a new political climate started blowing and in the panchayat - based society, many things have been, and are being, done through the Sabhadhipati (President of the Zilla Parishad) and the Advisory Committee meant for the tribals. Inspite of all these attempts the actual progress is to be properly assessed. But constant killings of the Lodhas during this time has actually left a blot on the Indian democracy, and the remedial measures suggested on this regard are very expensive and quite fruitless.

Year	*Location*	*Lodha victims*	*Persons blamed*
1961	Dhanghari/Dhansola P.S. Binpur	1 (entire village were set on fire)	Santal, Mahato, Bhumij
1968	Jhargram P.S.	5 (18 villages were set on fire)	Santal
1979	Patina, Naagram P.S.	(19 killed a few All deformed & mutilated)	tribes and castes
1981	Ganua P.S. Narayangarh	(8 killed, a 12 deformed & mutilated)	Local people of all castes
1982	Ninuntegeria P.S., Jhargram	(2 killed, a few deformed & mutilated)	Local people Santal
1984	Soro, Bagjhapa	(6 killed)	Local People
1986	Keshiary & Kharagpur	(4 Killed)	Local people
1989	Pingla	(many deformed and mutilated)	

TABLE A1
ASHRAM HOSTELS

Sl. No.	Name and Particulars	Meant for and Quota	Rs. Sanctioned
1.	Daharpur, Unit 1, Samaj Sewak Sangha Narayangarh-1964	Boys : 30	Rs. 20,000/-
2.	Badalpur Ashram Hostel Unit l, Sabong-1966	Boys : 20	Rs. 20,000/-
3.	Pukuria Ashram Hostel Bharat Sevashram Sangha Jhargrama - 1966	Boys : 25	Rs. 25,000/-
4.	Chaksahapur Ashram Hostel Unit 1, Debra-1976	Boys : 25	Rs. 20,000/-
5.	Daharpur Samaj Sevak Unit 11, - 1968	Boys : 30	Rs. 20,000/-
6.	Badalpur, Unit 11,	Boys : Secondary level (Lodha and other tribes)	
7.	Chaksahapur Unit 11, Debra - 1989	Boys : 30	No grant for construction
8.	Krishnarakshitchak Ashram Hostel, Kharagpur-1980	Boys : 30	Rs. 50,000/-
9.	Satsol Ashram Keshiary - 1980	Boys : 20	Rs. 50,000/-
10.	Singdui Ashram Nayagram - 1980	Boys : 20	Rs. 50,000/-
11.	Pathardahara Nayagram - 1980	Boys : 20	Rs. 50,000/-
12.	Raiberia, Nayagram - 1980	Boys : 20	Rs. 50,000/-
13.	Chandabila, Nayagram - 1980	Boys : 20	Rs. 50,000/-
1.	Daharpur Samaj Sevak Sangha, Narayagarh-1970	Girls : 20	Rs. 20,000/-
2.	Chaksahapur, Debra, Unit 3 - 1984	Girls : 40	Rs. 1,21,000/-
3.	Kharikamathani, Nayagram - 1980	Girls : 30	Rs. 50,000/-
4.	Ramakrishna Sarada Hostel, Jhargram-1980	Girls : 30	Rs. 1,56,000/-
5.	Chaksahapur - 1991, Unit-4	Girls : 30	Rs. 1,50,000/-

It is needless to consider the situation more critically taking into account the cultural background on the one hand and the formulation of the welfare programmes and their implementation on the other. With such a backdrop a critical analysis of the culture of the Lodha is needed in order to examine how far this group is in a position to receive the assistance and utilise it fruitfully. The nature of welfare activities leading to development and for minimising the prevailing social and economic distances should be considered objectively. But it appears that the inadequacies of the implementing authority and of the programmes together give a gloomy picture of the total development scenario. Lack of experience and a kid-gloves attitude of the planners are responsible. For reaching at the root of the tribes cultural constraints no positive breakthrough could be made in the matter; no perceptible dent could also be made to fathom the depth of the existing pnenuries of the people. The plans already made in this regard are faulty, misdirected and so they failed to bring about any perceptible change in the life of these luckless people of the Lodha tribe. It requires the ability to use a new technology to be implemented by dedicated workers along with the introduction of a sound and fruitful education system suited to their needs.

IV

Welfare Programmes for the Chenchus

Culture of a particular community of a specific region changes appreciably due to various factors at work of which Development undertaken by them or introduced by other agencies, at different stages, are most important. This is generally a long historical process and takes a long time to bring about an overall change in the existing conventional cultural patterns, as well as the values and concepts of a particular society, Such changes are largely influenced by the input of the supervisor cultures of the neighbouring communities, in general, absorb consciously or subconsciously in course of time. As the Chenchus are treated as one of the most primitive tribal groups, many welfare measures have been undertaken for them by the Government in order to effect an accelerated development. It has been observed that such welfare activities among the Chenchus were given priority since the pre-independence period by two different administrations, e.g., the British Administration in the Nallamali Region, i.e., erstwhile Madras Presidency and the Nizam Administration Telengana in the Plateau of Amrabad in Hyderabad state. It is to be mentioned that the former welfare scheme was implemented by the Forest Department and the latter by the Tribal Welfare Department, for which the experience and services of

Prof. Haimendorf was utilised. He served the Nizam as an Advisor for sometime for dealing with the tribals living in Hyderabad. An attempt has been made in this section to discuss the impact of such welfare measures on the traditional life-style of the Chenchus.

The Chenchus villages situated in Nallemalai region of Kurnool and Prakasam districts were treated as 'Reserve Forest villages' and were placed under the control of the Forest Department for administration purposes. The welfare of the Chenchus of Nallamali was a major concern of the Forest Conservation Laws of 1860 and the encroachment of the plains living agricultural population resulted in curtailment of their area of peregrination and subsistence of these foodgathering people. However, certain rights were granted to them in Section 26 of the Madras Forest Act, 1885 permitting the tribals to free grazing of cattle in the forest areas, utilisation of bamboo for house construction etc.

Various Welfare Schemes framed and implemented by the Forest Department, from time to time, with a view to wean them away from their nomadic foodgathering life, by way of settling them in larger and planned habitation areas and providing them the benefits of various welfare measures, such as giving land for cultivation, plough, bullocks etc. as also the right to use all minor forest products for domestic purposes, as well as for sale. Taking advantage of the permission to collect certain specified forest products for use and sale by the Chenchus and their ignorance, a large number of private traders used to purchase these at a throw-away price from them, mainly by the tactics of advancing them loans in times of distress and thus winning their sympathy, thereby denying them the benefits of this concession, in addition to the loss of income by the Forest Department as a result of granting this concession, for which it had to stop the annual auctions of logs and trees. Thus, deprived of its income, the Forest Department waived the permission given to the Chenchus for collection and sale of minor forest products in 1883.

Since the initiation of the Planning Era, it was not until the 2nd Fifth Year Plan that the Government of India sanctioned a scheme of 'Land colonization of Chenchus' at Byrlwti and Nagaluty gwdems. as centrally sponsored projects. Under this projects a

Co-operative Land Colonization Scheme was started in March, 1957 for settling 100 households by providing them the following amenities:

1. Reclamation of 500 acres of land for cultivation purpose, providing 4 acres of dry land and 1 acre of wet land per family.
2. Irrigation facilities
3. Construction of huts
4. Purchase of plough and bullock at the rate of 1 pair per family.
5. Supply of agricultural implements
6. Supply of improved seeds
7. Sinking of wells
8. Common civic amenities
9. Construction of staff quarters

The society started functioning with 40 members on the roll, with a share capital of Rs. 5/- per member. A senior co-operative Inspector from the Co-operative Department was placed in charge of the society under the general guidance of a Board of Directors consisting of 7 members, including the Deputy Tehsildar, Atmakur, Forest Range Office of Byrluti. Agricultural Demonstrator of Atmakur and four Chenchus non-official members.

During 1959-60 an area of 150 acres of land was made fit for cultivation and the society itself took up cultivation as the Chenchus were not willing to cultivate the lands individually. Initially 72 acres of land was brought under cultivation and it suffered, a loss of Rs. 5,279/- as against the investment of Rs. 543,200. During 1960-61, too, land was disturbed to the members of the colony. But the response was again poor due to lack of technical know-how, for settled cultivation. Again, the society took up the cultivation and incurred heavy loss. From them onwards, the society caused to function and the land was left for cultivation to the Chenchus themselves. But majority of them leased out their land to the plain cultivators of the nearby villages.

The causes for the failure of this scheme were as follows:

1. As the Chenchu-economy was forest-oriented for ages, they did not acquire the skill or aptitude towards cultivation.

2. There is another important factor, which was neglected by the officials while planning and implementing the programme. Chenchus mostly earn their livelihood by the wages earned through working in bamboo and timber couples and forest plantations. When they do not get work in the coupes, they go in for collection of roots and tubers, while interviewing the Chenchus to take up individual cultivation, the officials did not provide any means of subsistence to the tribals, who were compelled to bestow their time and energy continuously for two or three months for ploughing, sowing and harvesting. So, they left this job.
3. There was a long-standing revelry between the two groups of Chenchus belonging to Nagaluty and Byrluti gwdims, who were inducted into the scheme as beneficiaries. Lack of social cohension among the people in the colony and the failure on the part of the officials to create strong leadership contributed to some extent to the failure of the programme.
4. 100 huts were constructed - 50 at Nagabuty gwdem and 50 at Byrbluty gwdem, under the programme. The pattern of streets and the design of the huts in the colony were decided upon by the administrators. The pattern of huts was not compatible with the traditional value-system of the people and the ecological conditions of the region. With the result the Chenchus did not accept. So all the families deserted the huts within a short space of time and constructed their traditional type of huts very near the colony.
5. Weeding operation in the fields compelled them to forego all wage-bound employments elsewhere, which they would have secured during the period. So, they did not show any inclination towards cultivation which they did not know, as failure of crops would have thrown them into the jaws of virtual starvation.
6. Even after the society took up cultivation, it was alleged that it did not employ any Chenchus labourers out the agricultural operations on the ground that they were in experienced an, at the same time, demanded advance

payment as their wages. Instead labourers were drafted from the neighbouring villages in the plains, thus bearing all opportunities before the Chenchus to learn the methods of cultivation. This has induced them not to take up cultivation during the subsequent years.

7. There was a tank called 'Gosaikatta' in the colony for providing irrigation water into the adjoining farm lands. It was silted and needed re-excavation. The society did not do this work.

For this Chenchus living in Telengana region of the erst while Nizam's Domination, Prof. Haimendorf, the then Adviser to Nizam's Government on Backward classes and Tribal groups evolved a special programmes for their development after conducting a study into the life and problems of the Chenchus, as part of a larger programme for the development of back-ward and tribal groups of the region. In the former Hyderabad State, secured Schemes were introduced to settle the Chenchus as cultivators of land. In 1942 sincere efforts were made to improve the education and economic standards of the jungle (forest-dwelling) Chenchus. In the same year, the Nizam's Government created a 'Chenchus Reserve Settlement' and certain ameliorative schemes were started for the benefit of the Chenchus living on the Northern side of the river Krishna. An area of 7,56,000 acres was declared as the 'Chenchus/Reserve'. They were permitted to hunt and collect forest products. No outsider was allowed to settle in the 'Chenchus Reserve'. They were permitted to hunt and collect forest products. No outsider was allowed to settle in the 'Chenchus Reserve'. A schedule of wages was fixed for the Chenchus working under the Forest Contractors. A provision was also made for rendering them medical facilities Employment rules were also relaxed to appoint Chenchus in the forest department (Plan for development of chenchus 1976:40). An area of 6,000 acres was earmarked as 'Chenchus reserve' in upper plateau of Amrabad region. Other than chenchus was not allowed to settle in this reserved area and no money lender was allowed to do his business in the 'Reserve'. Within this demarcated area, the Chenchus were allowed to cultivate their lands, free of any revenue. The Chenchus colony at Mannanoor was established with an agricultural farm, a co-operative society, a school and a Rural Dispensary. Under this scheme, 262 acres of land was given to 19 Chenchus families for collective farming. Another Chenchus colony at Vatwarlapalli, located at a distance of 18 miles gron Mannanoor was established in the year 1951-52 for the Chenchus living in the jungles. 800 acres of land was earmarked for the rehabilitation of Chenchus. But in these Chenchus colonies, several non-tribal had settled and garbled the land from the tribal people. In former days, Chenchus cleared jungles at Vatwarlapalli colony at the rate of 5 acres for each family. But later on, local non-tribal groups burnt the houses of the Chenchus and drove them away.

In view of the limited financial resources and the scattered distribution of the population, it was not possible to have a separate Administrative unit for implementation of these programmes. So, to reduce administrative 'overheads', the existing administrative machinery is utilised for implementation of these programmes. The Integrated Tribal Development Agency was established during 1975-76 with its headquarters at Hyderabad. The Director of Tribal welfare has been nominated as Ex. Officio-Chairman and one of the officers of Tribal Research Institute was nominated as Ex-officio project officer and subsequently, the joint director, Tribal welfare has been nominated as Ex-officio project officer at the project level. An advisory committee has been constituted with the Director of Tribal Welfare as Chairman, The committee consists of heads of various departments or their representatives as members to advise the project authority on formulation of various programmes institutional locations etc. within the project area. As the intended beneficiaries are scattered over six districts (Kurnool, Prakasam, Mahbubnagar, Guntur, Nalgonda, Rangareddi) and local needs and problems vary, a district level sub-committee was also constituted in each district. The committee consists of the collector as Ex. officio chairman and the conservator of forest concerned. District level officers, the District Tribal Welfare Officer, Social Welfare Officer (concerned with tribal welfare schemes), the concerned Members of Parliament/Legislative Assemblys the Chenchus leader of the area and the project officer. This committee formulates and implements the programmes within the broad framework of the fixed Chenchu action plan.

The programme is implemented exclusively with the funds made available from Special Central Assistance. These development programmes from Special Central Assistance. These development programmes are being implemented by the Assistant Project Officers with the concurrence of the Collectors of the Projects.

It was felt that the Chenchu can be developed economically only when they were settled permanently at a particular place. Earlier, efforts in this regard were made by the Nizam government in Amrabad plateau and by the former Madras Government in Nallamalal Range of Kurnool district by bringing the Chenchus who were scattered occur small gwdems across a wide area, into some re-grouped centres like Mannanoor, Vetawarlapalli, Byrluti, etc. were educational institutions and basic amenities like wells for providing drinking water, housing colonies etc. were made available to make the Chenchus depend on a steady and assured source of income, it was planned to teach them agriculture, and accordingly land reclamation, supply of plough, bullocks and milch-animals were provided. However, the Chenchus, who lacked the tradition of cultivation were not able to adapt themselves with the simple methods techniques of cultivation. Ultimately, these schemes seems to be failures. Cultivation done without proper initiative and interest, coupled with lack of irrigation facilities and pest control means, resulted in very poor yield and forced the Chenchus top revert to collection of forest product for subsistence. Thus, the lands which were reserved for the Chenchus and were reclaimed at huge costs lay barren. Some non-tribals were brought to teach the Chenchus the art of cultivation, who subsequently encroached upon their lands at secular places. Even the Chenchus living outside the forest area did not derive the benefits of agricultural development programmes, as they are mostly landless and sparsely distributed in the interior areas. Though the Chenchus were not able to take up agriculture by using plough, bullocks etc. they are used to raising food crops suitable to their environment using the traditional digging sticks. Since time immemorial, every chenchu clears a patch of land around his hut and dilable it with a digging stick to plant seeds and their personnel consumption. The plots are marked and guarded by fencing them with bamboo wattle walls.

In pursuance of tribal development policy adopted during the Fifth Year Plan, an Integrated Tribal Development Agency for (Primitive Tribes) Chenchus was established during the year 1975-76 for implementing intensive and systematic developmental programmes for the benefit of Chenchus.

A state level committee with director of tribal welfare as chairperson, representatives of state level developmental departments as members and project officer as member secretary was constituted to formulate broad policies for implementation of development programmes in six identified districts. In order to implement the various programmes formulated for promoting accelerated development of Chenchus the ITDA for primitive tribes (chenchus) was shifted from State headquarters to Srisailam, the central place of Chenchu habitat. This agency has been implementing poverty alleviation schemes for Chenchus in all the six districts viz. Kurnool, Prakasam, Guntur, Mahbubnagar, Nalgonda and Rangareddi with 80 per cent subsidy (both central assistance and state plan funds) and 20 per cent Margin money from A.P. Scheduled Tribes Co-operative Finance Corporation. In deserving cases cent percent subsidy is also allowed in case margin money is not available. In addition to special central assistance, state plan funds. T.S.P. and D.R.D.A. funds are also utilised in order to cover more number of Chenchu families.

During Fifth Five Year Plan period (1975-76 to 1979-80) an amount of Rs. 43,500 lakhs was allotted to six identified for implementation of schemes for welfare of Chenchus. Approximately more than 6,000 Chenchus were benefited. In the sixth plan period, an amount of Rs. 50,690 lakhs was allotted and this amount was incurred for the development of 5,160 Chenchus. The average expenditure per beneficiary during V and VI Five Year Plans were Rs. 691.40 and Rs. 982.36 respectively. This investment for each family under poverty alleviation programme should not be less than Rs. 10,000/-. During VII Five Year Plan, an amount of Rs. 428.77 lakhs was allotted out of which an amount of Rs. 340.406 lakhs was spent and 9,473 families were assisted to cross the poverty line. The average expenditure for each beneficiary is not sufficient to create durable and immovable assets capable of improving the conditions Chenchus families. Unlike all other developmental activities among Scheduled Tribes, the subsidy pattern for primitive tribal groups is different. In implementation of schemes under poverty alleviation programmes, cent percent subsidy is granted to Chenchu families as no other financial institutions are coming forward to advance loans. Further only very few branches of nationalised banks are located in tribal areas. From establishment of I.T.D.A. for Chenchus, altogether an amount of Rs. 427,791 lakhs was spent in project area on various schemes for the benefit of 20,910 persons. The emphasis on poverty alleviation started from middle of Sixth Plan only and hence the per beneficiary expenditure increased from Rs. 982.36 to 4,000/- at the end of VII Five Year Plan.

Some of the important schemes with wide range programmes implemented for the development of Chenchus are as follows:

1. *Land based programme.*
   (a) Assignment of Govt. waste lands b. Cultivation of lands in earmarked 'Chenchu Enclosures'
   (b) Purchase of private land for distribution to landless Chenchus
   (c) Supply of plough bullocks and agricultural implements, bullock carts and supply of seeds, fertilizers and pesticides.

2. *Minor Irrigation*

Provision of bore wells and open wells, energisetion of irrigation wells and supply of oil engines and electric motors.

3. *Animal husbandry*
   (a) Supply of milch animals and sheep/goat units
   (b) Pig rearing
   (c) Calf rearing

4. *Fisheries*
   (a) Fish ponds
   (b) Supply of boats and nets to Chenchus living at Dam sites

5. *Training Programmes.*
   (a) Farmers training programmes to chenchus
   (b) Training in tailoring, embroidery and plastic wire baskets, toys etc. and leaf plate making

(c) Training programme in light motor vehicle driving
(d) Training in Typewriting and computer operations

6. Schemes under I.S.B. Sector

The Chenchus entrepreneurs are sanctioned the following schemes:

(a) Kirana shops
(b) Beedi and cigarette bunks
(c) Tea stalls
(d) Sweet meet shop
(e) Soda shops
(f) Cycle rickshaws
(g) Cycle shops
(h) Coconut selling shops at temples
(i) Preparation of rose water shops
(j) Vegetable vending
(k) Small cloth shops
(l) Supply of carpentry & blacksmithy equipment
(m) Fancy shops etc.
(n) Tailoring
(o) Lime kilm
(p) Supply of mike sets

7. Medical and Health services

(a) Conducting periodical medical camps in Chenchu settlements
(b) Immunization programme
(c) T.B. Beruming and treatment
(d) Malaria treatment
(e) Chlorination of drinking water wel^ls in Chenchu gudems
(f) Drinking water supply
(g) Digging of bore wells
(h) Digging of open wells

The Chenchus living in Vikarabad division of Ranga Reddy district were rehabilitated in full fledged housing colonies. Permanent houses were provided, land were either purchased or government lands were assigned. Plough bullocks were supplied. All other agricultural inputs were supplied at the beginning of the settlement. For such colonies with minimum 40 Chenchu families were rehabilitated in each colony. The Chenchus who were earlier subsisting largely by eating tuburs roots, jungle fruits of as agricultural labour are now able to produce foodgrains for themselves. They are also rearing milch cattle and selling milk. Housing colonies and land assignment programmes have proved a success among Chenchus of Rangareddi district. From inception of I.T.D.A. from 1975-76 till 1989-90 an amount of Rs. 46,498 lakhs was incurred for the benefit of 1069 Chenchus.

The Chenchus in Mahbubnagar district are living in 199 villages. They are provided with irrigation wells, electric motors oil engines in addition to plough bullocks and carts. Lands from private owners were purchased and assigned to landless Chenchus. Permanent housing colonies were constructed at Jangareddipalli, Chenchugudem, Vatawarlapalli etc., Several Houses constructed at Vatawarlapalli are collapsing and Chenchus have to construct that houses by the side of dilapidated houses. The housing scheme at chenchugudem, Jangareddipalli is successful. Some of the Chenchus contributed and constructed good permanent houses. Under individual business and industrial ventures, Kirana shops, mini flour mills and cranes were stones normally while digging wells. The Chenchu beneficiary gets hire charges of Rs. 50/- to Rs. 70/- per day. An amount of Rs. 128.946 lakhs was allotted from inception of project till the end of VII Five Year Plan out of which an amount of Rs. 106.012 lakhs was spent in order to assist 4071 Chenchu beneficiaries to improve their economic conditions.

Chenchus in Prakasam district are mostly living in and around nallamali forest ranges spread over, mainly in former Yerragondapalem. Markapur and Giddlur taluks. Schemes like supply of plough bullocks, carts, irrigation wells, electric motor/ oil engines, sheep units were implemented. In Garapenta village alone, 22 oil engines were supplied and oil of them are utlising the oil engines and cultivating their lands with irrigation facilities. Irrigation wells are also taken up on large scale in Marripalem, Chintala villages. Chenchu farmers are taking up commercial crops like groundnut, chillies etc. An amount of Rs. 107.401 was incurred from 1976 to 1990 (till March) for various developmental activities and family oriented schemes.

The Chenchus living in Kurnool district especially at Bairluti,

Nagaluti, Narapareddikunta Ahobilam etc. have been cultivating forest lands leased out to them. The plough bullocks, carts sheep units, cows were supplied with a view to reform he Chenchus indulging in robbery and thefts. A housing colony for 45 Chenchu families was constructed at Panyam village near Nandyal, Kurnool district. In addition to a semi-permanent house, one poultry unit of 200 birds was also provided to each family. The women folk were taught to weave the mats. The bore wells are dug at bairluti is brought under cultivation. Government are taking various steps to assign government lands to chenchus in the proximity of forest area. An amount of Rs. 80,738 lakhs was allotted from Fifth Plan period till the end of Seventh Plan; out of this amount, Rs. 65,148 lakhs was spent for the benefit of 3439 chenchus. The Chenchu settlements are some of them are also found living under the trees. The housing problem is very acute in pilgrim and tourist centres like Srisailam; Ahobilam. The chenchus in the past not holy places in nallamali hills but they protected temples and shrines. But Chenchus are totally replaced and displaced in their habitat. The pilgrims are provided all the facilities but local Chenchus are deprived of the basic facilities. Chenchus of Srisailam town have been demanding for permanent housing scheme but this scheme is not yet implemented even though temple authorities have earmarked land in the western part (Mekala banda area).

There are 41 Chenchu settlements spread in Veldurthi, Macherla and Duri 'Mandals of Guntur district. Two Chenchu villages, i.e., Jandapenta and Batakulapai are situated in Tiger Sanctuary of Nallamali hills and rest are outside Tiger Project. A permanent housing colony was constructed at Bellamkondavaripalem and 75 Chenchu families living at different places were settled. The Chenchus living in Chinaparla paya (75 families), Sivalingapuram (25 families), Yerrabalam (15 families) were assigned 5 acres of land to each family and they have been cultivating commercial crops like cotton, groundnut, chillies etc., like any other plain area farmers. It is difficult to distinguish Chenchu farmer and other non-tribal farmers. Bore wells and Electric motors are provided to progressive farmers and they have asking for power sprayers to progressive farmers and they have asking for power sprayers to protect their crops from pests. There is great demand for assignment of land to landless agricultural labourers belonging to Chenchus.

It is significant to note that total allotment of Rs. 43, 400 lakhs during Fifth Five Year Plan increased to Rs. 428.877 lakhs, nearly 10 times, by the end of Seventh Five Year Plan. The investment for development of Chenchus has been multiplied at Tribal Welfare Department, Government of Andhra Pradesh has been allotting substantial amount from its plan budget in addition to Special Central Assistance in view of destitute conditions of Chenchus.

The achievements under various scheme in six districts for the years 1985-86 to 1989-90 are furnished in Annexure VIII. An amount of Rs. 340.406 lakhs was spent for the benefit of 9473 Chenchus. The young Chenchus are being encouraged to take up business ventures like starting of flour mills, fair price shops, fishing with improved equipment. It is observed in the field that Chenchu benefits are able to utilise properly the inputs given to them and getting extra income.

Literacy levels and educational attainment of Chenchus is extremely low. The percentage of literacy among Chenchus is only 5.9 per cent as per 1961 Census reports and it increased to 6.59 per cent according to 1971 Census reports. During the entire decade, the literacy has not increased even by one percent. There is marked increased from 5.59 per cent to 9.73 per cent as per 1981 Census reports but this is still extremely low when compared to State literacy levels of general population. There are no Chenchu candidates who passed Matriculation as per 1961 reports. The female literates constitute roughly one third increased. There are no Chenchu candidates who passed Matriculation as per 1961 reports. The female literates constitute roughly one third increased. There are 21 male and 2 female matriculates and two graduates in six project districts. Chenchu candidates who studied Matric and above more that doubled among males and increase five fold among females. But during entire decade only one became graduate. Altogether there are three graduates, one each in Kurnool, Prakasam and Mahbubnagar districts. It is gratifying to note that there are two female graduates in Kurnool district but no other district in the project area produced female graduates. This trend indicates that most of the candidates are stopping with matriculation and seeking jobs and they are also not aspiring to go to professional courses. Only one candidate from Kurnool district belonging to Chenchu tribe studied M.B.B.S. and working as Physician in Kurnool district and another candidate from mahaboobnagar became Ayurvedic doctor and working as Vaid in Ayurvedic dispensary in Mahaboobnagar district. In Guntur, Nalgonda and Rangareddi districts, there are no graduates at all. Female matriculates are nil in these three districts. There was only one male matriculate as per 1961 Census reports in Kurnool districts but after two decades, there are 45 male candidates and 11 femàle candidates who studied matriculation and above but below graduation. This increase who has greater awareness about importance of Education among Chenchus. Improvement in educational levels are also due to introduction of various schemes especially starting of number of Ashram Schools, hostels in Chenchus are as.

After recognition of Chenchus as Primitive Tribal Group, number of Ashram Schools, hostels and Residential schools were established. The tribal welfare department has been running 43 Ashram schools with total strength of 266 in the project area. All these Ashram schools are located in Chenchu area and most of the children belong to Chenchu tribe only. Similarly, 18 hostels are being run where there are high schools in the vicinity of chenchu habitat. Four prestigious Residential Schools exclusively for chenchu children are established in central places in the Chenchu habitat. Approximately, an amount of Rs., 1 crore is being spent towards construction of school buildings, dormitories, teachers quarters etc. in an area of 20 to 30 acres of land. Quality education is being imparted though these institutions. There are approximately 1200 candidates mostly belonging to Chenchu tribe studying from Class III to Class X. Within a decade, all these special institutions established during V, VI and VII Five Year Plan periods will certainly produce more educated Chenchu children an properly motivate them to go to professional courses like medicine and Engineering.

In order to further boost up literacy levels of Scheduled Tribes to State and National standards, State Government have started a crash educational programme during 1985-86 in the Tribal sub-plan areas of the state. All the school less tribal habitations were identified after field survey and Government established 2,090 single teacher schools in the entire suit-plan area of the state. The educational qualifications for teachers and norms for establishment of schools were also relaxed. All the teacher posts are reserved to local tribals under the provisions of the V Schedule of the Constitution so as to teach tribal children in their own mother tongue in first two classes. This scheme also aimed at creating more job opportunities to educated youth who could not continue their studies further. On the same analogy, 40 single teacher schools were established in school less Chenchu habitate in different districts of project area during 1988-89 and all the posts of 60 teachers are filled in by candidates belonging to Chenchu educated youth who failed or passed matriculation. Another 46 posts were also created during 1989-90 and Chenchu candidates were appointed in Ashram schools and single teacher schools. Orientation Training Courses are organised in teaching methodology before they are posted as teachers. It is proposed to depute them to regular training course for one year to the Teacher Training Centres established exclusively for training Scheduled Tribe candidates. The main aim of this scheme of recruiting local tribal candidates as teachers is to really make the teachers as relations, friends, philosophers and guides to local tribals. As chenchus are at subsistence level of economy the parent take all the children into the forest while engaged in collection of gum and other minor forest produce. The children assist the parents in collection of not only minor forest produce, but also edible roots, tubers and fruits. During entire season of availability of various kinds of minor forest produce, Chenchu families live in the forest without any kind of basic facilities. The children are exposed to all kinds of hardships and minimum basic facilities are not available to them. They are exposed to unhygienic conditions and malnutrition. It is unfortunate that integrated child development scheme is not extended in this food gathering and hunting tribe. There is urgent need to extend this scheme before much damage is done to health and nutrition conditions of Chenchus and their children.

In view of extremely low literacy levels and heavy drop out rate among girls, it is essential to establish atleast one Residential high school exclusively for Chenchu girls in Srisailam and one Residential Junior College at Dornala, Prakasam District.

Wild Life Sanctuary and Chenchus

The Nagarjuna Sagar, Srisailam Sanctuary (Tiger Project) spreads in Guntur, Prakasam, Kurnool, Mahbubnagar and Nalgonda districts and boundaries of this sanctuary are more or less co-terminus with the traditional habitat of Chenchus. The total project area is 3568.00 sq.kms. and there are 124 villages located in the sanctuary area. Out of these 124 villages, 24 villages are situated in the core area of the project consisting of 432 Chenchu families with more than 2,000 population. The total cultivated area in the sanctuary is 12,457.50 acres, out of which, 1,478 acres of land is situated in the core area of the project. This land is cultivated by Chenchus and by few other Scheduled Tribes and some of the Chenchus are having pattas (legal titles) to these lands. All kinds of activities are prohibited by Forest Department under the provisions of Wild Life Protection Act of 1972. The Forest Development as well as the Tribal Welfare Department stopped all kinds of developmental activities within the core area. The Chenchus who were living in the core area are not rehabitated. In the past, Forest department used to employ them for bamboo and wood cutting and pay them wages. But presently all kinds of exploitation of forest resources are stopped and consequently Chenchus are denied of their daily wages.

Chenchus earn substantial amounts by sale of minor forest produce like honey, gum, broom sticks, myrabolams, chirongi (Buchanania latifolia) Mohua flowers (Bassia latifolia). Adda leaves (Bahaunia Vahuli), Abnus (Diospyrs Melanoxylon), Tamarind, Medicinal roots and plants etc. Presently, they are afraid of going to interior forest because of wills animals like Tiger Bears etc. The plough bullocks and other livestock supplied by Tribal Welfare Department are falling a prey to the wild animals. The Chenchus are not getting proper compensation. Human beings killed or mauled by carnivores within the core are of the Tiger project are not adequately compensated either. Even though this projects was introduced in 1981 under Wild Life (Protection) Act, 1971, so far no rehabilitation programmes for Chenchus living in the core area of the project are taken up. Wild Life Protection, afforestation schemes are essential but lives of human beings living in these habitate are more important and precious.

The details of deaths, injuries to both beings and animals upto June 1990 are as follows:

1. Number of human deaths.	:	5
2. Number of human being injured	:	13
3. Number of domestic animals killed	:	408

In case of death of human beings, the maximum limit of compensation is upto Rs. 5000/-. The victims are eligible for compensation if the attack is outside the core area only. The victims are eligible for half compensation if the attack is outside the core area but within the sanctuary limits. In addition to above compensation, the injured persons are paid Rs. 10/- per day during period of hospitalisation for maximum period of 50 days in addition to cost of medicines, treatment, travel subject to maximum of Rs. 200/-. As Chenchus have been living in the Nallamali hills from time immemorial before introduction of forest conservancy act and wild life act and some of the Chenchus are also having *patta lands* within the core area, some of the restrictions have to be relaxed in case of Chenchus who larger subsist by food gathering and collection of minor forest produce.

The present rates of compensation are extremely low. The rate of compensation should be enhanced to Rs. 2000/- in case of death caused by carnivores. The forest department has to pay minimum Rs. 50/- per day to injured during hospitalisation in addition to the total cost of medicines and treatment. An immediate relief or Rs. 500/- may be paid in all cases of injury to meet medical expenses which may be deducted later from total amount of exgratia.

It is observed that cases of T.B. among the Chenchus have been on increase after introduction of sanctuary. Earlier Chenchus hunt small game like rabbits, wild fowls etc. But all kinds of hunting are prohibited. The bowls and arrows are confiscated from them. They are denied of proteins in their-diet and consequently they are suffering from diseases. The project officer of I.T.D.A. for Chenchus has been organising medical camps to treat specially T.B. patients. Confiscation of bows and arrows from food gathering tribe not only deprived them of their important food but also rendered them helpless when wild animals or thieves attack them.

Sri Varadarja Swamy project, a medium irrigation project has been taken up for construction on Munimadugulavagu, a tributary to river Bhavanasi which is in turn a tributary, to River Krishna. Before completion of the construction of a dam, Chenchus of Pacheruvugudem were shifted in the month of December, 1985. Out of 181 families in this village, 132 belong the Chenchus. An housing colony was constructed at Kottalacheruvu village in Atmakur Mandal of Kurnool district. The authorities have promised assignment of 5 acres of developed lands to outsets. But till the end of 1990, only 2 to 3 acres of developed lands was assigned and these lands are yet to be developed. The Chenchus and other uprooted families are not provided adequate means of livelihood. The local Chenchus reported that the medium irrigation project authorities have into employed any Chenchu person even as unskilled labourer. The project authorities have not taken care to provide employment, at least to one member in each family, threatened by submersion. The Chenchu families at rehabilitation centre are going to their original place of habitation (Pecheruvu) and collecting gum, minor forest produce and another edible fruits and tubers. Some of them are again temporarily residing in the old place during season of collection of gum. It is very difficult to cut their invisible bonds of territorial affiliations with ancestral lands. Even though Chenchus were brought to new place more than four years back, they were not properly rehabilitated. Unless Kottalacheruvu rehabilitation centre is developed as model colony, with all basic facilities and assured means of livelihood, it would be difficult to persuade Chenchus of core area to come out voluntarily to settle down in the rehabilitation centres on the periphery of Tiger Sanctuary. Efforts should be taken to create original habitual environment at new place of settlement.

The tribal families who mainly depend upon sale of minor forest produce have to be imparted scientific skills in collection of forest produce and processing. It is observed that gum yielding tree species are becoming extinct because of unscientific methods of cutting the bark of trees for gum production. They are not able to get adequate returns for their labour. Simple and appropriate technology has to be introduced in preparing leaf cups, plates, deseeding of tamarind basket making processing of various herbal medicines. The local Chenchus have to be involved in regeneration and afforestation scheme. The minor forest produce yielding and edible tubers, roots, rhyzomes have to be extensively propagated in afforestation programmes. These species should become renewable and regular source of income and food till the Chenchus become progressive cultivators.

Housing Programme and Land Assignment

As Chenchus are emerging from their 'primitive' enclaves, permanent housing programmes coupled with assignment of cultivable or developed lands are essential programmes of action. These programme are successful in Ranga Reddy district but same schemes are not properly implemented in Mahbubnagar, Kurnool, and Prakasam districts. The housing scheme implemented in plain are as where land is scarce, is implemented in stereotyped manner in tribal areas where land is abundantly available. The limited land of 100 to 150 square yards assigned for house sites in plain areas is also earmarked to tribals. The stereotyped single room housing pattern is also being implemented in Chenchu villages. The permanent houses constructed for Chenchus at Vatawarlapalli village of Mahaboobnagar and Bairlutigudem of Kurnool district are almost reject by Chenchus. Few houses constructed at Vatawarlapalli have already collapsed. They constructed their own traditional houses by the side of these so called permanent houses because of poor standards of construction. The new houses have become permanent liabilities. They require sufficient space for keeping their cattle, goats, fodder etc. Each family should be provided atleast minimum 1000 square yards keeping in view the present as well as future needs of each tribal family. The place, design, material structure of the houses may be taken in consolation with local Chenchus. Each family has to the provided minimum 3 to 5 acres of land. The programmes of rehabilitation of Chenchus who are displaced due to wild life sanctuary or irrigation projects should be very comprehensive and acceptable to the beneficiaries.

TABLE
PRIMITIVE TRIBAL GROUPS AND THEIR POPULATION IN FROM 1961 TO 1991

(Figures in actual)

Sl. No.	*States/UTs*	*Name of PTG*	*Population in*			
			1961	*1971*	*1981*	*1991*
(1)	*(2)*	*(3)*	*(4)*	*(5)*	*(6)*	*(7)*
1.	Andhra Pradesh	1. Chenchu	17609	24178	28434	40869
		2. Bodo Gadaba	21840	25108	27732	33127
		3. Gutob Gadaba				
		4. Dongria Khond	21754	34382	39408	66629
		5. Kuttia Khond				
		6. Kolam	16731	26498	21842	41254
		7. Konda Reddi	35439	42777	54685	76391
		8. Kondasavara	-	28189	-	-
		9. Bondo Porja				
		10. Khond Porja	9350	12347	16479	24154
		11. Parengiperja				
		12. Thoti	546	1785	1388	3654
		Total	**123269**	**195264**	**189968**	**286078**
2.	Bihar	13. Asur	5819	7026	7783	9623
		14. Birhor	2438	3464	4377	8083
		15. Birjia	4029	3628	4057	6191
		16. Hill Kharia	108983	127002	141771	151634
		17. Korwa	21162	18717	21940	24871
		18. Mal Paharia	45423	48636	79322	86790
		19. Parhaiya	12268	14651	24012	30421
		20. Sauria Paharia	55606	59047	39269	48761
		21. Savar	1561	3548	3014	4264
		Total	**257289**	**285719**	**325545**	**370638**
3.	Gujarat	22. Kolgha	-	29464	62232	82679
		23. Kathodi	-	2939	2546	4773
		24. Kotwalia	-	12902	17759	19569
		25. Padhar	-	4758	10587	15896

(1)	(2)	(3)	(4)	(5)	(6)	(7)
		26. Siddi	-	4482	5429	6336
		Total		**54545**	**98553**	**129253**
4.	Karna-taka	27. Jenu Kuruba	3623	6656	34747	29371
		28. Koraga	6382	7620	15146	16322
		Total	**10005**	**14276**	**49893**	**45693**
5.	Kerala	29. Cholanaikayan	-	306	234	-
		30. Kadar	-	1120	1503	2021
		31. Kattunayakan	-	5565	8803	12155
		32. Koraga	-	1200	1098	1651
		33. Kurumba	-	1319	1283	1820
		Total	-	**9510**	**12921**	**17647**
6.	Madhya Pradesh	34. Abujhmaria	11115	13000	15500	-
		35. Baiga	-	6194	248949	317549
		36. Bharia	-	1589	1614	-
		37. Birhor	513	738	561	2206
		38. Hill Korwa	23606	67000	19041	-
		39. Kamar	-	13600	17517	20565
		40. Sahariya	174320	207174	261816	332748
		Total	**209554**	**309295**	**564998**	**673068**
7.	Mahara-shtra	41. Katkari/Kathodi	-	146785	174602	202203
		42. Kolam	-	56061	118073	147843
		43. Maria Gond	-	53400	66750	-
		Total	-	**256246**	**359425**	**350046**
8.	Manipur	44. Maram Naga	-	5123	6544	9592
9.	Orissa	45. Chuktia Bhunjia	-	-	-	-
		46. Birhor	-	248	142	825
		47. Bondo	-	3870	5895	7315
		48. Didayi	-	3055	1978	5471
		49. Dongria-Khond	-	2676	6067	-
		50. Juang	-	3181	30876	35665
		51. Kharia	-	1259	1259	-
		52. Kutia Khond	-	3016	4735	-

(1)	(2)	(3)	(4)	(5)	(6)	(7)
		53. Lanjia Saura	-	4223	8421	-
		54. Lodha	-	1598	5100	7458
		55. Mankirdia	-	133	1005	1491
		56. Paudi Bhuyan	-	4424	8872	-
		57. Saura	-	2845	2917	-
		Total	-	**30528**	**77267**	**58225**
10.	Rajasthan	58. Seharia	23125	26796	40945	59810
11.	Tamil Nadu	59. Irular	79835	89025	105757	138827
		60. Kattunayakan	6459	5042	26383	42761
		61. Kota	833	1188	604	752
		62. Kurumba	1174	2754	4354	4768
		63. Paniyan	4779	6093	6393	7124
		64. Toda	714	930	875	1100
		Total	**93794**	**105032**	**144366**	**195332**
12.	Tripura	65. Riang	56597	64722	84004	111606
13.	Uttar Pradesh	66. Buksa	-	-	31807	34621
		67. Raji	-	-	1087	1728
		Total	-	-	**32894**	**36349**
14.	West Bengal	68. Birhor	-	-	658	855
		69. Lodha	-	45906	53718	68095
		70. Toto	-	-	675	-
		Total	-	**45906**	**55051**	**68950**
15.	A&N Islands	71. Great Andamanese	-	-	42	32
		72. Jarawa	-	-	31	89
		73. Onge	-	-	97	101
		74. Sentinelese	-	-	-	24
		75. Shompen	71	212	223	131
		Total	**71**	**212**	**393**	**377**
	All India	**Grand Total**	**773704**	**1403174**	**2042767**	**2412664**

Source: Census of India, 1961, 1971, 1981 & 1991.

Concentration of Tribal Population (1991)

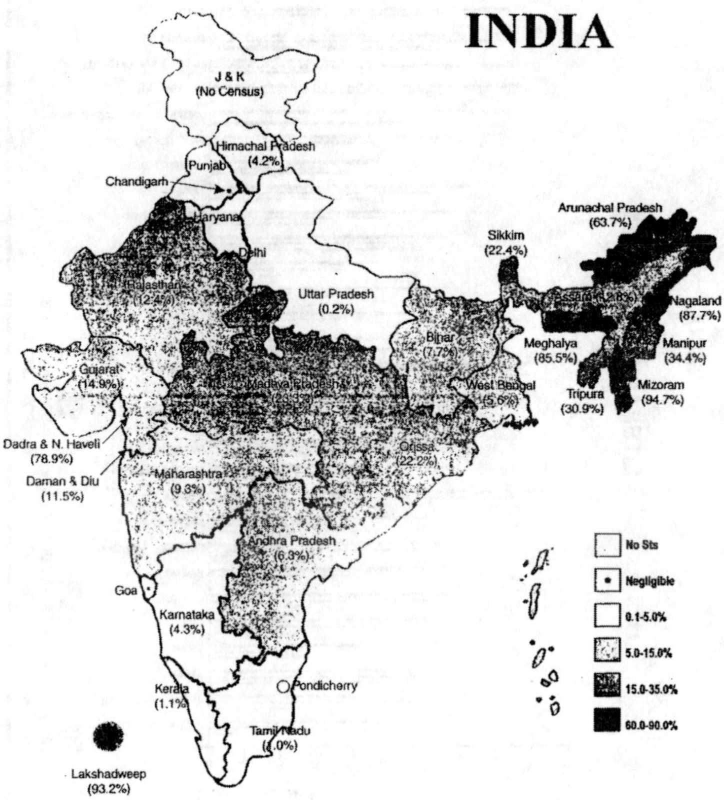

Source: ***Planning Commission (Backward Classes and Tribal Development Division)***
Government of India, New Delhi - 110020

INDIA

LITERACY RATES, 1991

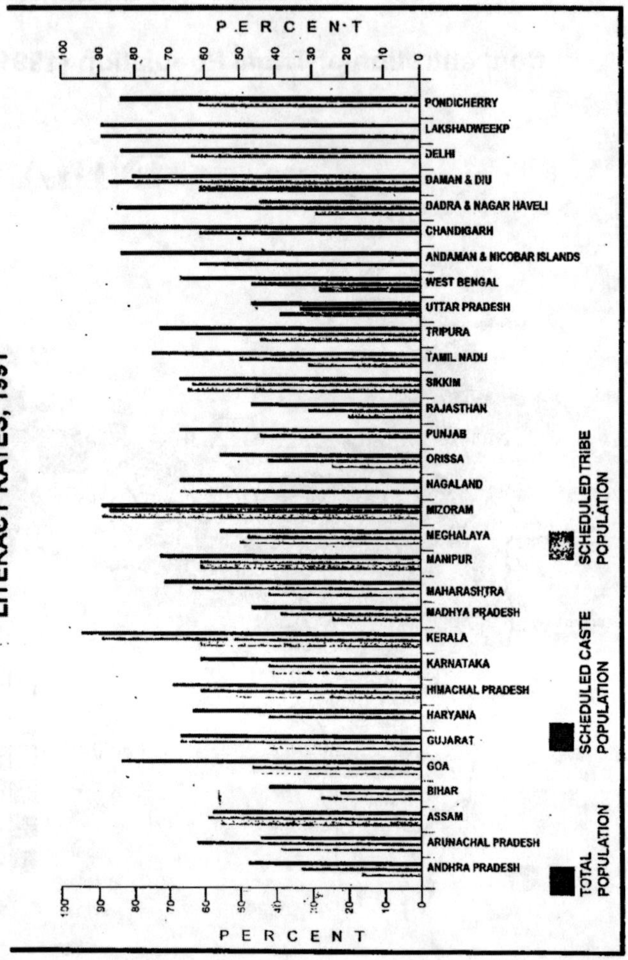

Sex Ratio (1961-1991)

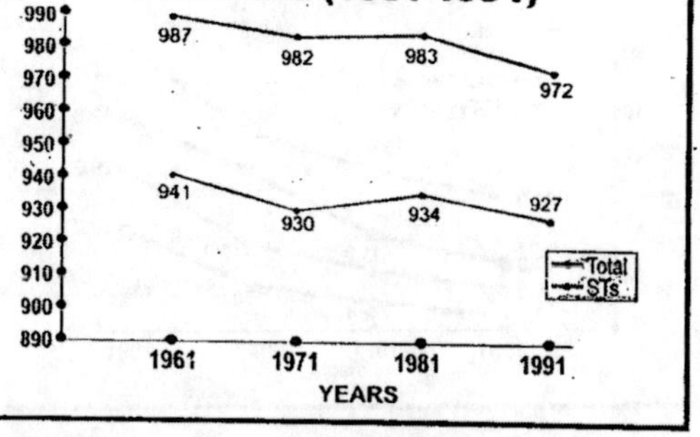

Work Participation Rate (1961-1991)

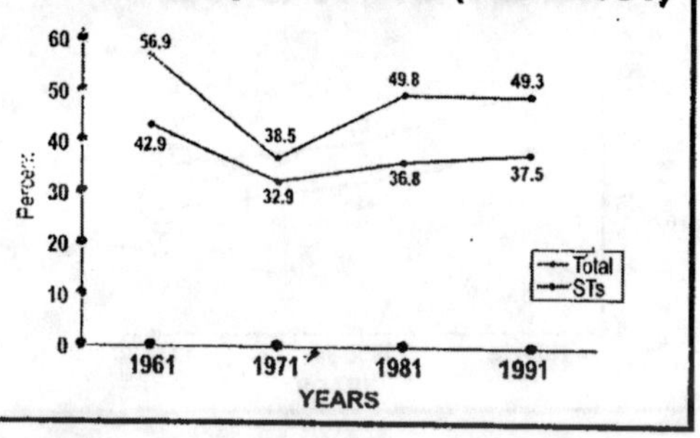

Displacement of Tribals (1951-1990)

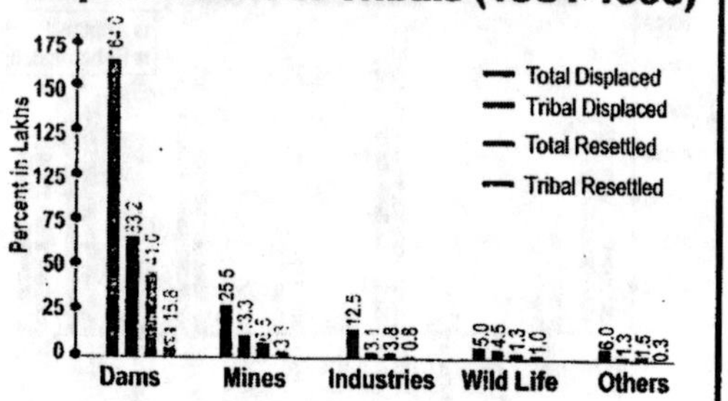

Source: Ministry of Rural Development, Government of India

Literacy Rate (1961-1991)

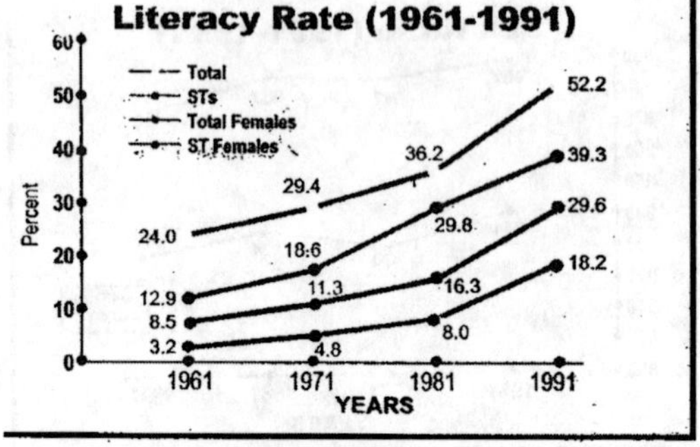

Below Poverty Line (Rural : 1977-78 to 1993-94)

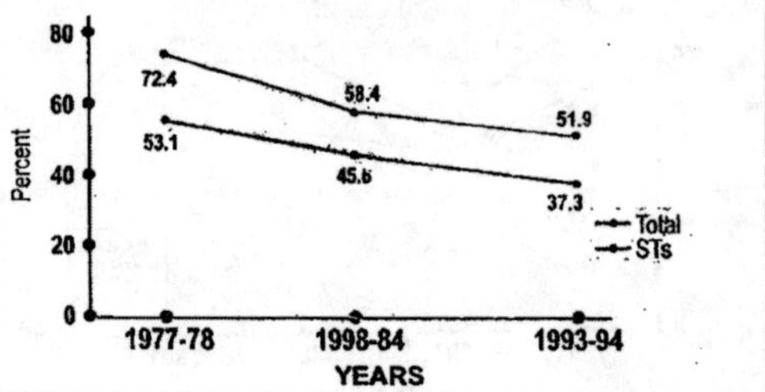

Bonded Labour (1993)*

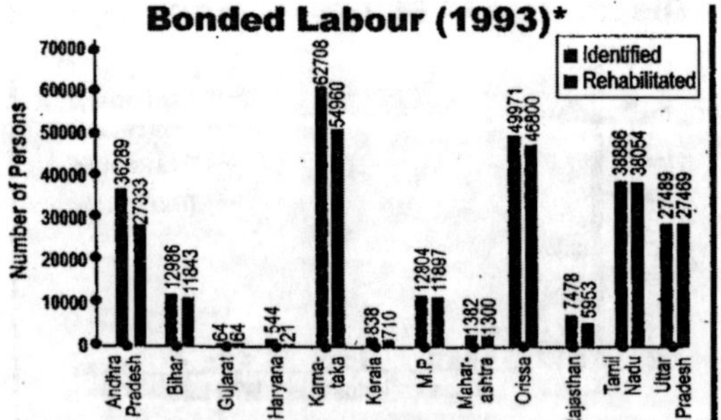

** STs are estimated to be around 25% of the cases reported*

Source: Report of the Working Group on STs of the Ninth Plan (1972-2002)

Seven

Conclusion: Transformations and Change

Considering the nature of welfare or development programmes with reference to the Totos, the Lodhas and the Chenchus, a conclusion can be drawn in this section through analysing the various impacts which are responsible for bringing about socio-economic transformation leading to development and change. Before.we discuss transformation and change of the selected tribal communities, let us have a clear-cut meaning of the term and its importance in the real context.

The unfolding dialects of world history is now entering its most comprehensive and perhaps most problematic phase. The phase in which the so-called peripheries of the country's political structure and responding to the concepts of self-determination, self-reliance and sovereignty of peoples which the leaders of ruling party need proclaimed but which they themselves superficially ignored the forces of change. They are doing this with all the available resources and skills at their command. It is a phase in which the social structure of the existing societies were being deeply established, with the poor and the oppressed both rising in revolt and also being controlled by the state apparatus. It is a phase in which the struggle for human rights was drawing upon the deeper springs of identity and authenticity, against domination and alienation and for human and cultural dignity. It is a phase in which the conflict between tradition and modernity, primitivism and settled agriculture was being turned upside down.

The basic import of the word 'development' is a process which means movement from one condition towards another, a process of gradual unfolding or 'growth' or state of 'advancement'. It sums up and designates the most important aspects of change concerning the 'well-being' or 'uplift' of the people in general, and it ensures stability-cum-comfort in their living processes. Undoubtedly, developments an active policy which refers to 'mature economy' and 'self-sustaining growth' and the related action pattern will no doubt generate an increased productivity which, in course of time, will improve the quality of life, namely, elevating the people from poverty to prosperity and opening up more employment opportunities.

It is a patent fact that primitivism persists side by side as an adjunct to modern society. Thus most of the Primitive Tribal Groups categorised as such have till date the archaic style of living in spite of the respective welfare projects pursued for their benefits by the Government since Independence. Accordingly, successful evaluations of the conditions of the tribal communities of our country made by many teams of experts, though their observations and suggestions convey that they are at the 'lowest rung' of the societal ladder even among the tribal groups, and therefore they deserve special attention, still some sort of a process of transformation has been observed due to launching of the many more welfare programmes.

As these selected tribal communities are primitive tribal communities, initially the rehabilitation schemes includes the housing facilities; but other facilities such as purchase of bullocks, goats, other implements and seeds along with the purchase of land and their reclamation have to be provided. The main object or rehabilitation is to provide the beneficiaries a stable economic background, so that by getting such benefits they might equate themselves with other more progressive communities of the country, gradually narrowing the economic and social distances so long prevailing amongst them. With the passage of time no doubt the process of transformation has been notices, but that is not permanent in nature. That may be due to the faulty approach of the government; but the people's cultural attitude also acts as a barrier. The Chenchus living in Vikarabad division of Rangareddi district were rehabilitated in full-fledged housing colonies. The same was done in the case of the Toto at Totopara of Jalpaiguri district and the Lodhas at Daharpur and Pukuria of Medinipur district. For all the cases permanent houses were provided. Lands were either purchased or Government lands were assigned. The plough and bullock inputs were supplied at the beginning of the settlement.

With the process of literacy campaign and the introduction of other educational programmes these communities are gradually becoming literate. With the introduction of Ashram school for these tribal communities a new healthy environment is being offered to these communities to change their mental outlook. Though the result is not so satisfactory it cannot be denied that the signs of change are at the process.

A good number of voluntary organisations are doing good work for these tribal communities in their respective areas. With their active involvement these communities are showing their interest in keeping themselves in a healthy and hygienic atmosphere and also doing well economically by raising their yearly income out of income-generating programmes.

Now-a-days, these communities are becoming too much politically conscious which is quite visible in the case of the Lodhas and the Totos in the State of West Bengal. And in the case of the Chenchus of Andhra Pradesh also this type of change has been noticed due to influence of the naxalite movement.

Finally, it can be said that any development programme can bring some sort of transformation with a variance degree. But it is also true that for bringing transformation the total responsibility does not lie either with the government machinery or with the voluntary organisations. The communities, for whom this socio-economic transformation is necessary concerned should be more conscious for themselves. Then the process of transformation will be much more easier, otherwise it will a very difficult task for any change-agents.

As the present study is not a fact-finding one, it attempts to find out the various factors responsible for greater participation and involvement of the selected tribal communities. On the contrary, it further tries to find out the factors which are not that much conducive to generate the participation process among the tribal communities towards development programmes. Whatever policy recommendation has been made in the following pages will be going waste or will remain on paper only unless the government shown keen interest to make the people more participatory in nature. With this in view, a few development strategies can be suggested which have he derived from this study:

(a) People's participation can be ensured while selecting the right beneficiaries by providing them the scheme they feed necessary.
(b) For the sake of spending money on fulfilling the government target in a haphazard way the scheme should not be provided.
(c) While formulating the scheme by an method the beneficiaries concerned should be allowed to propose their own choice of scheme which will be helpful to them while implementing the scheme to get a good return.
(d) To make the people's level of participation and involvement in a most effective way the government officials as well as the panchayat functionaries should monitor and evaluate all programmes.
(e) The people can be more participatory in nature provided they receive their project amount in time without any delay.
(f) The needed scheme can be provided to the beneficiaries of different blocks by taking into consideration the available raw materials along with basic infrastructural facilities.
(g) The total cost of the scheme can be enhanced from time to time as per the present market value.
(h) A line of development cadre can be built up within the Panchayati Raj system to make the people aware of the different schemes. The present CPI (M) - dominated government on the democratic basses ignore these factors.
(i) Government officials of the development department concerned should ensure joint responsibility by taking other functionaries from Banks, Schools, Health centres and Voluntary organisations into confidence to have awareness camps in different villages to highlight the need and importance of participation to make the programme a successful and realistic one.

Eight

Suggestions & Recommendations

The earlier chapter attempted to explore the different development programmes and their impact on the selected primitive tribal communities, with reference to the Totos, the Lodhas and the Chenchus for their overall socio-economic transformation. Inspite of various plan programmes and projects taken up by the Government machinery, Panchayati Raj Institutions and Voluntary organisations the transformation process is not satisfactory causing lack of qualitative development, even though from the Government's point of view, the programme is successful. This is due to faulty schemes and half hearted support of the people in this programme. Constitutional provisions and various development strategies during the development plan period from the very beginning of the First Five Year Plan to the Eighth Five Year Plant clearly indicate the action pattern of the welfare state of India but some mention may be made here about the term 'welfare' and 'developments'. The following points are important in this respect:

(a) For the socio-economic development of the tribal communities, especially the tribe mentioned above, a number of development programmes through different developmental agencies have been introduced in order to bring up the backward communities on a par with the mainstream of the society. Consequently, we have agricultural development programme, Animal husbandry programme, Rural cottage industries programme etc. in respect of inputs for the basic infrastructural facilities of the tribals. But the investigation made in this project reveals that these ameliorative measures have not yielded the desired result. This is due to the people's lack of participation and the development functionaries, failed to make the people more participatory in nature.

(b) The majority of the tribal communities depends on agriculture. Naturally, emphasis has been laid on it in various plans and programmes. In most cases, however, it has been found that this programme could not evoke satisfactory response, though in some cases the people responded to it rather nicely. Therefore, we get a mixed kind of reaction.

(c) Besides agriculture there are other programmes too. These are animal husbandry, rural cottage industry programmes etc. Here also the picture is by and large the same indicating an unequal degree of success.

(d) If we look back to our plan documents it will be seen that the government is spending a lot of money for the uplift of the tribal communities. In reality, however, the output is very meagre. This is due to the government's faulty approach towards their development and also for giving wrong priorities to the schemes for their benefits. Lastly, the apathetic attitude of the different tribal communities towards the various tribal development programmes and also the hegation of the socio-cultural-political aspects are further constraints for implementation of the programmes.

(e) A good number of voluntary organisations are carrying out various developmental work about the tribal communities, with their limited financial resource among the tribal communities. In this connection, the benefits produced by two - the government agency and the voluntary organisation in the task of involving the tribal communities in the involvement and participatory process, major keys for the success of the development programme, if much better than that of the Government, inspite of their constraints. The Seventh Five Year Plan recommended that a considerable amount of the development programmes would be implemented by different voluntary organisation in the country and the same recommendation is being carried out in the Eighth Five Year Plan also.

(f) From the very beginning of the community development programme it has been emphasized that people's participation is a must to make any development programme a successful one. But from the present study it has been found that mostly the development programmes remain only 'Government's programme' rather than 'people's programme. It has been observed also that during the course of investigation the term participation is restricted here only by saying "I do, you participate" by allotting the scheme which are not at all need-based or by releasing the project amount not fully but some portion of that only.

(g) To make the participation process an institutionalised one, obviously one can say that the Panchayati Raj institution is an effective mechanism through which the participatory process will be more meaningfully and more realistically achieved. The present study is the context of West Bengal state with reference to Medinipur district, where Panchayati Raj institution is very much effective due to strong political will-force, reveals that the participation process of the tribal communities, expected to be more effective but in reality is not satisfactory at all.

The above points suggest the formulation of the following need-based policy recommendations for a better realization of tribal development in the study area with reference to the nature of their participation and involvement.

Recommendation Agricultural Development

The economic pursuit of most of the tribals is agriculture. Agriculture and allied activities constitute the mainstay of their livelihood. To make the fullest use of the agricultural assistance given to them the following recommendation are made for tribal people:

(a) Though the sizable tribal area received fairly good rainfall the run-off losses are very high on account of the undulation topography, and as a result, low production. Soil conservation in this regard with an effective water management system can be introduced.

(b) With the introduction of a better water management system the land can be brought under double and multiple cropping system.

(c) For its effective utilisation the people can be imparted the skill formulation training.

(d) Field demonstration should be arranged by introducing the simplest method of extension technique, which will be helpful for the tribals to gather different technical know how about agriculture.

(e) To make co-operative institutions, mainly LAMPS, stronger by which the tribal people will get assistance financially as well as by selling their products in the market through these institutions in order to get rid of the wily middlemen.

(f) The agricultural department should organise a tribal cell to monitor the progress of programmes in the tribal areas through the joint process of participation.

Recommendations for Animal Husbandry and Livestock Development

Though in tribal villages the major thrust of the economy is in agriculture their income may also be supplemented by cattle rearing including the rearing of small animals like goats and seep. This programme will benefit the scheduled tribes considerably. Under the family-based programme milk-cattle, goats, sheep and pigs were made available by the government. The tribal sub-plan discussions reveal that there was only a partial success in such attempts. This has been due to following reasons:

(a) Regarding the supply of milk-cattle under animal husbandry programme the tribals were unable to get substantial benefits out of it owing to their inability to feed the cattle properly. In a few cases the supplied cattle quickly changed hands illegally for money without any supervision either by government functionaries or by panchayat officials.

(b) This scheme was in general most liked by the scheduled tribes because it increased their family income and helped them when they were in pecuniary difficulty.

(c) As regards the supply of animals malpractices in the matter of selection of right type of animals and also in fixing their reasonable price were reported. Therefore, necessary steps may be taken when the beneficiaries are invited to purchase the animals from the market in the presence of the livestock officer and panchayat members. During survey it was observed that the livestock officer and panchayat members concerned failed to fulfil their normal duties by maintaining their day-to-day official records without going deep into the matter.

In order to minimise the existing inadequacies the following recommendations are made:

(a) The first and foremost need at present is to strengthen the animal husbandry sector for meeting the needs of the tribals.

(b) Any varieties of goats, cows, pigs, can be supplied to the tribals only after assuring medical aids.

(c) With the help of veterinary centres proper health measures are to be taken to check the epidemic or such animals. In this connection mobile veterinary services can be provided in each of the blocks.

(d) Proper marketing facilities should be arranged through co-operatives so that the exploitation by the middlemen can be effectively stopped.

(e) The tribal should be motivated to rear the supplied animals in a scientific way.

(f) Pastureland should be so organised that it can supply the optimum amount of fodder in each block area.

Recommendation for Forest Development Programme

Land and forest are the twin economic sources of the tribal communities. Tribals living in and around the forests should, therefore, be allowed to utilise them to the fullest extent. Naturally the forest department in collaboration with the tribal welfare department should observe certain major objectives for the growth of the tribal economy. For the development of the forest a few recommendations are given below:

(a) There should be a close link-up the forest policy and

programmes on the one hand, and the tribal and other forest-dependent communities on the other.

(b) There should be more concession for the tribals for making use of the forest for fuel, fodder requirements of small timber etc. for house-building and also for the supply of agricultural implements more liberally through the forest participatory management process.

(c) Some schemes like crafts and village-based industries connected with forest and forest produce should be given top-most priority.

(d) Social forestry should be encouraged in such a manner that the tribal people themselves feel enthused to grow the species of the trees and plants relevant to their needs, like food, fodder, fuel, fibre, timber etc. in and around tribal villages.

(e) Keeping in view the ecological balance increased forest production is necessary. The local tribal community which has a symbiotic relationship with the forest should be accepted as partner in local forestry development programme.

Recommendations for Cottage/Small-scale/Households Industries

The location of the major industries of the country will continue to be guided by overall national interest. Similarly, greater attention should be paid to the development of households industries in the area where these people, by virtue of their traditional skill, can develop their own small-scale industries and crafts. The following recommendations are made for this sector:

(a) There should be provision for imparting training to the local artisan in various ways.

(b) Marketing facilities should be arranged in such a manner that the tribal people without the help of middle-men can sell their products.

(c) There should be enough supply of raw material to the tribals to encourage them to develop their own skills and industries.

(d) Encouragement should be given to develop forest-based industries, like:

(i) Beekeeping and honey extraction
(ii) Collection of leaves and leaf-plate-making
(iii) Collection of Tendu leaves and biri-making and marketing the same.
(iv) Babui grass, bamboo and cane crafts
(v) Carpentry and wood craft
(vi) Extraction of fibre from different sources

Recommendations for Basic Infrastructure and Facilities

To carry out any development activities, there is an urgent need of extending basic infrastructural facilities like roads, transport, irrigation, health, education and other recreational facilities. Here a few recommendations are made as follows.

(a) To make the production system full-proof, the infrastructural needs of the industrial unit irrespective of their size should be met. Power supply, supply of water, provision for transport, marketing and financial aid in time, should be handled by proper authorities.
(b) Provision of field canals to carry for the purpose of irrigation should be made.
(c) Proper location of wells, tube-wells, pumps and other sources of water supply will have to be made in such a way that parity can be maintained among the different tribal groups of people.
(d) Communication net-work in terms of approachable roads to the nearest block office to be extended to the inaccessible tribal pockets.
(e) A source of potable drinking water within a distance of one kilometer of the tribal habitation should be made available.
(f) Efforts should be made to arrange power supply in such a way that wherever the tribal communities need it most for small or minor irrigation purposes, or for the group of artisan of tribal communities for production, it should be made available to them there.
(g) The most important aspect of the education system is to bring down to a minimum the drop-out rate among students in order to utilise the existing facilities to the maximum possible extent.

(h) More job-oriented education should be introduced in the field of maintenance of rural tools and power machinery, scooter repairing, carpentry, printing press etc.

(i) Existing health facilities should be strengthened in terms of delivering the health facilities to the door step of the tribal people.

(j) Mobile camp should be introduced for providing medical facilities to the tribals in the inner countryside where the communication system is very unsatisfactory.

(k) The tribal research institute should encourage the local tribal youth clubs to initiate different cultural activities like drama, music, dance, printing etc. to preserve their individual culture which may be helpful to bring them together more closely.

Recommendations for People's Participation

The main concern for tribal development appears to be oriented towards bridging the gap between tribals and non-tribals, so that the former can become partners in the new productive processes and development programmes. Development of the tribal population should receive special attention as their problems are different from those of the other backward communities. Accordingly, since independence and especially during the plan are the task of overall development of the tribal people was given utmost importance. Plan provisions for the welfare of the tribals were made, either directly by the central government which sanctioned funds of by the state government which spends money for their amelioration. Accordingly, many more schemes were introduced and executed through different government machinery as well as numerous voluntary organisations. The beneficiaries of any welfare administration should not merely be 'receivers' with government taking up the role of the 'giver', but should actively associate themselves in the project administration. The Panchayati Raj institution, the autonomous development authorities in the tribal region, the project implementation advisory committee at various levels with tribal representation have all been some of the ways of associating the tribal people in the tribal development administration. Though attempts have been made in this direction, the result is not that much satisfactory. Here a few recommendations are being proposed to strengthen the participation process for the overall success of tribal development.

(a) Before the formulation of any scheme a thorough survey about the socio-economic, cultural and political factors of different tribal communities has to be undertaken.

(b) Different communities having their different occupational pattern and cultural set-up, require community-based development or family benefits scheme.

(c) While formulating a scheme for any tribal community the tribal communities concerned should be involved actively.

(d) A need-based and family-oriented scheme should be introduced.

(e) Before implementing any scheme technical possibilities and other possible infrastructural facilities should be examined.

(f) Wherever in this region there is concentration of the Lodha and Kora families there should be provision for diverting of Jawahar Rojgar Yojna funds. The qualitative aspect of the unit of any scheme should be checked and verified while monitoring the scheme either by the beneficiary themselves or by the Panchayat officials or by government officials so that solution can be offered on the spot.

(g) Opinions of different voluntary organisations and other research institutes at the time of formulation of the scheme should be obtained.

(h) While implementing the scheme by the communities concerned the implementing agency should supervise the work periodically so that the qualitative aspect of any scheme can be checked and verified.

(i) The beneficiaries concerned should be made aware of the need and importance of monitoring and evaluation from time to time either in the Panchayat office or in the Block development office.

Recommendations for Organisation and Administration

The existing organisation for tribal development consisted of a five-tier body *viz.* State level body, District level body, Block level body, Gram Panchayat level body and Voluntary Organisation level body, having different functionaries bearing various responsibilities at their respective levels. To make it an efficient organisation a few policy recommendation are given below.

(a) A single line of administration either managed totally by the Govt. functionaries, is recommended which will assume overall responsibility for the development of the area and can take care of all aspects with a view to reducing the harassments faced by the tribal people.

(b) The feeling of proper co-operation and co-ordination of the department personnel should be ensured for the welfare of the tribals.

(c) There is a need for developing the quality of leadership among the tribal communities.

(d) To make the Lodha cell more active the educated, Lodha youths should be posted by providing them necessary training about the development programmes meant for Lodha community.

(e) Unnecessary political interference during the implementation and the selection of should be avoided.

(f) Voluntary organisations should be encouraged to carry out development programme.

(g) Though the Panchayat is one of the most organised institutions, the government should not give a long rope to them with regard to development programmes and to over ride the government officials in a majority of the cases.

(h) In any government organisation, particularly in the district and the block, there should be provision for absorbing a group of social scientists.

(i) Some rules, compelling the officials to stay in the tribal areas should be framed.

(j) Ignoring the party affiliation, the actual development work should be entrusted to the Panchayat, so that the different communities, irrespective of their political identity should not be deprived of getting legitimate benefits of development programmes.

(k) At the grass-root levels the Panchayati Raj is a well-organised institution. Naturally, the Panchayat has to take a greater responsibility for the overall development of the different communities, rather than spreading political propaganda by providing governments scheme to the like-minded people.

(l) The Government's attitude towards development programme should be such that people might not take it as a relief measure or dole.

Nine

Present Programmes and Policies: Identified Primitive Tribal Groups in India

The tribal development involves development of a number of groups which are at different stages of socio-economic development. At one extreme are groups which are indistinguishable from the general agricultural communities in the more backward areas while at the other extreme are the groups which still lead a secluded and archaic mode of life. The situation of large difference in the levels of socio-economic development of various communities has always posed important issues before the planners and administrators. Therefore, there has been an effort to identify the more backward communities and make special programmes for those groups. The Scheduled Areas and Tribes Commissions, the Shilu Ao Committee and a number of other bodies in their reports have listed the such backward groups. In some states, special programmes and special facilities have also been provided for these groups.

Backwardness and Poverty

2. On the eve of the Fifth Five Year Plan formulation, the entire range of programmes under tribal development was reviewed. The problem of the more backward tribal communities was also discussed in considerable detail. While considering these problems, it was noted that backwardness itself needed a closer scrutiny. Amongst the backward are those groups who are distinctly earlier stages of economic evolution like hunters, food gatherers, and shifting cultivators. These groups have to be distinguished from those more backward communities which are economically worse off, compared

to the general tribal population. In earlier discussions, no clear distinction had been attempted between poverty and conditions ascribable to a prior stage of economic development. The groups which are at the pre-agricultural level of technology are not necessarily poor. The food gatherers, who may entirely subsist on the forest, may not be poor because his stage of economic development is different, where poverty in the conventional sense has no meaning. There may be deprivation and consequent sense has no meaning. There may be deprivation and consequent 'want' if his natural resources are being encroached upon. This 'want' has to be differentiated from 'poverty' of the modern context.

Definition of Primitive Tribes

3. In the new strategy of tribal development, therefore, the two concepts, viz. a very backward stage of economic development and a lower level in the economic structure have been clearly distinguished. Those groups, which fall in the former category, have been categorised under primitive tribal communities while those in the latter category are terms as the more backward tribal communities.

4. Agricultural economy has been taken to be the water-shed for identification of primitive tribal communities. The pre-agricultural economic groups generally have been included in the primitive communities. The highest form of technology in the case of these groups can be said to be practised by shifting cultivators. Shifting cultivation is a stage of graduation from food gathering and hunting to settled agriculture. Even here, there are no clear boundaries. It is well know that process of change may not inform all facets of community life simultaneously. In the North East, all shifting cultivators are not entirely dependent on it. They depend on shifting cultivation in varying degrees. There are groups who are only nominally or partially dependent on this form of cultivation. Many of these groups, however, have advanced educationally and socially as a result of continued effort in social services. In their case, shifting cultivation does not represent a pre-agricultural stage of socio-economic life, it is, more appropriately, one of the means of livelihood in their peculiar situation. It is as good a source of livelihood as agricultural or

mechanized agriculture or any other form on which a community may subsist. Therefore, in defining primitive tribal groups, some more distinguishing features have to be identified. It appears that literacy is an important criterion which may reasonably indicate the general level of social development of a community. Therefore, besides the stage of economy criterion, level of literacy has also been taken as a characteristic to identify the groups which need special attention and could be properly categorized as primitive tribal communities.

The following are the most important criteria:—

(a) Pre-agricultural level of technology;

(b) Extremely low level of literacy, i.e., below 2 per cent; and

(c) Near stagnant or diminishing population.

5. The tribal communities so identified which are backward and deprived must receive adequate attention to joint the mainstream of society. With this end in view, 75 communities have been identified so far in 15 States and UTs. A list of identified tribal groups scattered over States/UTs is placed at Annexure I. The population and literacy of these groups are placed at Annexure II and Annexure III.

Health

6. The health condition of the primitive tribal groups is precarious. It has been seen that diseases like goiter, yaws, malaria and guinea worm are endemic in tribal areas. Some of the diseases are due to insanitary conditions, poor hygiene and lack of safe drinking water. The children are prone to nutritional deficiency and diarrhoea and females suffer anaemia. The Onges of Andaman & Nicobar Islands suffer from infertility as per study conducted by ICMR. The State Governments of Rajasthan, Karnataka, Tamil Nadu, Maharashtra, Tripura, Gujarat have not given details of specific diseases suffered by the primitive tribals. However, as per available information in Kerala Cholanaikayans one of the identified primitive tribal groups, there are no medical institutions within a radius of 25 km. Further, they are not in the habit of approaching health centres for treatment of their illness. The State Governments of Kerala, Madhya Pradesh have given details of specific diseases suffered by the PTGs. The Action Plan reports

does not contain details of Sub-centres, PHCs etc. in their habitation and their requirements.

Education

7. Education is one of the key inputs for social and economic status in society. As we generally know that the primitive tribes' greatest handicap is the low literacy level which is a stumbling block in the development. The State Governments do not send information non female literacy and even the literacy position for other primitive tribal group is not complete. The literacy position of some of the tribes is placed at Annexure IV.

Housing

8. Some of the State Governments like Gujarat, Rajasthan, Kerala, Tamil Nadu, Madhya Pradesh have scheme for houses. However, the details regarding the condition of the houses in which the primitive tribal groups in habitat is not available.

Family Income Generating Schemes

9. The Annual Plan report of the State Governments show that the scheme for the development of PTGs are of general nature like agriculture, soil conservation, animal husbandry, fisheries etc.

Shifting Cultivation/Collection of Minor Forest Produces

10. The tribal communities are placed in the list of primitive tribal groups on the basis of fixed criteria and one of the criterion is tribals practising shifting cultivation/collection of minor forest products. The reports of the State governments are silent on number of tribals weaned from shifting cultivation to settled cultivation.

Preparation of Project Reports

11. The State Governments were requested in 16 July, 1993 and 22nd August, 1994 to prepare comprehensive project report and action plan for each identified primitive tribal group keeping in mind socio-economic developmental aspects of their lives. The project were to clearly indicate after proper survey/studies of their felt needs and their capacity to absorb new technology and resources.

12. The available information indicates that only the State Govts. of Rajasthan, Karnataka, Tamil Nadu, Maharashtra, Kerala, Gujarat, Tripura, Andaman & Nicobar Islands and Madhya Pradesh have sent the action plan/project report. These reports except Madhya, is not in accordance on the lines suggested. Information from other State Govts. like Andhra Pradesh, Bihar, Orissa, Manipur, Uttar Pradesh and West Bengal are still awaited.

13. The State Governments were also requested to give the following details in their Action Plan:—

(i) Clear physical location of the primitive groups;
(ii) Their present economic and health condition;
(iii) Urgent problems facing the group needing immediate action;
(iv) Administrative arrangements proposed keeping in view special requirement of dedicated persons and flexibility in operations;
(v) Financial requirement with annual phasing with physical targets and achievements etc.

However, the information on these are lacking.

14. The field visits have revealed that there is lack of basic facilities like safe drinking water, irregular attendance by teachers in schools, inputs given to farmer not in accordance with their needs. Lack of proper supervision of agriculture programmes. In spite of old age pension scheme, the villagers are not aware of it. Liquor vending is still prevalent in the villages. The houses were very small and in a dilapidated condition resulting in moisture giving raise to fever and other ailments. Employment assurance scheme has not been launched in some of the areas inhabited by PTGs due to the restriction imposed by the Forest Department. Very few households own lands and even the land owning families face food insecurity problems due to poor productivity of land. The poor productivity of land is due to combination of acts such as non-availability of plough bullocks, agricultural implements etc. It was noticed that ITDAs are not enough concerned for this major food problem. Hence, the ITDA must act as per its aims and objectives and help the tribals in improving their economic condition through creating a revolving fund. Tackling the food insecurity problem of the PTGs thus becomes the most important

intervention for the ITDPs concerned. The general approach for development of the tribals below poverty line is followed for the PTGs as well. But the problems of PTGs are very different from the other tribes. The typical approach for development of the people below the poverty line is followed even for the PTGs, which has been counter-productive. The Thrift Societies could be run by tribal women. ITDA can arrange training programmes for farmers for agriculture and allied activities and also for other income generating activities in which tribals have skills and aptitude. Grain Bank scheme can help them in times of food scarcity and in lean seasonal months. Organisation and management of grain banks should be left to village community. The primary education should be remodelled to suit the needs of children. The approach to primitive tribe development should form habitat specific programmes keeping in view their local conditions. After food security problem, delivery of Health services is of paramount important in the strategy for development of PTGs. The multi-pronged approach like health, education, mobile, medical facilities etc. may be adopted to tackle these problems.

Recommendations Made in the Working Group Reports on Tribal Development

15. The Working Group Reports for the Sixth, Seventh, Eighth and Ninth Plan period have made many useful recommendations with regard to PTGs.

(i) There should be unique programme/project reports taking into consideration the environmental aspect including education, health, nutrition, drinking water, transport and communication.

(ii) Development should aim at conservation and reorganization of traditional skills of the groups.

(iii) The administrative structure should consist of separate organizational structure with project officers with specific responsibility of handling and developing these communities.

(iv) Special regulations should be promulgated to protect the command over resources of the group.

(v) ICDS programmes in blocks having primitive tribes should receive topmost priority.

(vi) Special allowances to the Govt. staff deputed to work in primitive tribal areas under finance Commission Award.
(vii) Dedicated voluntary organisations should be induced to work in this area.

Recommendations SOF the Study Sponsored by the Ministry

16. The Pan-Asian Management on Rural Research Organisation undertook a study on Primitive tribes with special reference to Chenchus of Andhra Pradesh, Katkaris of Maharashtra and Seharias of Rajasthan. The objectives of the study were to-

(i) understand their anthropological position in contemporary India;
(ii) assess various programmes that are being implemented especially for the primitive tribes; and
(iii) highlight the successful programmes in the three States by comparing the methods used in each State.

17. A critical analysis of the report indicates that the implementing Agency has not gone into the guidelines issued by the Government of India in regard to excise policy in tribal areas, whether Chenchus brewing their own country liquor or there is prevalence of commercial vending of alcoholic beverages. It is also silent whether there is any awareness campaign about it. The Organisation in the report of Katkaris of Maharashtra have not clearly pointed out whether they came across any case of forced labour in brick kilns, coal kilns, agriculture and sand quarries where they are employed. Very little information has been given about child labourers.

Recommendations made in the Conference of Ministers/ Secretaries of State Govts./UT Admns. held on 2nd - 3rd February, 1996 in Vigyan Bhavan, New Delhi

18. In the two days conference held with Ministers/Secretaries of Social Welfare of State Govts. and UTs it has been recommended that the five year action plan for PTGs should incorporate total good security. The Action Plan of the State Govts. should have in built flexibility to cater to the specific needs of each tribe and its environment, committed officials, dedicated workers, NGOs, anthropologists should be associated with their programmes

including those of rural development for this purpose. The implementation of the action plan should be on the top of the agenda of Tribal Development Department and concerned District collectors.

19. Assuming the criteria to be valid still, on the whole, it appears there is little likelihood of discovery of more such groups. On the other hand, there is a possibility of elimination of some groups who might show progress in socio-cultural, socio-economic, educational and related fields. It will also depend on post-1971 population and demographic data becoming available indicative of the trends. As such, their progress needs to be monitored on a continuing basis for different purposes, including for the purpose of assessing the need for continuation of a particular group in the list. Review and revision of the criteria also should be kept under scrutiny.

20. The present occasion offers an opportunity to make a review of the criteria mentioned. It will be conceded that during the nearly three decades elapsing between the time the four coordinates of identification were evolved and now, events have marched ahead and changes have taken place even among the isolated groups under consideration. Thought even now there are hunting and gathering groups, may have taken to cultivation. However, some of them are in the rudimentary stage of agriculture, some in shifting cultivation stage and a few may have gone even beyond. The scenario is varied. Hence, "pre-agricultural level of technology" may not be satisfied as a test, though a particular group may fall into the present slot otherwise.

21. The difference between the general run of tribal groups and the primitive tribal groups under consideration stands out in bold relief on account of two dimensions. Much more than the common scheduled tribal groups, they stay in more interior pockets which are generally, even less accessible than the habitat of the common tribal groups. Secondly, the cultural gap between the primitive tribal groups and the non-tribal societies is wider as compared to that between the common tribal societies and the non-tribal societies. Outstanding examples in this context are the bay-Islanders like the Shompen, Jarwa, Sentinelese of the Andaman & Nicobar Islands. Even

some of the main land groups can be cited in this context, e.g., the Bondo of Orissa, Cholanaikayan of Kerala, the Abujhmarias of Madhya Pradesh, the Birhor of Bihar.

22. The scenario of the 75 identified PTGs is a lesson in diversity. Some of those groups which stand out as 'most primitive' have been mentioned in the preceding paragraph. But there are those who come within the ambit of acculturation in the three States of Bihar, Orissa and Madhya Pradesh. We considered the question whether it is possible and, indeed, useful, to admit classification of these groups into a few neat categories. Each group may be studied carefully in its manifold aspects and project reports are prepared for improvement in the health, education, economic and other sectors. In fact, tribe-wise approach is required in other contexts also.

23. Before proceeding further, one question which might be regarded as minor in one context but which has significant implications in understanding of these groups, having also a psychological bearing on these groups themselves, pertains to their nomenclature.

24. Before embarking on ideas concerning approach, policy, paths of development and other conceptual matters, it is necessary to have a look at the situation as it prevails on the ground. The report of the Eighth Five Year Plan Working Group does not embody the profile and status of each of the groups as it existed then. But we have no doubt that they would have had before them a broad appraisal. On enquiry, we find that few project reports on these groups in the country are available. In fact, information available is scanty, sketchy and inadequate. It generally indicates funds received by a State government and the expenditure therefrom. Reference to the demographic, sociological, environmental etc. features are casual. Even the plan programmes and their physical impact, particularly on the socio-economic conditions of the families, are dealt with cavalierly. It is not know what evaluation studies have been undertaken. According to the Ministry of Tribal Affairs sources, they do not posses adequate material on the demographic, economic, educational, health and other sectors of individual group on account of non-receipt of data, information, statistics from the concerned State

Governments. Thus, we are handicapped in appreciation of the position of each of the group under consideration. The results of evaluation would have enabled us to build up suitable plans and programmes. We have mentioned earlier the lack of even population data. It seems that the deficiency is much larger. We are perturbed to find ourselves and the entire administrative and planning machinery in this predicament. Constructive steps need to be taken for building up urgently a comprehensive data base and building up urgently a comprehensive data base and status sketches. We can not exaggerate the importance of intensive survey and studies of each of these groups covering every single aspect of their life and after life. The need for individual studies becomes more apparent in the light of the fact that each of these communities is different from the other in significant particulars e.g. socio-cultural, economic, environmental. The unique attributes of each call for unique treatment in planning and implementation. The availability of project reports based on intensive studies would enable us to proceed to erect a plan superstructure. Wherever necessary, the government of India and State Governments should commission intensive studies preceding preparation of project reports.

25. In the Sixth and Seventh Plan period, it had been the guideline that a separate Project Report should be prepared for each tribal group, taking into account its unique features, particularly, cultural, environmental and socio-economic. It was prescribed that the first phase of development should aim at conservation and re-organisation of the traditional skills of the groups, while the second phase should spell out the development programmes. Rehabilitation of the eco-system was given a high priority. Above all, it was emphasised that each blue-print should be prepared based on the group's own proclivity expressed by the group's representatives in consultative assemblies. We find that this pivotal function of preparation of one Project Report for each tribal group has fallen into arrears, betokening a state of neglect. We feel that the first and foremost need is preparation of Project Reports for these communities in dialogue with them, reflecting their ideas of needs, aspirations, development, etc. For the purpose, it is necessary to strike a rapport with them.

26. This takes us to the question of strategy to be followed for improvement of the socio-economic consideration. Conscious or unconsciously, ambivalence has persisted and decisions which can be characterized as more or less adhoc seem to have been taken. In this context, the most prominent example that comes to the mind is that of the tribes of Andaman & Nicobar Islands. For too long, these tribes have been the subject of adhoc treatment. It is time to consider the matter in depth in its different ramifications, and in a relatively long-ranged perspective for all the primary groups. For the purpose, we suggest formation of an Expert Committee comprised of experienced administrators (retired and serving), social scientists, social workers, tribal leaders and dif necessary, others to go into the entire gamut of this question and render appropriate advise to the concerned authorities.

27. Since this may take time and pending the availability of considered counsel of such expert body, some broad lines of action are chalked out here.

In the first instance, one has to proceed on the premise that each tribal community has to be considered as unique and the approach, consequently, has to be specifically tribe-wise. It has been found that out of the 75 identified Primitive Tribal Groups, some have a reasonably high rate of growth, some are more or less stagnant, in their numbers and some others have a negative growth-rate. Secondly, some continue to live in, comparatively speaking well-preserved environment, while some others have slid into impoverish state gradually on account of degradation of their environment over a period of time. Thirdly, those groups who still live encysted in un-tampered physical environment on account of its inaccessibility may have escaped exploitation, but others whose lot it has been to get "civilised" on account of culture contact through accessibility have been badly exposed to all manner of exploitation. The different scenarios would need to be reckoned with in dealing with formulations for them.

28. Subject again to the proviso of policy or policies and that may be evolved by the committee proposed earlier, we feel that there are two soft entry points for the groups under consideration i.e. health and education. Many of these groups are in a poor state of healthy and nutrition. Further, many live in sanitary conditions.

It is necessary to provide to them adequate health security and nutrition security. Their own system of medicine has given them relief over ages and should be encouraged. Further, steps may be taken to ensure that preventive and promotive measures as per the modern system do reach them. In the same category, safe drinking water supply, sanitation, primary school etc. are basic needs and require to be attended to on priority basis. Drinking water is the most fundamental requirement and is the prime requisite for building up health and sanitation levels. In effect, the minimum needs programme is the highest priority.

29. After consideration of these social sectors, attention to infrastructure like link roads, rural roads, market roads needs to be given. In some areas, mobile medical and essential commodities vans have gone well on account of outreach. The infrastructure items have to be considered from the point of view of local tribal community's perceptions, interests, needs, aspirations etc. It has been diagnosed by some analysts that a major failure in the field of tribal development in these four decades has been the more or less total reliance on the bureaucratic machinery for execution of planned programmes. Moreover, the prospective beneficiaries themselves have stood aloof. These two deficiencies have to be removed. The role of the administrative machinery should to help the community in formulations and implementation of plans and programmes. In other words, it is felt that the best vehicle would be the endogenous institutions and organisations who should be entrusted both formulation and implementation with the aid of concerned official experts. The Bhuria Committee in its report (1995) suggested making the Gram Sabha strong, as traditionally it has been conducting the affairs of the tribal communities. It is endorsed that the Gram Sabha should become the fulcrum of development activities. The difference spelt out here in the reversal of the roles of the two should be clearly appreciated. To drive the point further, it is envisaged that the official agencies should no longer be formulators and executants of the programmes with the potential beneficiaries standing by and watching. Moreover, the scope and extent of the roles of each would need to be defined in the light of the conditions prevailing in each tribal community. From the official side, adequate managerial, technical and expert

back-up might be required. Provision of motor-worth roads would be warranted only on the basis of the specific circumstances which arise uncommonly. Otherwise, such roads opening up interior areas all of a sudden are responsible for cultural and economic shocks.

30. In the third category and in that order of priority, it is felt that economic scheme should come in. In the entire canvas of planned development, economic schemes in different sectors like agriculture, horticulture, animal husbandry, fishery, industry, co-operation etc. have sprouted like mushrooms. There is a tendency to extend them indiscriminately, where be it scheduled tribes in general or even primary groups referred to here. There proliferation without having proved useful to the tribal context has led to confusion and loss of goodwill. A great context has led to confusion and loss of goodwill. A great deal of discrimination should be exercised in bringing the members of the groups into the fold of these schemes. In fact, the ends of development will be better served if a chosen few schemes german to the present context are selected and put on ground. These could be in the agriculture, forest (particularly minor forest produce) and cottage industries sectors. The tendency of loading big loans on them through loan component in subsidy-cum-loan schemes should be, by and large, avoided.

31. Considering all that has gone in herein-before, the important question is that all the agency or agencies which can be called upon to shoulder the task of implementation of plans formulated on the basis of the necessity. But the broad programmes and measures of development should be decided by the council of elders constituting the endogenous institutions, say the Gram Sabha. We also recommend that women bodies, youth organisations and other local organisations should be utilised to the fullest capacity.

32. In the new and changed orientation, the re-appraisal of personnel policies is necessary. Though it has been said so often before we reiterate that officials to be drawn for the purpose should not only be capable and competent, but should also possess sensitivity and dedication. For working in such difficult and remote areas a package of incentives needs to be attached. Further, and

importantly, realizing that official agencies along are not able to deliver the goods, the voluntary sector and the non-government organisations should be brought in as much as possible, only taking care to usher in the proven honest sincere, competent and dedicated ones. Their role will be crucial. Fortunately, their number is not as small today, as it used to be in the earlier days.

The implication of inclusion of new communities need to be understood in the present context. As it is, in the matter of reservations and other rights and privileges, the primary groups under consideration here receive only "left-overs". While the lion's share is appropriated by major and advanced tribes on account of their better economic and educational status. But if more number of communities were to share the same quantum of limited resources because of further scheduling, the fraction receivable by primary groups shrinks further. We should prevent the compounding. Alternatively, sub-reservations should be earmarked for each of the primary groups on the basis of some rational formula.

33. It is emphasised that the project report should reflect integration of all the programmes and should be a well-coordinated package. Inter-alia, it should dwell on protective measures like laws which prevent loss of land, safeguards against usuary, measures against bondage, steps against sharp trade practices and have instruments against social and sexual exploitation and others concerned. Further, it should dilate on the means and ways in which the tribal community's own institutions and mechanisms are brought into play in the effort towards improvement. Fourthly, funding should be indicated very clearly and the instructions should be spelt out in detail. The concerned State Governments might consider separate administrative outfits for these groups at the community level and State level.

34. Now it has come to the important question of approach to and philosophy for the primary tribal groups. This question is reserved till the end of the report as we felt that a reverse of the landscape we have so far covered equips one better for its comprehension and appreciation. Essentially, it is one of letting the tribal groups more forward in life the way they have done during the past decades or intervening to accelerating change

among them. The former approach can be described as a laissez faire or conservationist approach and may be based on one's conviction that no alien agency has the moral right to dictate to a community in whatever circumstances placed, to adopt a direction and speed different from the innate. Endogenous forces should rule change. The second solicitous and concerned, would not like to allow any section of the society to lag behind markedly in socio-economic, educational and other fields. Undoubtedly, each has its strong points, Apart from the moral standpoint, the former is moved by the consideration that induction of forced change may upset the internal dynamics related not only to environment and economics, but also to their social and individual psyche culture etc. It may create distortions diverse sorts to the point of rending the age-old fabric of the community for introducing morbidity. One can not brush aside these consideration lightly. The second school of thought also has its logic. Assuming change to be in-built by nature, it would like those lagging behind to move faster in directions set by modern forces through exogenous impulses. It also feels morally called upon to actively help the strugglers to join the mainstream on what it regards as the road to progress. There are obvious pitfalls in both. An attitude of aloofness may perpetuate relative stagnation, while aggressive intervention may trigger back lash and aberrations. It may be difficult no to err. But the blunder can be Herculean if deliberations are conducted to the exclusion of those who are the subject of the approach and the strategy and who have to bear the brunt of development. It is not only desirable but also essential that they have the final say after consideration of all the pros and cons.

35. Needless to say, there are certain tribal groups who are yet not in a position to articulate themselves on such issues. The Sentinelese still people a world of their own bereft almost wholly of contact with other people. The contacts of the Jarawa are limited. Some Shompen have contact but most (in fact, we may not even know how many) live in forest fastnesses. We are not aware which other groups can be included in this bracket. It is possible that policy for this category may have to be worked out almost without their association.

36. Then there are hunter-gatherers with elementary

agricultural pursuits, like the Birhor, Cholanaikayan. Their culture-contacts might have been minimal, but have not been totally absent. They may be able to convey in howsoever vague and subliminal terms what they would like to do, what their concept of "development" and how they see themselves fitting into the universe around. These would be invaluable leads for evolving relevant formulations and frame-work.

37. We visualize a large number of the primary groups to express themselves more or less adequately on the issues involved so that the outlines emerging there from can become the bulwark of the approach or the philosophy. A common perception is that they favour socio-economic advancement of the kind they are around. If so, and this should specifically be confirmed in consultation with each, it calls for interventionist approach. The degree and nature of intervention have to be determined in the light of status of each group.

38. Thus, though some broad categories of primary groups can thus be conceptualized, in the ultimate analysis each group's own situation, status and stage needs to be studied carefully for evolving approach, strategy and developmental paradigms. In this regard, we venture to express these broad and tentative views in anticipation of and without prejudice to the considered conclusions of the committee we have proposed in para 10 foregoing. In fact, we do so only ad interim, so that the process in the Ninth Plan can be set in motion. As and when the recommendations of the proposed committee are received, appropriate action should be taken.

39. Finally, there is the question of the role, duty and responsibility of the State towards the primary tribal groups. In a democracy, and particularly welfarist democratic state, it is taken for granted that the good of the people is the State's first concern. Among the people, the subject tribal groups should deserve the foremost attention and care. We have proceeded on this assumption so far. But the winds of economic liberalism that have been blowing in the country during the past half a decade and concomitant re-orientation of the role of the State give rise to the apprehension that these remote and fringe entities, of little consequence in the game of electoral politics may fade out of national consciousness

in the new harsh world of competitive market forces. Some of them have been gradually declining in number and are, presently, very small. One should not be surprised if they become extinct before long. Others are vulnerable in different ways. If not looked after, their survival also, such as it is in want and misery, may be at stake. It is, therefore, essential to reappraise the situation and take a conscious decision that the shrinking State will not for sake its full-fledged part of nursing and fostering these marginal communities.

40. Since Fifth Five Year Plan, under SCA, funds have been provided to States and UTs for development of STs in the TSP areas. These PTGs are almost all residing in the ITDP areas. The State Governments have been utilizing funds out of SCA for the development of these groups. The erstwhile Ministry of Welfare/ Social Justice & Empowerment had requested the State governments to take up development of PTGs on a project basis and funding is being provided by the State Governments out of SCA for the purpose. It has, however, been found from experience that projects or even specific schemes for the development of PTGs have not been forthcoming from the States. Further, though a part of SCA is being utilised by the States/UTs, specifically for PTGs, the feed back on results achieved is inadequate. The exact amount utilised for the development of PTGs out of SCA as well as State Plan funds has not been reported by the State Govts./ UOT Admns.

The objectives are to achieve total development of the entire population of PTGs. There are some burning issues relating to these groups - (i) The cause of decline in the population of certain PTGs should be investigated and causes removed; (ii) While maternity and child health facilities are extremely important for them, family planning measures for limiting the family size are not relevant in their case and (iii) the areas specific or tribe specific multi-sectoral projects should be taken up for development of PTGs.

41. Priority should be given to—

(a) Primary education and adult education.

(b) Health services.

(c) Schemes for economic development of families.

(d) Provision of the minimum needs already identified under MNP to the extent these have not been or can not be provided under States' TSP or other Centrally Sponsored Schemes.

(e) Provision of social services should not be delayed or avoided merely because per capita cost is high on account of low population density or difficult terrain.

42. Erstwhile Ministry of Welfare/Social Justice & Empowerment have evolved guidelines to provide 100% subsidy for individual benefit schemes for PTGs. It was also emphasised that Project Administrators of the ITDPs should give adequate emphasis for development of these groups. Guidelines were also issued to provide monetary and non-monetary incentives to the personnel working in this Ministry by different schemes should be encouraged to take up developmental projects for specific PTGs. Funding for the projects should also include the administrative cost of the NGO concerned. In regard to elimination of exploitative practices, Project Directors of the ITDPs should be actively involved for overall development of these groups.

43. During discussions with the Planning Commission, it was observed that adequate attention has not so far been made by the State Govts./UTs for the development of PTGs funded out of SCA, State Plan resources, schemes for NGOs, vocational training for tribals, educational complexes for the low literacy pockets etc. The National Development Council while finalizing the Ninth Five Year Plan document, observed the following -

> "While the all-round development of STs, in general, will be addressed through the continuing programmes but with added thrust and support, the PTGs, who are leading an extremely precarious life and some of whom are on the verge of extinction due to hunger, starvation and diseases, will be attended to, on a priority basis, in the Ninth Plan. As the ongoing programmes have not been able to alleviate the conditions of the PTGs, direct programmes for the welfare and development of PTGs, will be launched in the Ninth Plan through an integrated action plan incorporating supply of safe drinking water, food and nutrition security, health coverage, educational facilities etc. The proposed

Action Plan for PTGs will have an in-built flexibility to cater to the specific needs of each tribe and its environment".

44. During 1998-99, a Special Central Sector Scheme was introduced after doing exercises through series of discussions with the Planning Commission and Finance Ministry. The objective of this newly introduced Central Sector Scheme in 1998-99 is reproduced below-

"The funds under the Central Sector Scheme for the Development of PTGs would be available only for those items/activities which though very crucial for the survival, protection and development of PTGs, are not specifically catered to by any existing schemes, State or Central or by guidelines governing the utilisation of funds under SCA to TSP and Article 275(1) of the Constitution. Such items/activities can not be exhaustively identified at the Central level as they may differ from State to State and within a State from project to project. However, funds under the scheme could be used for helping the beneficiaries of the project to cope with extremely adverse pressures which threaten their survival and protect them against various forms of exploitation and thereby bringing them to a stage when they can demand and receive specific assets and services. The activities under the scheme may include measures such as awareness generation and confidence building, training for skill development of tribal youth organisations of self-help groups and provision of services/inputs not covered by an existing scheme. In terms of beneficiaries, the scheme will cover only members of PTGs".

45. According to the Planning Commission, adequate funds are kept in the budget of the Ministry for implementation of the programmes through the State Governments. Very small portion of fund has been kept for NGO schemes as Ministry has adequate provision under different schemes like vocational training, educational complexes in low literacy pockets and grant-in-aid to NGOs. Very small amount has been kept for NGOs and UTs. The details of the budget provision for States/UTs and NGOs since 1998-99 are given below—

BUDGET OUTLAY UNDER THE CENTRAL SECTOR SCHEME OF DEVELOPMENT OF PTGs

(Rs. in Crores)

Year	*States*	*UTs/NGOs*	*Total*
1998-1999	3.00	1.00	4.00
1999-2000	8.00	2.00	10.00
2000-2001	9.70	2.80	12.50

46. It is felt that participation in scheme prepared by the beneficiaries based on their felt needs of paramount importance. After the schemes are so formulated, it is equally important to empower the beneficiaries, so that they actively participate in implementation and deem it as their own project, rather than it being thrust on them. It is here that the NGOs can play a crucial role to create awareness about various needs and involve them in participatory management. Due to their long track record of working amount the weaker sections sof the society, they can motivate and organize these people by organizing self-help groups from among the PTGs. The views of the NGOs working in the tribal areas will be of immense help for devising suitable programmes for implementation among PTGs.

STATEMENT SHOWING THE STATE-WISE TOTAL POPULATION, MAIN OCCUPATION, LOCATION OF ALL 75 PRIMITIVE TRIBES AS PER 1971 AND 1981 CENSUS

S. No.	Name of State/UT	Name of Primitive Tribe	1971 Census	1981 Census	Location: Distt.	Location: Block	Main Occupation
1	2	3	4	5	6	7	8
1.	Andhra Pradesh	1. Bodo Gadaba 2. Gutob Gadaba	25188	28049	Visakhapatnam	Chintapalli, Araku Anantagiri, G. Madugula, Paderu	Food Gathering
		3. Chenchu	24176	28297	Rangareddi, Nalgonda, Mahabubnagar, Kurnool, Guntur, Prakasam	Vikarabad, Devarakonda, Atchampet, Kolhapur, Atmakur, Nandyal, Allagadda, Macherla Markapur	Agriculture
		4. Bondo Porja, 5. Paranji Porja, 6. Khond Porja	12357	16374	Visakhapatnam	Chintapalli, Pedabajalu, Munchingput, Araku, Anantagiri, G. Madugula, Paderu	Food Gathering
		7. Kolam	26498	30352	Adilabad	Adilabad, Asifabad, Khanapur, Boath	Food gathering
		8. Konda Reddi	42777	54473	East Godavari	Rampachodavaram, Rajayammangi, Addateegala	Shifting Cultivation
					West Godavari	Polavaram, Buttayagudem	

1	2	3	4	5	6	7	8
					Khammam	Bhadrachalam, Kunavaram, V.R. Puram, Aswaropeta, Suddimalla, Yellandu, Venkatapuram, Burgapipahad	
		9. Konda Savaras	3000	18189	Srikakulam Vizianagaram	Seethampeta, Bhadragiri	Food gathering
		10. Kuttia Khond, 11. Dongria Khond	34875	50726	Visakhapatnam	Anantagiri, Araku, Munchangiput, Paderu, Chintapalli, Pedabayalu, G. Madugula	Food gathering
		12. Thoti	1785	1753	Adilabad	Untur, Asifabad, Laksheltipet	Misc. Occupation
		Total	167578	228213			
2.	Bihar	1. Asur	7020	8683	Patna, Siwan, Ranchi, Dhanbad, Giridih, Palamau		Food gathering
		2. Birhor	3464	4277	Patna, Gaya, Nawada, Saran, Muzaffarpur, Munger, Bhagalpur, Santhal Parganas, Dhanbad, Giridih, Hazaribagh, Ranchi, Palamau, Singhbhum		Food gathering

1	2	3	4	5	6	7	8
		3. Birjia	3628	4057	Patna, Aurangabad, Purnia, Katihar, Bhagalpur, Dhanbad, Giridih, Hazaribagh, Ranchi, Palamau and Singhbhum		Agriculture
		4. Hill Kharia	10241	14177	Patna, Saran, Purnea, Bhagalpur, Santhal Pargana, Dhanbad, Giridih, Hazaribagh, Ranchi, Palamau, Singhbhum		Shifting Cultivation
		5. Korwa	21637	21940	Patna, Rohtas, Bhajpur, Muzaffarpur, Kathihar, Monghur, Bhagalpur, Santhal Parganas, Dhanbad, Giridih, Hazaribagh, Ranchi, Palamau, Singhbhum		Shifting Cultivation
		6. Malpaharia	48636	79322	Patna, Gaya, Aurangabad, Paschimi Champaran, Madhubani, Saharsa, Purnea, Katihar, Monghyr, Bhagalpur, S.P., Dhanbad, Giridih, Hazaribagh, Ranchi, Palamau, Singhbhum		Shifting Cultivation

1	2	3	4	5	6	7	8
		7. Pahariya	14651	24012	Gaya, Bhojpur, Saharsa, Purnia, Katihar, Bhagalpur, S.P., Giridih, Hazaribagh, Ranchi, Palamau and Singhbhum		Food Gathering
		8. Sauria Paharia	59047	39269	Patna, Gaya, Monghyr, Bhagalpur, Purnea, Santhal Pargana, Ranchi, Hazaribagh, Dhanbad		Shifting Cultivation
		9. Savar	3548	3014	Patna, Saran, Purnea, Bhagalpur, Santhal Pargana, Dhanbad, Guridih, Hazaribagh, Ranchi, Palamau, Singhbhum		Shifting Cultivation
		Total:	171872	198751			
3.	Gujarat	1. Kathodi	2939	4360	Dangs Valsad Surat Bharuch Panchmahal Sabarkantha	Dangs Vansda Mandvi Songadh Rajpipla Dahod, Khedbrahma	Misc. Occupation

1	2	3	4	5	6	7	8
		2. Kotwalia	12902	15837	Dangas Valsad Surat Bharuch Panchmahal Sabarkantha Vadodara Kheda Ahmedabad, Mahesana	Dangs Vansda Mandvi Songadh Rajipla Dahod Khedbrahma Chhotaudepur	Misc. Occupation, Bamboo Work
		3. Padhar	4756	9322	Surendranagar, Ahmedabad		Shifting Cultivation
		4. Siddi	4482	5600	Amreli, Surendranagar, Rajkot, Bhavnagar, Jamnagar, Junagadh		Shifting Cultivation
		5. Kolgha	29464	26060	Dangas Valsad Surat Bharuch Panchmahal Sabarkantha Banaskantha Vadodara Kheda Ahemedabad, Mehsana	Dangs Vansda Mandvi Songadh Rajpipla Dahod Khedbrahma Palanpur Chhotaudepur	Misc. Occupation
		Total:	54543	61179			

1	2	3	4	5	6	7	8
4.	Karnataka	1. Jenu Kuruba	15401	17865	Mysore and Kodagu	H.D. Kote, Gundlupet, Hunsur, Periyapatna, Nagarahole, Kattambella, Murkul, Anekodu, Kushalnagar	Misc. Occupation
		2. Koraga	13627	15810	Dakshina Kannada	Udipi, Coondapur, Mangalore, Karkala, Belthangadi	Misc. Occupation
		Total	29028	33675			
5.	Kerala	1. Cholanaikayan (A section of Kattunayakan)	5565	8803	Malappuram	Nilambur	Food Gathering
		2. Kadar	1120	1503	Palghat Thrissur	Chittur, Mukundapuram Taluk, Chalakudy Block	Food Gathering
		3. Kattunaickns	5565	8803	Wayanad	Manantoddy, Kalpetta, S. Battery	Food Gathering
		4. Kurumbas	1014	1283	Palghat	Allappady	Food Gathering
		5. Koraga	724	1503	Kasaragod		Misc. Occupation
		Total	8773	13374			
6.	Madhya Pradesh	1. Abujhmarias	13327	15500	Narayampur, Bijapur & Dantewada Teshils of Bastar, Orcha Block		Food Gathering
		2. Baigas	113677	139665	52 villages of Baigachak in Samnapur, Bajag & Karanjia T.D. Blocks of Mandla and additional areas		Shifting Cultivation

1	2	3	4	5	6	7	8
		3. Bharias	1300	1589	Patalkot area of Block Tamia, Chhindwara Distt.		Misc. Occupation
		4. Hill Korwas	13488	16860	T.D. Blocks Bagicha & Manora of Raigarh, Shankargarh, Kusmi, Lundra & Rajpur of Surguja and Korba of Bilaspur.		Shifting Cultivation
		5. Kamars	12418	13500	Gariaband, Manipur, Chhura & Nagri Blocks of Raipur Distt.		Food Gathering
		6. Sahariya	173618	207600	District of Gwalior & Chambal Division viz, Gwalior, Guna, Shivpuri, Datia & Morena		Misc. Occupation
		7. Birhor	738	886			Misc. Occupation
		Total:	328466	395600			
7.	Mahara-shtra	1. Katkari (Kathodia)	146785	174602	Thane District		Misc. Occupation
		2. Kolam	56061	118073	Yavatmal Nanded	Yavatmal, Kelapur, Wani Nanded, Hatgaon, Kinwat, Bhokar, Biloli, Beglur, Mukhed, Kandhar	Food Gathering
		3. Maria Gond	40000	66750	Gadchiroli	Etapalli, Aheri, Sirencha	Food Gathering

1	2	3	4	5	6	7	8
8.	Manipur	1. Maram Nagas	4539	5972	Senapati (Formerly Manipur North Distt.)	Tadubi & Kengpoki	Agriculture
		Total:	4539	5972			
9.	Orissa	1. Birhor	98	142	Sundargarh	Lahunipada	Food Gathering
		2. Bondo Poraja	4431	5895	Koraput	Khairiput	Shifting Cultivation
		3. Didayi	2161	1978	Koraput	Kudnuguma, Khairput	Misc. Occupation
		4. Dongria Khond	1041	1145	Koraput	Bissamcuttack Muniguda	Shifting Cultivation
		5. Juangs	3834	4217	Keonjhar	Bansapal	Shifting Cultivation
		6. Kharias	1392	1531	Mayurbhanj	Jashipur	Shifting Cultivation
		7. Kutia Khond	4735	5208	Phulbani, Kalahandi	Tumudibandh	Shifting Cultivation
		8. Lanjia Sauras	5687	6255	G. Udaigiri Mayurbhanj	Lanjigarh Popular	Shifting Cultivation
		9. Lodhas	3891	5100		Suliapada Marada	Food Gathering
		10. Mankirdia	333	205	Mayurbhanj	Jashipur	Food Gathering
		11. Paudi Bhuyans	6495	7145	Ganjam, Dhenkanal	Gumma, Nuagarh, Pallahara	Food Gathering
		12. Soura	5651	6216	Ganjam	Mohana, R. Udaigiri	Food Gathering
		13. Chuktia Bhunjia	-	2164	Sonabeda Platum in Nuapada Distt.		Shifting Cultivation, Collection of Timber, Bamboo
		Total:	39749	47201			
10.	Rajasthan	1. Seharias	22069	33978	Kota	Shahbad, Kishanganj	Misc. Occupation
		Total:	22069	33978			

1	2	3	4	5	6	7	8
11.	Tamil Nadu	1. Nattu Naikkose	5042	26383	Madras, Chingleput, North Arcot, South Arcot, Dharmapuri, Coimbatore, The Nilgiris, Madurai, Tiruchirappalli, Thanjavur, Ramanathapuram		Food Gathering
		2. Rotas	1183	604	Madras, The Nilgiris, Chingleput		Misc. Occupation
		3. Kurumbas	2754	4354	The Nilgiris		Misc. Occupation
		4. Irular	89025	105757	Madras, Chingleput, North Arcot, South Arcot, Dharmapuri, Salem, Coimbatore, The Nilgiris, Madurai, Trichy, Thanjavur		Food Gathering
		5. Paniyana	6093	6393	Chingleput, South Arcot, Dharmapuri, Salem, Coimbatore, The Nilgiris, Madurai, Thanjavur, Tiruchirappalli,		Shifting Cultivation
		6. Todas	930	875	Madras, Chingleput, South Arcot, Dharmapuri, Coimbatore, The Nilgiris		Misc. Occupation
		Total	105032	144366			

1	2	3	4	5	6	7	8
12.	Tripura	1. Riangs	64722	84004	North Tripura	Kanchanpur, Panisagar, Choumanu, Kumarghat, Salema	Shifting Cultivation
					South Tripura	Udaipur, Amarpur, Dumburnagar, Bagafa, Rajnagar	
					West Tripura	Klowai, Taliamura, Bishalgarh	
		Total:	64722	84004			
13.	Uttar Pradesh	1. Buksa	23317	30938	Bijnore	Nazibabad, Kotwali, Afzalgarh	Agriculture
					Dehradun	Doiwala, Sahaspur	
					Nainital	Kashipur, Bajpur, Ramnagar, Gadarpur, Rudrapur	
					Pauri Garhwal	Dugadda	
		2. Raji	1918	478	Pithoragarh	Dharchula, Didihat, Kanalichhina, Champewat	Food Gathering
		Total:	25235	31416			
14.	West Bengal	1. Birhor	154	214	Purulia	Bagmundi, Jalda	Food Gathering
		2. Lodhas	45906	53717	Medinipur, Jalpaiguri, Bankura, Hugli, Puruliya, Darjiling, Maldah		Food Gathering
		3. Totos	650	716	Jalpaiguri	Madarihat	Agriculture
		Total:	46710	54647			

1	*2*	*3*	*4*	*5*	*6*	*7*	*8*
15.	Andaman & Nicobar Islands	1. Great Andamanese	24	28	Andamans Middle Andamans		Food Gathering
		2. Jarwas	250	200	South Andáman, Middle Andamans		Food Gathering
		3. Onges	112	98	Little Andamans		Food Gathering
		4. Sentinelese	50	80	Little Andamans		Food Gathering
		5. Shompens	92	214	Nicobar (Great Nicobar)		Food Gathering
		Total:	528	620			
		Grand Total:	1311690 (13.12 lakhs)	1692421 (16.92 Lakhs)			

themselves, using the local material. The basic need is that something to live in must be available right in the beginning. The emphasis has to be on the benefits directly accruing to the tribals as early as possible. The road link may also not be necessary in each settlement and it need not be a part of primitive group programme. It can be a part of sub-plan programme.

6. In settlement programmes, generally some subsistence allowance is given. Subsistence allowance without counterpart labour input is likely to be misused and demoralizing. It creates a sense of dependence in the community and a sense of bestowing a benefit by the Government functionaries. Such a relationship cannot be healthy. A mechanism has to be found whereby the community should be given the feeling that they are earning their subsistence and nothing is being paid to them ex-gratia. For example, an arrangement could be worked out whereby their wage could be say Rs. 2.50 per day, out of which certain amount say 50p could be deducted as a token payment for the goods which have been supplied to them free. A free supply should have been taken as an initial advance without interest, which could go to form a corpus of the community, which they draw upon in the case of needs and which could be reimbursed by the group from their earnings in the project. In the case of supply of seeds, this principle has already been incorporated. The seeds, which have been given initially will go to form a grain-hold in the community from which they will be taking advance year after year and paying back seeds with 25 per cent extra, which is their conventional method of payment.

7. The programme should be prepared on the basis of providing working opportunity for a period of 300 days in a year on minimum wages. The principle of converting the manpower of the group into capital assets has to be followed. Thus, the entire land reclamation work can be taken up by the beneficiary group itself. The work programmes of 9 months in a year can be chalked out. Agricultural implements can also be provided. It is expected that once the lands get developed, each family will be able to have an income of about Rs. 2,000/- per annum.

8. Programmes like construction of community halls and huts need not be taken up immediately as only construction

programme, not built around economic programmes will become infructuous in case the community shifts its habitat again. The question of establishing processing units can come up only when there is sizeable raw-material to be processed, warranting establishment of such centers. It is not unusual that processing units get established and there is no raw-material available. The infrastructure has to follow programmes of direct benefits rather than to precede it.

9. Irrigation programmes can be taken up provided bulk of the land belongs to the primitive tribes. Provision of irrigation facilities must be accompanied by a very careful extension support of extension agency assuming responsibility for successful agricultural operation. If this is not ensured, it is likely that they may loose whatever land they have.

10. In the plantation programme, the approach has to be to give ownership on the trees to the tribals while the land may continue to belong to the State. The labour cost of the plantation should be met from the project fund keeping cost of capital investment to the bare minimum.

11. Bee keeping and similar other cottage industries may have a good potential. The Khadi and Village Industries Commission may be requested to work out a sizable programme particularly for the more interior areas, so that a substantial number of primitive tribes could be benefited.

12. It may be possible for the State Government to give contact of fishing in the tank to the tribal cooperative development corporation, who can organize cooperatives of fishermen in the areas. Cooperatives for the supply of raw-materials to the primitive tribes (like bamboos) should be arranged, which will also undertake marketing of the finished goods. The large size multi-purpose society will be a functional society catering to the needs of the tribals rather than an area society. Those activities which have relevance to the members can be taken up. A suitable programme for advance of consumption credit may be drawn up linking it up with certain specific economic activities.

13. The fuel wood collectors are the weakest group in any community. They have no means of livelihood. It will be useful if a programme for fuel wood collectors is taken up which should

include organisation of cooperatives, provision of consumption credit and planting of special fuel wood series.

14. The coverage of programme could include health education and economic activities. Provision of social amenities should form a part of the village development programme. Similarly, provision of drinking water could be taken up in State sector, because these are the weakest groups.

Health

15. Among the primitive groups, the first problem is that of health. The entire primitive community should be medically checked up by a team to be organized by the Health Department and they should be given medical care according to a time schedule. Unless the medical check up is done in the first instance, they may not be able to take up physical labour which they will have to do if agriculture is going to be their primitive economic activity.

16. In general, tribal populations are fraught with an assortment of health problems such as anaemia, tuberculosis, leprosy, etc. compounded with the situation of lack of nutrition, (hunger) which leads to poor infant health or even mortality. All this is further compounded by the problem of untrained 'Dais' (traditional midwife or birth attendants) supervising deliveries.

Tribal Health Status and Service Delivery System

17. Reported data suggests wide variability - regionally and between the tribes. On one hand-while some tribal communities have adopted more or less the way of life of non-tribal at one end of spectrum, there are 75 Primitive Tribal Groups (PTGs) with varying population growth rates (increasing/declining-most declining)

18. On the other hand, the health indicators of tribal populations in North Eastern States are comparatively better than their counterparts elsewhere in the country due to high literacy, better awareness and utilization of available health services. Albeit populations exhibit an increasing trend.

19. Earlier Strategies to Improve Health Care in Tribal Areas has focused:

- Ensuring availability of adequate infrastructure and personnel;

- Area specific Reproductive Child Health (RCH) programmes;
- 100 per cent Central Plan funds for National Anti Malaria Programme;
- Focus on effective implementation of the Health & Family Welfare (FW) programmes;
- Close monitoring under Tribal Sub-Plan, early detection of problems in implementation of all ongoing programmes and mid course correction.

20. Studies in the area of health care in tribal areas have pointed out that there are three major factors responsible for low achievement of health care programmes:

- Weak government infrastructure both in terms of physical facilities and manpower;
- Poor means of communication,
- Low education and awareness levels among tribals in addition to deep-rooted socio-cultural traditions.

21. **Gaps in Health Infrastructure are:**

- The present pattern of health and family welfare structure is based on 3-tier system, the primary, secondary and tertiary levels. Services are delivered through a network of sub-centres, Primary Health Centres and Community Health Centres at the peripheral level.
- The present norm for setting up of infrastructure is solely based on population. The norms for establishment of sub-centres, PHCs and CHCs have been released for Tribal areas. A Sub-centre is opened for 3000 instead of 5000 populations in non-tribal areas. Similarly a PHC in tribal area is opened for 20,000 population instead of a norm of 30,000 population and a CHC for 80,000 instead of 1,20,000 population.

22. In view of the above, there is a need to have a fresh look at the existing rigid population norms for these areas.

- All weather accessibility, minimum possible distance from the residential area (should be within 3 Kms to access to a sub-centre) and a flexible population norm would be more appropriate.

- The States have to work out the exact number of sub-centres, PHC, CHC, on this basis through a process of consultation at micro level involving Panchayati Raj Institutions, and local functionaries.
- The population figures of Census 2001 should be taken into consideration. Efforts should be made to fill up the gaps.

The flexible approach undertaken by the Department of Women and Child Development in their ICDS Scheme in tribal areas may be taken as an example.

Education

23. The tribal groups under consideration have to be equipped mentally and psychologically so that they are able to withstand the degradation among them of external agencies. This will be possible by instilling in them a sense of confidence, giving them a feeling that they have a distinct personality and cultural individuality, and educating them in a way which does not erode these features of their personality. In other words they need to imbibe education of a sort different from the conventional type. Where there are schools available in the neighbourhood, the children of the primitive groups may be encouraged to join them. For this purpose a suitable incentive for attendance may be given as an indirect compensation to the parents for the loss in the earnings of the family as a result of the child going away to the school. At the primary school level, scholarship will not be suitable. The assistance has to be mostly in kinds, school uniform, text books and exercise books. It would be desirable to work out a system whereby children also get some nourishment. It will be difficult to adopt mid-day meal programme only for a section of the school. Children could be given a certain quantity of gram every week of every month which they could eat before coming to school. It will be useful if the community is involved in this programme, so that it could be ensured that the gram given for children is eaten by the children. Another incentive could be to give cash awards at the end of the year on the basis of attendance in the schools. This will help in maintenance of minimum attendance in the elementary class.

24. Establishment of Ashram Schools can also be thought of. Ashram Schools could function as a multi-purpose complex where consumer articles could be made available to the people and even minor forest produce from the tribals is purchased. But Ashram School is not a solution for all kinds of situations. Even when it is decided to have an Ashram School, the emphasis initially should be on the services rendered to the primitive tribes than on buildings etc. In the initial stage provision should be made for a Kacha thatched ashram type building rather than a pucca building. Full provision, should be made for maintenance of the children and teachers for these institutions.

25. A substantial adult education effort should also be made amongst the primitive tribes. In the first instance reading material should be prepared keeping in view their own local situation and their problems.

26. Yet it has to be borne in mind that in the past, modern education cannot be deemed to have held much relevance for them since they were out off from the outer world; their awareness and insight of the world around sufficed for their life and culture. However, the intrusion of the external forces has exposed them and thrown challenges which can be met only through an understanding of the working of the modern world which comes through modern education. They have, therefore, to be introduced to such education, while not allowing them to be alienated from their own culture. In other word, they have to be initiated into progress towards higher levels of technology, economy, health, education, etc. This will automatically draw them into the national main stream. But considering the simplicity of their organisation if the transitional phase is made too abrupt there is likelihood of resulting distortion which would be trying for them. So much so, that some of them might fight shy of the change and there should be no attempt to force its pace unduly.

27. We have been urging that a project report should be prepared for primitive tribal community. Each of them should be unique related to the lifestyle, needs and aspirations of each of the groups. It bears emphasis that there cannot be stereotyped project reports for the various tribal communities. Further these project reports may be drawn up in a long range perspective of say 10, 15

or 20 years. The project report should incorporate possible sources of finance. An integrated approach aimed at improving the life and economy of the target group within a time schedule should be the key factor.

28. The numerical strength of each of the tribal communities varies from a few hundreds to a few thousands. Of course, there are some tribal groups in the Andaman & Nicobar Islands like the Great Andamanese, the Shompen, the Sentilinese, the Onge who number less than a hundred, each while the Jarawa are estimated at a couple of hundreds. The financial outlays required of their development would not be much. In fact, the absorption capacity would also not allow large-scale investment. The full financial requirements will continue to be met by the government of India. But the low financial outlays have to be counter-balanced by a much larger human and physical effort for their agriculture, forest, irrigation, etc.

29. This brings us to the question of suitable administrative machinery for effecting development of the primitive tribal groups. While programmes have got to be appropriative and suitable as stressed above, no emphasis can be strong enough for creation of competent, dedicated and sensitive personnel manning it. Some States have already created separate administrative structures for these tribal groups. In some States, societies under the Societies Registration Act have been constituted. Each State may have to figure out what is best in the given circumstances. Both the type of structure needed and the quality of personnel to be posted require close attention of the State government at very high levels. A review of the programme indicates the urgent need for paying special attention to these groups. It is suggested that primitive tribal groups programme may be taken up as a priority item and identification, preparation of project reports, establishment of administrative machinery and initiation of programme may be completed expeditiously.

Professor A. Aiyaupan's Views and Suggestions on Development of Tribal Population in India on the basis of his Field Work in India and abroad during his Life Time

30. An attempt is made here to show that the slow, piece-meal effort now made to develop tribal areas will not be effective

in bridging the gap in progress between tribal and non-tribal communities.

31. Instead of frittering away scarce resources on fragmentary and ill-planned programmes, concentrated use of funds for large-scale agro-industrial projects, as suggested by the Malayappan Committee in Madras and for Orissa tribal areas by the National Council of Applied Economic Research may be more useful and productive of good for the tribes and the nation as a whole. Comparative data from other parts of the world show that the arguments of those who suggest that our tribals may not be able to participate in large-scale projects are baseless.

32. India has a tribal population of about 7 crores. In other words, out of every 100 Indians, 6.8 are Adibasis. Few other countries of the world have such a large population of tribesmen. USSR, China and USA have tribal communities, economically and educationally backward in comparison with the rest of their peoples and speaking languages and practising customs different from those of the majority communities, but in none of these countries are the tribal groups so numerous as in India. There are over two hundred major tribes and more than twice this number of minor tribes distributed in the most inaccessible and wild hill and forest tracts of India. On account of their distinctive ways of life, their general isolation from the currents of our national life and their economic and educational backwardness, these tribes are to be regarded as the weakest of our minorities. While other minorities are nationally organized, vocal and led by effective leaders, the tribal minorities are generally without pressure groups and leaders. (Exception should, of course, be made of tribes that have come under the influence of Christian missions). For this reason, the Adibasis are extremely dependent on the goodwill and sympathy of the majority communities, the Central and State Governments and the welfare agencies. Their future depends very largely on the understanding with which the people at large and the administration approach the tribal question.

In the Political Melting Pot

33. Some people regard the problem of the Adibasis as one of the many new post-Independence problems. While it is true

that far more attention is now being paid to the Adibasis and the Government is now more concerned about their welfare, the British Indian Government were also interested in giving some measure of special protection to the tribal people. In areas where there is a large concentration of tribal population, there were simplified types of administration and there were special laws to protect the tribesmen from exploitation. This policy of the British was one of insulation; it was also a half-hearted policy which was first discussed in the open at the time of the Round Table Conference (1934). There are now no special areas and no question of simplified administration except in NEFA. Politically all the tribes have been brought under the general administration to sink or swim with the rest. Except reservation of a few seats in the legislatures and reservation of a certain percentage of Government jobs, and scholarships for students there are no special privileges given to them. Politically and administratively, the tribes are now little insulated; they have been more or less thrown into the melting pot of national politics.

34. The Government of India, however, has been keenly aware of the need to protect the tribes from exploitation and of the need for giving special grants for the development of tribal areas. Briefly, we might say the present Government's policy is one of gradual integration without radically altering their traditional ways.

35. In furtherance of the Government's policy of bringing the tribal areas from their present backwardness to the general level of development reached by the progressive areas there is the programme of intensive development in the Tribal Development Blocks for which the Government of India is committed to give special grants.

Widening Gap

36. The objective of bridging the gap between the tribes and the rest of the population is not possible of achievement at the present slow rate of development. The gap, instead of closing, tends to grow wider and in the handicap race the tribes will be left further behind. My suggestion, therefore, is that we have to anticipate the Fourth or Fifth Five Year Plan developments in

agriculture and rural industrialization, and make an earlier beginning of these developments in the tribal areas and thus give them an earlier start.

37. The National Council of Applied Economic Research has made a suggestion in its Techno-Economic Survey of Orissa that agricultural estates should be started in the predominantly tribal areas of that State where land is available in sufficiently large blocks. The Andhra Government also have their plan for a Rs.10.00 crore coffee plantation in the Aruku Valley Mechanised farms of the type started with Russian aid in Rajasthan are also worth considering.

38. I have had informal discussions with the Additional Development Commissioner, Orissa, on the practicability of Agricultural Estates in Koraput district. Since climate, etc. there are not different from those of the Aruku valley where coffee growing experiments have been successful, coffee estates are agriculturally feasible. The Additional Development Commissioner suggested that cash crops such as cashew and potato, rice, and tobacco at the lower levels of the hill slopes and valley can be tried in addition, so that instead of coffee alone we may plan multi-crop agricultural estates. Ways will have to be devised to involve the tribal communities in these large-scale agricultural schemes nor merely as labourers, but as partners who, in due course, will run the whole business themselves.

39. The tribesmen of the western and southern districts of Orissa now grow a number of commercial crops. But they suffer because of exploitation by middle-men, lack of capital, and lack of knowledge of modern ways of increasing output. They have neither credit nor marketing organizations. The middle men advance credit and but or rather capture the produce at prices fixed by them.

40. Both the Elwin Committee on tribal blocks and the Dhebar Commission have made recommendations about the urgent need for credit and marketing corporations to help the tribals. With their primitive methods of production the proposed credit facilities and marketing organizations by themselves will be of little use. Will they get enough from their little holdings to meet the needs of a fuller life? Hence, it is essential that plans for modernized agricultural development, that is, agriculture as an industry should

be considered for the tribal areas, and this should be done earlier than elsewhere for the reasons already stated.

Unfavourable Stereotypes

41. When I first made this suggestion in the course of a brief personal discussion with UN Dhebar, he told me that in the new steel towns and in Tatanagar, the Adibasis are engaged only for the most unskilled types of works as they are not considered fit to handle more complicated jobs. This is a case of giving the unwanted underdog a bad name and hanging it. The recruiting agencies in all these places have not given the Adibasis a chance. I am told there is a Santhal who is now working as a University Professor. That means he was given a chance to prepare himself for such a career. Adibasis work in the Accountant General's Office in Orissa. There are Adibasis in the Indian Administrative Services who are as good as any other government employees. Is not the translation of a tribal youth from his rural home to offices in the State capitals a sudden change? Are they not adapting themselves to the new situation? If the Government were not generous to them and if they had not been given the chance, unsympathetic critics would have continued to say that the Adibasis are unfit for high Government jobs. Several Konds are employed as skilled workers in the Rayagada Sugar Factory, Oraons and Mundas as machine men in the Bonai iron ore quarries and in the Cement Factory at Rajgangpur in Sundargarh district. The, Adibasis in Tatanagar, etc. have not been given a chance under fair and sympathetic conditions.

42. In other parts of the world, aboriginal peoples have in recent years undergone rapid transformation from very primitive conditions. Backward Papuans in New Guinea area, far more backward, primitive and isolated than any of our tribes have, during the last few decades made tremendous progress. Prof. Firth of the London School of Economics mentions of a particular Papuan Co-operative society which owns a small ship to import and export goods. There are Polynesian tribal estate owners and ship owners. If these primitive populations can make good progress, our Adibasis, too, can do likewise, but they should be given the chance, initial help and encouragement.

43. The old belief that simpler folk cannot make rapid adjustments to change is found to be only partially correct. Many are the cases we know of tribes whom contacts and changes ruined but the circumstances of each case would show that it was not change as such that created disorganization but the failure to reorganize. In her re-study of the Manus people (north of New Guinea) Margaret Mead has shown how under the dynamic leadership of Palieau, a community of about 4,000 people who lived a generation back at the stone age level gave up its old ways of life and modernized itself on the western patterns acquired by contact with American forces stationed in the area during World War II. Their housing pattern, family pattern, sex relationship and local government were all changed radically in the course of 25 years.

44. In India itself, the transformation by Christian missionaries of the ways of life of minority communities such as Khasis, Garos and Nagas did not take long. The changes have been quick and since the cultural traits taken over included English language, Christianity and several western values, the transformation meant also modernization. Individuals as well as groups can and do change without deleterious effects. Both psychological and sociological theories have been veering to this point of view.

45. In the course of a dozen years, a serf population of Peruvian Indians, living under miserable condition were transformed to a modern community, so progressive as to serve as a model for the whole of Peru. These Vicosinos were able to change and make adjustments because the programmes were goal-directed and guided, deliberately chosen and planned. The scientific resources of Professor Allan Holmberg and his team, and the cooperative spirit of the Peruvvian and American technicians and careful organisation did the job in spite of initial doubts and suspicions.

46. Every one with some education knows now a days that on the proper conservation of our forests depends the agricultural and, to a very great extent, the industrial prosperity of our country. Now, what is the relation between these all-important forests and the jungle tribes? These people are the only community who can stand the rigours of the Malaria of the mosquito infested jungles,

your forest officials, conservators, rangers and foresters from the plans, may, in your view, be conserving, protecting and exploiting the forests for your benefit; you are thoroughly mistaken. The real workers are the lowly, despised and neglected jungle people whom you and your forest officials take for granted as part of the jungle wealth. The jungle inen have been blessed by nature with a greater amount of resistance to malaria, and it is no exaggeration to say that had it not been for the large number of hill tribes who toil for you in the forests they would not be what they are now. Now what do we do for the tribes? Money-lenders and other kinds of human, pests are exported from the plains to the jungle areas; they suck the blood of the hill-men; accounts of how these sowcars deprive the jungle men of the fruits of their hard work, would make a harrowing story. Living on the verge of starvation, the jungle tribes are rapidly losing their efficiency and, in course of time, if the exploitation continues, the situation will get definitely bad. I hope the logic of what I just now said will not be lost upon you. Neglect the junglemen, and you cut at the root of your agricultural economy.

47. People lacking understanding are likely to look with contempt upon hillmen; the more you know them and the more intimate your contacts with them, your attitude will change. One of our chief human weaknesses is our inability to see the "other" man's point of view. A vegetarian, for example, is very apt to mistake most non-vegetarians for minor carnivores; when the difference extends to language, mode of living and clothing, the difficulties in properly understanding the "other man" become all the more greater. You and I, so called civilized men, clothed and with out hair cut and combed, often fail to see the noble spirit in individuals differently draped or not draped at all, and with unkempt hair. Several of our hill tribes speak languages or dialects which we do not understand. Many of them go half naked. They live in miserable huts and eat animals which most of us consider repugnant. It is no wonder, therefore, that thoughtless men tend to regard jungle people no better than animals, but let me however tell you that the hill people have been reduced to this pitiable condition as a result of centuries of exploitation. But look at the marvels which education and better opportunities have done in

the ease of some tribal people. In Assam where Missionary agencies helped the tribesmen to stand on their own legs there are cabinet members belonging to the tribal population. There is no significant point of difference between the plainsmen and the so-called aboriginal tribes. The difference between us and the tribes is chiefly a matter of economics. This world witnessed several economic revolutions before the industrial revolution of which you read so much. The discovery of the plough and of the domestication of cattle was responsible for the greatest agricultural revolution in human history. As a result of these two new factors, early men took to intensive cultivation, to settle in large colonies and to the exchange of commodities on a commercial scale. Certain tribes who refused to adopt the new methods of cultivation involving the use of the plough and cattle, clung to the primitive digging sticks and hoes and also remained stuck up in jungle habitats where they were not put to the necessity of competing with their more go-ahead compatriots. Several of our hill people are the remnants of this conservative section of our ancient population. Even now, in certain parts of India, there are aboriginal tribes to whom the use of the plough is taboo. These tribesmen who refused to accept innovations were acting in the same manner as some of our orthodox neighbours do in several vital matters, but the consequences of conservatism in the case of most of these tribes people were catastrophic. As you all very know, in this world, people who get mastery over neighbours with less efficient tools. Communities of people whose most effective weapons of offence were bows and arrows were conquered by those who had fire arms. No doubt we may blame the tribesmen for their lack of adaptability. Let me leave aside old history; talking of the present situation, we have to deal with the economic and social problems, of the weakest and the most defenceless of our minorities, namely our tribal Indians. Civilised nations will judge us not so much by our industrial progress or administrative efficiency as by the way in which we treat the weakest among us. The rehabilitation of the tribes, from this point of view, is not merely a human or social problem but a national problem. We have communities of jungle people, fellow-Indians, living on roots which they gather from the jungles and on the vermin which they trap. We have other groups which cultivate the slopes of the hills with their digging sticks after burning down patches of the forest. Some come so degraded on account of poverty that they do not hesitate to take to crime. Several tribes, as for example, the Paniyans of Wynad, are practically slaves.

48. No time should be lost in doing something for these poor people, for, in fact, if you really care to understand them you will be surprised to find our tribesmen are first rate human material still harbouring several of our ancient virtues, which we have lost due to our having become civilized. Basic virtues, such as honesty, kindness, neighbourliness and fellow feeling are nowhere found in a better measure than among our jungle tribes.

Other Important Areas of Concern Need to be Handled

Economic Deprivation

49. Tribals have been subjected to poverty and economic deprivation mainly due to erosion in their subsistence based economy. Their subsistence, sustenance and survival essentially based upon land, water and forest which form their 'life-line as they provide source for agriculture, shifting cultivation and other natural resources for their day to day living. Weakening of the subsistence base has been adversely effecting their self-sufficiency and threatening their very existence. The situation had further deteriorated, since the administrative restrictions have been imposed on collection/utilization of forest land and forest resources that the tribals traditionally dependent upon.

Shifting Cultivation

50. The assessment of the situation indicated that Tribals primarily depend upon agriculture which constitutes their mainstay. According to 1991 Census, 42.4 per cent of the ST population are Main Workers. Of these, 54.5 per cent were cultivators and 32.7 per cent were agricultural labourers. Thus, more than 87 per cent of the tribal main workers are dependent on agriculture. The tribals generally live in most in-hospitable terrain and practice shifting cultivation on higher slopes and dry-land cultivation in plains and lower slopes where productivity and output are very low. Lack of proper irrigation facilities, decline in

fertility of soil and risks and uncertainties involving damages caused by the wild animals, pests, cyclones, droughts etc. have further deteriorated the agricultural yield. The growing tribal population and the declining agriculture productivity has become a serious threat to the subsistence base of the tribal communities, endangering their self-supporting food security system.

50.2 According to the Agricultural Census of 1990-91, of the total net sown area of 143.84 lakh hectares in the tribal areas, 13.2 per cent of the cultivated land is being irrigated through canals, tanks, wells/tube wells etc. Thus, the area of the un-irrigated land is very large. The provision of irrigation facilities is therefore the key to the improvement of their agriculture.

50.3 Shifting cultivation is still being practiced by the tribal population on higher slopes of hilly areas of the country. As estimated, more than 6 lakh tribal families in the States of North-East, Orissa, Andhra Pradesh, Bihar and Himachal Pradesh practice shifting cultivation, which is not ecologically sound. Yet, the shifting cultivation is integrally linked to the tribal economy in the areas where it is practiced and their social, economic and ritual activities are also centred around this practice. The problem of shifting cultivation is a very complex one involving economic, social and psychological aspects of the tribal communities. The Ministry of Agriculture has been implementing a scheme for Control and Transformation of Shifting Cultivation in the North-Eastern States, but the pace of its implementation has been very slow.

Deprivation of Forest Rights

51. Development of Forest Villages and successful implementation of Joint Forest Management since ages about 5000 forest villages exist within the boundary of reserved forest. Nearly 2 lakh tribal families were given heritable but inalienable rights on the lands which they have been cultivating in States of Madhya Pradesh, Chhattisgarh, Gujarat, Assam etc. Integrated development of these tribal people may receive urgent attention.

51.2 To strengthen symbiotic relationship between forest and forest dwellers, Joint Forest Management was started in the country in the year 1990. Concerted efforts are required to manage forest areas for regenerating the ecosystem and improving socio-economic conditions of the tribals.

Intellectual Property Rights

52. The tribal communities have a very close dependence on biological resources related to plants and animals/birds. Their livelihood and life style often depends upon and is shaped by these resources. Therefore, their survival and sustenance is intricately linked to conservation and utilization of these resources. Corporate protectionism in terms of patents and intellectual property rights (IPR) arising out of various international treaties/ instruments on trade and common property resources such as TRIPS under WTO represents a real threat to economic livelihood of these communities as well as a source of potential exploitation of their resource base as bio-diversity expressed in life forms and knowledge is sought to be converted into private property and treated as an open access system for free exploitation by those who want to privatize and patent it. There is an urgent need to provide appropriate legal and institutional arrangements for recognizing and acknowledging the rights of tribal communities to such resources and knowledge.

Land Alienation

53. Land is not only the most important productive resource base for the tribals; but also occupies an important place in their psyche as the main-stay of their social and religious practices. Over a period of time, this resource base of the tribal communities has tended to get eroded not only through acquisition for public purposes but also through fraudulent transfers, forcible eviction, mortgages, leases and encroachments. As per the information available with the Ministry of Rural Development in January 1999 while 4.65 lakh cases of alienation of tribal land covering an area of 9.18 lakh acres, were registered in the States of Andhra Pradesh, Assam, Bihar, Gujarat, Himachal Pradesh, Karnataka, Madhya Pradesh, Maharashtra, Orissa, Rajasthan and Tripura, only 2 lakh cases were disposed off in favour of 1.56 lakh tribal families covering an area of 5.38 lakh acres. Of these, the States affected by large scale tribal land alienation are - Andhra Pradesh (2.79 lakh acres); Madhya Pradesh (1.58 lakh acres); Karnataka (1.30 lakh acres); and Gujarat (1.17 lakh acres). As pointed out by various studies lack of political and administrative will continues to be the

cause for the perpetuation of the problem of land alienation amongst tribals as reflected in the reluctance to amend legal provisions to plug loopholes and swift administrative action to identify alienated land, and restoring it to the tribals with delivery of possession.

Displacement of Tribals

54. Rehabilitation of the Displaced Tribals is a serious problem which is yet to receive due attention. As per the information readily available, a total of 213 lakh population have been displaced during 1951-90 due to the various development projects like Dams, Mines, Industries, Wild Life Sanctuaries etc. of the total displaced, the tribals constitute 85.4 lakh representing 40.1 per cent. Amongst the total displaced tribals, only 21.2 lakh (24.8 per cent) could be resettled, so far.

54.2 As documented by various research studies, only a small percentage of tribal oustees could get the benefit of rehabilitation facilities. A vast majority of tribal people displaced by big projects are pushed into a vortex of increasing assetlessness, unemployment, debt-bondage and destitution. Women and children among them are the worst affected. The payment of compensation in cast directly dis-empowers tribals as the exploiters in the area exhaust their money through various unproductive expenditure and fraudulent practices. Any loss of access to traditional sources of livelihood viz - land, forest, sea, river, pasture, cattle etc. marginalizes women more than men in the labour market. It is only when land and other sources are replaced, tribals in general and tribal women in particular, can partially regain their economic status.

Indebtedness

55. The problem of indebtedness among tribals is not only an indication of their poverty but also reflects wider economic malaise, i.e., lack of education, low purchasing/bargaining power and lack of resources for engaging in gainful activity and meeting emergent expenditure. Under the Fifth Schedule of the Constitution, the Governors of States with Scheduled Areas were given powers for making regulations for placing restrictions on undesirable practices

like money-lending in such Scheduled Areas. Relevant Laws/ Regulations exist in 16 TSP States/UTs to regulate the business of money lending and to give debt relief. However, the legal measures to curb the activities of money lenders and traders have failed to have much effect on the severity of the problem due to the ineffective enforcement machinery and lack of alternative source of credits for meeting consumption and productive needs. Lack of informal technical institutions to extend especially credit to poor tribals forced them to depend upon usurious money lenders, which results in their debt-bondage.

Excise and Alcoholism

56. Alcholisms is one of the major causes for the prevailing tribal ill health, economic degradation and social disharmony which hamper their socio-economic development. However, tribal communities traditionally brew liquor from rice and other MFP products for their regular as well as occasional consumption related to certain rituals or social occasions and festivities. The initiation of commercial vending of liquor in tribal areas has started impoverishing the tribal population and leading them to suffer from indebtedness and exploitation of various types. In 1975, the then Ministry of Social Welfare issued guidelines to the States and UTs regarding Excise Policy in Tribal Areas which included discontinuing commercial vending of liquor in tribal areas; permitting the tribal communities to brew traditional rice beer only for their consumption; and weaning them away from the habit of alcohol consumption. Although the States and UTs have broadly accepted the guidelines, effective follow-up action was not taken for their revenue tend persist with and even extend commercial vending of liquor in the tribal areas ignoring the harmful effects on the tribal population.

Extinction of Tribal Culture

57. The principles of 'Panchsheel' specially adopted as an approach to the tribal development, recognize the importance of tribal culture and their traditions. As pronounced in the Second Five Year Plan, Welfare Programmes for Scheduled Tribes have to be based on respect and understanding of their culture and

traditions and an appreciation of the social, psychological and economic problems with which they are faced. Based on this principle, preservation and promotion of tribal culture has become the prime concern in formulating various developmental programmes for the well-being of the tribals. However, with accelerated development, tribals have been exposed/subjected to the rapid modernization and industrialization bringing them into sudden contact of non-tribal culture and social moves - which have had deep influence on the tribal life-style and culture, positive as well as negative. Therefore, along with various developmental policies and programmes initiated to improve the socio-economic conditions of tribal people, there is also an urgent need to preserve and promote various aspects of tribal culture and heritage, including their values of cooperation, community feeling, music, dance, literature, language, festivals/religion, knowledge and indigenous technology, skills, arts and handicrafts etc. The uniqueness, of the tribal culture which enriches the country's cultural mosaic, is fast disappearing and even getting distorted under powerful influences of the dominant culture.

Crimes/Atrocities Against Scheduled Tribes

58. Despite the enactment and enforcement of two Special Laws viz - Protection of Civil Rights Act of 1955 and the SCs and STs (Prevention of Atrocities) Act of 1989 and the Indian Penal Code (IPC), and other laws/legal provisions being in force for their protection, crimes/atrocities against the tribals, especially against women and children continue to be very high. Also, a large number of crimes committed against STs remain unreported because of their isolation and their reluctance due to fear and apathy of the enforcement machinery. Tribals are most harassed by judicial processes when they are involved in criminal/civil cases which are alien to their system of conflict resolution, and drag on for years and sap their energy, resources and erode their self-confidence and morale. Therefore, alternative arrangements for disposal of cases arising out of not very serious offences locally with the help of community and without the aid of lawyers and formal judicial/police procedures need to be evolved.

Ineffective Implementation of TSP and Utilisation of SCA to TSP

59. The special strategy of Tribal Sub-Plan (TSP) has been under implementation since 1975 both at the Central and State levels with the objective of ensuring that the benefits from various developmental sectors do not by-pass STs and accordingly funds, in population proportion, are earmarked for the development of STs. Only 18 Central Ministries/Departments and 20 States/UTs, are earmarking the funds for TSP. Despite the repeated suggestion to the State Governments to adopt the Maharashtra Model of resource allocations and utilization not many States have done so far. The strategy of TSP, as it is implemented, has also become very routinised. Its impact on improving the conditions of STs, is not being felt.

Panchayat Raj Institutions/Gram Sabha

60. The 73rd Amendment to the Constitution and its extension to the Fifth Scheduled Areas as per the provisions of the Panchayats (Extension to the Scheduled Areas) Act, 196 (PESA Act) ensures decentralized governance, planning and development ensuring categorical involvement of tribals there in. However, there are States who are yet to give affect to PESA Act, 196 to ensure effective participation to the tribals into the process of planning, implementing and monitoring various measures/programmes, besides ensuring the accountability of the public functionaries. Gram Sabha, in the tribal areas, being the grass-root level democratic institutions could ensure participation of the local tribals in preparing, implementing and monitoring of various welfare and development programmes and thus ensure development with equity and social justice. To this effect, the elected representatives of STs especially their women need to be empowered and sensitized by extending operational knowledge of the role and the functioning of the Panchayats and the Gram Sabhas as per the provisions made through the 73rd Amendment to the Constitution and the PESA Act, 1996. Unless such rigorous/ effective training and orientation are imparted to the tribal representatives, there would be neither any effective implementation of the programmes at the grass-root level nor

there would accountability of the efforts/investments for the well-being of the tribals.

Tribal Unrest

61. A long history of disruption of tribal communities, sustained and frequently brutal expropriation of tribal wealth and the resultant anger and despair has led to a situation in which many regions of tribal concentration are immersed in a cycle of violence. All States in the north-east have been ripped apart by violence. In many stretches of forested Central India, an array of outfits continue to channelise tribal anger into violent resistance to State power.

61.2 The impact of various poverty alleviation programmes put into action during the last two developmental decades has, no doubt, brought down the poverty levels amongst STs. Still, the incidence of poverty amongst STs continues to be very high and at 51.1 per cent in 1993-94, which is much higher when compared to 36 per cent in respect of general categories during the same year. Therefore, there has been an increasing unrest amongst the tribals and in tribal areas in the recent past. Radical/Extremist Movements are already operating in some parts of the country. The root cause for which is the perceived dissatisfaction with their existing conditions and failure to access benefits and facilities promised to them. There is an urgent need to critically review the approach and strategy of tribal protection and development followed so far and re-orient/change it wherever required so as to ensure flow of development benefits within a definite time-frame and restore their faith in the society and in the Government.

Need for a National Policy

62. Though the strategies of tribal development are expected to be based upon the principles of 'Panchsheel' which prescribes that 'the tribal people' should develop along the lines of their own genius and nothing should be imposed from outside; tribal rights in land and forest should be encouraged in conservation and promotion of their own traditional arts and culture; work through their own social and cultural institutions; and trained and build a team of their own people to do the work of administration and

development, but unfortunately these do not find their due position either in the frame of tribal development or various welfare and development programmes that are conceived and implemented by the Government. Many of the impediments/drawbacks experienced in achieving the intended goals in tribal development are fundamentally due to the reason that the Panchsheel principles were not taken into account in formulation and operational terms. Understanding of the social, cultural and economic systems of tribal societies is essential for formulating/implementing any strategy/programme meant for tribal development. Most of the developmental programmes as they exist today are extension of general rural development or poverty alleviation programme which have limitations in their applicability and effectiveness because these often do not get synchronized with the tribal way of life and hence loose relevance in the context of tribes.

63. Therefore, there is an urgent need to formulate a comprehensive National Policy for Empowering the Tribals of India with definite goals and targets to be achieved within a specific time-frame. Policy so adopted, should be able to provide a perspective which ensures that the status of the tribal population is raised to that of the rest of the society and they get their due share of benefit from development.

Eleven

Primitive Tribal Groups in States/UTs

1. Rajasthan

Sahariya PTG in Rajasthan

Sahariya are one of the most backward tribes of Rajasthan, who still follow most of the traditional way of social life. Sahariya means the companion of a tiger. According to legend they have been blessed by lord Shiva and live in the forest like sher (Tiger). The main customs and manners bear great resemblance with the caste Hindus; but they are considered as untouchables. There are 54,760 saharia in Rajasthan which is less than one per cent of total tribal population.

Distribution Pattern

Sahariya are mostly inhabited in Shahbad and Kishangunj tehsils of Baran district which constitute about 89.45 per cent of total sahariya population. A few Sahariya are also scattered in Udaipur, Chittorgarh, Kota, Jhalawar and Karauli districts. The living place of Sahariya's is mostly undulating hilly terrain covered with forest.

S.No.	*District*	*Population of Sahariya*	*Percentage*
1.	Baran	48,982	89.45
2.	Kota	2650	4.84
3.	Jhalawar	455	0.83
4.	Chittaurgarh	6.01	1.10
5.	Udaipur	284	0.52
6.	Sirohi	282	0.52
7.	Karauli	137	0.25
8.	Rajsamand	118	0.21
9.	Others	1251	2.28
	Total	54,760	100.00%

Literacy is very low in the community while only 8.5 per cent males are literate the number of female literates is as low as 0.7 per cent. Most of these tribe live in rural villages.

Occupational Structure

From economic point of view Sahariyas are living in insolated and physically unsuitable land. At places where plain land is available they do cultivation otherwise work as labourers in Land Lords fields. Only 36.3 per cent of Sahariya family do cultivation on their own land while 49.3 per cent work on others agricultural land as labourers. Sahariya also keep goat, cows, oxen, and also collect forest produces, fuel wood. Thus, 5.11 per cent of the workers are engaged in such allied activities. In other occupation like trade and commerce, transport services etc. only 8 per cent workers are engaged. This shows the poor economy of sahariya tribe in the state.

S.No.	*Occupation*	*Persons*	*Percentage*
1.	Cultivator	6128	36.32
2.	Agricultural labourers	8.325	49.34
3.	Live stock, mining, forestry etc.	862	5.11
4.	Household Industries	140	0.83
5.	Manufacturing	309	1.83
6.	Construction	233	1.38
7.	Trade and Commerce	386	2.29
8.	Transport and Communication	71	0.42
9.	Other services	418	2.48
	Total	16,872	100.00%

Social-Cultural Structure

Sahariya are Hindu by religion. They have no language of their own. Majority of them speak Karilahi and Haduati. A few also speak Brajbhasa. The important goods they worship are Kapa shiwala, valmiki. They were earlier bonded labourers but after the abolition of bonded labourer, they have been rehabilitated in different areas.

2. Karnataka

Primitive tribal groups are the Scheduled Tribes who practices Pre-agricultural level of technology, having low literacy percentage, with stagnant or diminishing population. In Karnataka state, Jenukuruba and Koraga tribes are recognized as primitive tribal groups.

Jenukuruba

Jenukuruba tribe peoples are short statured having a broad head with a broad nose and short face. The are non-vegetarians, Ragi and rice are their staple cereals. Collecting honey, herbs, roots and fruits are the traditional occupation of Jenukuruba tribes. Their language, locally called Jenunudi, a dialect of Kannada.

Jenukuruba tribe is concentrated in the districts of Mysore, Chamarajanagar and Kodagu.. As per the recent survey, total Jenukuruba tribe population is 23597. The district and taluk wise population is as follows.

(Rs. In lakhs)

Sl. No.	*District/Taluk*	*No. of families*	*Male*	*Female*	*Total*
(A)	Mysore				
1.	H.D. Kote	2423	4897	4368	9265
2.	Hunsur	1281	2746	2414	5160
3.	Nanjangudu	125	255	236	491
4.	Periyapatna	617	1077	1150	2227
	Total	4446	8975	8168	17143
(B)	Chamarajanagar				
1.	Gundlupet	248	416	412	828
(C)	Kodagu				
1.	Somwarpet	551	852	888	1740
2.	Virajpet	1206	2152	1734	3886
	Total	1757	3004	2622	5626
	Grand Total	6451	12395	11202	23597

Literacy

The total literacy among Jenukurubas is 17.09 per cent
The Female literacy among Jenukurubas is 19.29 per cent
The Male literacy among Jenukurubas is 15.10 per cent

Koraga

Koraga, a very quiet and inoffensive race, small and slight, the men seldom exceeding five feet six inches, black skinned, thick lipped, noses broad and flat and with bushy rough hairs. Their principle occupation is basket making. Most of them are labourers. It is generally believed that the Koraga speaks language of their own. In Dakshina Kannada they speak Tulu, Kannada, Konkani and Marati. Koragas have their own cultural practices. Drum and dance besides flute are the two aides that enable the Koragas to give expression to their cultural traits.

Koraga tribe is concentrated in Dakshina Kannada and Udupi districts. As per the recent survey the total population of the Koraga tribe is 11566. The district and taluk wise population is as follows.

Sl. No.	*District/Taluk*	*No. of families*	*Male*	*Female*	*Total*
(A)	Dakshina Kannada				
1.	Bantwal	170	296	267	563
2.	Belthangadi	98	152	136	288
3.	Mangalore	716	1372	1419	2791
4.	Sulya	47	77	74	151
5.	Puttur	104	170	174	344
	Total	1135	2067	2070	4137
(B)	Udupi				
1.	Udupi	959	1975	1875	3850
2.	Karkal	354	666	678	1344
3.	Kundapura	607	1135	1100	2235
	Total	1920	3776	3653	7429
	Grand Total	3055	5843	5723	11566

Literacy

Total literacy among Koragas is	38.12 per cent
The Female literacy among Koragas is	36.38 per cent
The Male literacy among Koragas is	39.82 per cent

LITERACY DETAILS

PTG	*Total Population*	*Total Literates*	*Male Literates*	*Female Literates*	*Percentage*		
					Male	*Female*	*Total*
Jenu Kuruba	23597	4033	1872	2161	15.10	19.29	17.09
Koraga	11566	4409	2327	2082	39.82	36.38	38.12

3. Orissa

Birhor/Mankirdia is an aboriginal group of people, simple and shy. They trap and eat monkeys and thus called as *Mankidia, Mankidi* or *Mankirdia*. In their tongue *Birhor* means *men of jungle*. The *jaggi,* settled group and the *uthulu,* nomadic group are the two main sections. The latter group is found in Orissa. They belong to Proto-Australoid group. They speak Munda. They speak Oriya and have multilingual in habit. They are of Kolarian origin. They claim to be the descendants of Sun. They are mostly found in forest areas of Sundargarh, Sambalpur, Keonjhar and Mayurbhanj districts. As per 1991 census their total population was 3468. Their sex ratio is 1001. In 1981 literacy was 3.4%. Birhor is a nomadic tribe. They are transhumants. They shuttle between market and forest. They repeatedly change their settlements, *tanda*. They select their settlement sites on the basis of proximity to sources of water and the local weekly market, and aboveboard, availability of *Siali* fibres, jutes and monkeys. They construct cone shaped leaf huts, *kumba,* and dwell there. The shrine for their clan god and dormitory houses is also made of leaves. They pursue hunting and gathering economy, make ropes and rope made crafts out of Siali fibres and *jutes,* and when needed they work as labourers. They have minimum assets like coarse clothes, a few silver bead ornaments. earthen and aluminium utensils, bamboo baskets, axe, knife, bow and arrow, monkey catching nets and date palm mats. They practise monogamy and proceed with marriage negotiations for adults only. Payment of bride price is prevalent. They believe in rebirth, bury the dead, observe life cycle rituals and lead a life of 'be happy and merry'.

Bondo otherwise known as Bondo Paraja is one of the most primitive tribes of Orissa. They call themselves as *remo,* which means 'man'. They speak *remo,* a south-Munda language. Once upon a time they were the warriors of the king of Chakrakote of Bastar in Madhya Pradesh. Thus they claim royal association and ancestry. Today they are found in the Khairpur Block of Malkangiri district on the north west of river machhkund bordering Andhra Pradesh. The Bondo numbered 2565, 3641, 4677, 5338, 5895 and 7315 in census 1941, 1951, 1961, 1971, 1981 and 1991 respectively. The corresponding decadal growth rate was 41.9 per cent, 28.4 per cent, 14.13 per cent and 10.43 per cent. This means that, over the years there has been a sharp decline in their growth rate. However, as per census 1991, the sex ratio is 1105 which is quite appreciable. In 1981 their literacy was 3.60 per cent. There are two culturally distinct groups of Bondo: lower Bondo and upper Bondo. The lower Bondo live in the foothill villages and are relatively acculturated. They are mainly settled agriculturists and wage earners. Whereas the upper Bondo live in the inaccessible mountainous areas with an elevation varying from 1500 ft. to 4000 ft. well known as the Bonda-hills. They are distributed in 31 villages in an area of 130 sq. kms. They continue to maintain their primitive customs and traditions. Their villages are situated on hilltops nearer to perennial streams. The houses are quite spread out. A village is an important social unit, members of which are related to each other as *soru bhai,* meaning *dining brothers.* Marriage within the village is strictly forbidden. They have two roomed thatched houses having cattle-shed close-by. The megalithic platform called *sindibor* is found in the centre of the village. It serves as a community centre for the village elders and sociopolitical and religious heads. The village deity resides in *hundi,* their main shrine. The girls' dormitory is called *selani dingo* and that of the boys' dormitory, *Ingersing dingo.* Monogamy is commonly prevalent whereas the relatively well to do prefer polygyny. In most cases the wife is older than the husband. Bride-wealth is paid in shape of cattle, liquor and a rupee in cash. The women are free to accept or reject a marriage proposal. They pursue shifting cultivation in addition to growing rice in the stream beds and raise other cereals, pulses and oil seeds by ploughing the upland. The Bondo rice is fine, scented and delicious. Besides they domesticate cows, goats, pigs and poultry birds. They have their traditional village council where *naik*, village headman, *challan*, assistant to headman, and *barik*, messenger are the main functionaries. A sword, *patkhanda*, kept hidden in a banyan tree at village Mudulipada is a royal insignia that gets worshipped every year in January-February. The believe in sorcery and black magic. *Dissari* is their astrologer-cum-medicineman. The Bondo men are very suspicious and they always move armed with bows and arrows, and knife. They are well known for their aggressiveness. On the contrary, the Bondo women are very affectionate, loving, responsible and industrious. They are respected and honoured in the society. The Bondo women used to have their shaven heads, wear scanty self-woven scarf, *nodic*, prepared out of *kereng* fibre, adorn themselves with colourful bead necklaces and ornaments, and decorate their shaven heads with flowers and jungle beads.

Chenchu a nomadic tribe. They mainly inhabit Guntur, Prakasam and Mahabubnagar districts of Andhra Pradesh and are sparsely distributed in the bordering areas of Orissa and Karnataka. They have synonyms like Chenchuvaru or Chenchwar. Guha (1933) classified Chenchu as of Prot-Australoid stock. They speak a Dravidian dialect for both inter and intra group communication. According to 1991 census their population in Orissa is only 275. Sex ratio is 599. Literacy in 1981 was 7.70 per cent. They are mainly concentrated in the districts of Kalahandi and Sundargarh. Chenchu settlements are generally uniclan and homogenous comprising consanguineal and affinal relatives of both male and female lines. Family is mostly nuclear patrilocal and patrilineal and inheritance of properly follows the rule of male equigeniture. The tribe is divided into two broad divisions like Konda (Hill) Chenchu and Adavi (Jungle) Chenchu. Each broad group is again divided into numbers of exogamous totemic septs (Kulam) viz. - Gurram (Horse), Arati (Plantain tree), Manla (tree), Tota (Garden), Mekala (Goat), Indla (House), Savaram (Gold coin), and Gundam (Pit), etc. In the Chenchu society monogamy is the general rule and marriage by negotiation is an ideal practice. Marriage by service and by elopement are also in vogue. Cross-cousin marriage is preferred. Marriage of widows, widowers, divorcees, junior levirate, junior sororate are allowed. Bride price is prevalent and is paid both in cash and kind. A Brahman priest officiates in wedding rituals. The Chenchu observe puberty rites for girls. The pollution period lasts for five days. Birth pollution is observed for eleven days. A newborn baby is given a name by a woman sorcerer on the fourth day and tonsure is performed when the child is three to five years old. The Chenchu practise burial for the dead. Each clan has its separate burial ground. They observe death pollution for a period three to eleven days. Purificatory rites such as the *Chira dinamu* is performed on the third day and the *Padda dinamu* or Peddadivasam ceremony on the eleventh day. They also observe death anniversary with a feast given to lineage members. Chenchu are traditionally hunters and food gatherers. They supplement their economy by agricultural and non-agricultural pursuits in addition to selling forest produces and rearing livestock. At present, a few of them have taken up settled cultivation. They are non-vegetarians. Jawar, ragi and rice constitute their principal diet. They are addicted to country liquor and smoking cheroots and tobaccos. Their religion is Hinduism. They celebrate many Hindu festivals like Ugadi, Sankranthi, Dusara, Sivarathri and make pilgrimage to sacred shrines like 'Tirupati, Simachalam, Srisailam, etc. They also worship their traditional deities and believe in existence of soul and spirits and supernatural entities. The Chenchu have very elaborate traditional community council known as *Kula Panchayati* headed by Raju (King) of *Bhumin Kulam* assisted by *Pradhani* (minister) of *Kudumala Kulam* and *Kollagudar* (whip attender) of *Uttaluri Kulam*. It settles inter and intra community disputes. However the chenchu have retained their beautiful folk songs which are sung by both men and women during festive occasions.

Chuktia Bhunjia is a small and little known tribe of Western Orissa. They consider themselves as a pure and clean section of the Bhunjia tribe. Their mother tongue *Bhunjia* is a mixture of Oriya, Hindi and Chhatisgarhi languages. As per 1991 census they live in 17 villages in Sonabera plateau with a population of 1579. Their villages are located in they sylvan hill ranges. They have linear pattern of houses, arranged in rows. The shrine of *sunadei,* the supreme deity is located at the heart of the Sunabera village. A Bhunjia dwelling consists of one large living room, an open verandah, a kitchen-shed, one cattle shed and a goat pen. The kitchen is separately built at a little distance. The houses are made up of wooden poles and mud walls, the roof thatched with wild grass. The kitchen is the most sacred place for them and they entertain the belief that their ancestral spirit dwells in there. No unrelated person, not even the daughter of the family, especially after her marriage is allowed to enter into kitchen. Consequent upon the defilement of the kitchen it is levelled to the ground and the roof is burnt and a kitchen is built anew. The tribe is divided into two exogamous moieties, markam, affines, and netam, kins. Each moiety is again split into a number of lineages, barags. They prefer cross cousin marriage. Men wear hand-woven clothes, *dhoti* and *gamuchha* and women wear sari. The women adorn themselves with ornaments of brass, aluminium, silver and imitation ornaments and put on tatoo marks. They observe birth pollution for six days, Pre-puberty rite, kundabera, is significant for the maiden. It is a ritual of arrow marriage celebrated for a group of girls of the same age-set. No girl can marry before that. They bury the dead and observe death rituals on the third day and organize and partake mortuary feast. The maternal uncle plays a vital role in all the life cycle rituals. The Chuktia Bhunjias are settled agriculturists and depend on minor forest collections. Rice is their principal crop. Besides, they cultivate pulses, oil seeds and vegetables. Due to lack of regular market and communication facilities the middlemen exploit them. A Chuktia Bhunjia can marry a Chinda Bhunjia following a rite called dudhpani in which an affine washes the mouth of the bride with milk. The Chuktia Bhunjia worship sunadei, Budharaja, Dharani mata and Budhimai for the wellbeing of one and all. They have been influenced by Hinduism and worship Hindu gods and goddess like, shiva, Jagannath and observe festivals. Bhudharaja and Sunadei are their main village deities. Chaitra Jatra is their main festival. They also worship ancestral spirits, natural and supernatural objects. Pujari, priest, chhaturiya, umbrella holder, and katariya, animal sacrifier are the religious functionaries. Their village council is called 'bhunjia baithki'. 'siyam' is the headman of the village and Badamajhi is the chief adjudicator of the inter-village council called 'Kuraha'.

Didayi is a small community of hill dwelling tribe of south Orissa, mostly confined to Malkangiri district. Their neighbours call them 'Didayi' - the wild people. But, they themselves give their identity as *Gatar* - "the people". They recount the legend that they are the younger brothers of the neighbouring tribes, such as, the Bondo, the Gadaba and the Paraja. They are found only in 42 settlements scattered over a compact patch of remote hill country in the Kondakomberu ranges of the Eastern Ghats. Their population according to 1991 census is 5471. Their sex ratio is 1031. In 1981 their literacy was 3.20 per cent. The area of habitation comes under the jurisdiction of Khairput and Kudumulguma Blocks of Malkangiri district. Didayi settlements have scattered houses located adjacent to hill streams. The houses are enclosed with bamboo wattle fencing. The central place inside the village where community activities like rituals, dances and meetings are organized is called gulisung. The Didayi men wear the simplest loincloth and women put on colourful saris. Women love to put on various kinds of ornaments, beads etc. Agriculture is the mainstay of Didayi subsistence supplemented by hunting and food gathering. While the hill-dwellers practise shifting cultivation, their plains-living counterparts have adopted settled plough cultivation. They rear animals like cattle, pig, dog and poultry birds. Traditionally, they are skillful in making bamboo baskets for domestic use as well as for sale in the local market. The staple food of Didayi is rice and millet. Other seasonal food crops and edibles as forest produce supplement their diet. Addiction to mohua liquor, salap juice and rice beer, landha, is quite common to them. Five totemic clans, bonso, exogamous segments characterize the social structure of Didayi. In a clan there are agnatic lineages, brea. Marriage is the most important and colourful event in Didayi life. Men and women are relatively free to choose their mates. They acquire mates by negotiations, elopement, instrusion and service. Widow remarriage, levirate and sororate are in practice. Adult marriage and monogamy is common among them. The custom of bride price is prevalent. Didayi perform elaborate mortuary rites. Mourning is observed for ten days. Purificatory rites, dasa, is observed on the tenth day in the company of kinsmen and fellow villagers. Socio-political affairs in Didayi village are managed by the traditional village council called *lepar.* The traditional village priest, palasi, the secular chief *naik* and messenger challan are the functionaries. Today the role of Ward Member and Sarpanch has assumed importance. They observe festivals, like, lendi pande, soboloy hia, jugulubar hia, dosae hia, gasendia hia, singati hia, ghia pande, bhairo puja, rokdia, hini hundi, golota, aloli hia, gimder pande sanraik hia, etc. These festivals are associated with different phases of agricultural operations, eating of first fruit, onset of first rainfall and the like. They believe in ghosts and spirits and follow shamanistic as well as herbal medicinal practices for healing.

Dongria Kondh is one of the primitive groups of the Kondh tribe. As the name signifies it is a community of hill dwelling (dongar means high-hill land) people. They inhabit exclusively the wooded Niamgiri hill ranges (from about 1500 ft. to 4500 ft. above sea level) of Koraput (undivided), the major tribal district of Orissa. They inhabit in 116 villages having a total population of about 7000. They are distinct in their language and culture from the neighbouring population of tribes and castes in the plain. Unaffected by Christianity in particular, they have continued to maintain age-old forms of economy, social organization, rituals and beliefs, and have persisted in the seclusion of hill regions separated by formidable natural barriers. Although the Oriya call them 'Dongria Kondh' they call themselves 'Dongran Kuan' or 'Drili Kuan'. They put a long narrow piece of cloth round the waist in such a way that the two embroidered ends of the cloth remain hanging one in the front and the other at the back. The piece of cloth is termed in their Kui language as *drili*. It is nearly 20 to 28 ft. long and one-ft. in width. It is men's wear. The women wear a cloth of four to five ft. in length and nearly two-ft. in width. They use another piece of cloth, which covers the front side like an apron. The striking unity of the Dongria Kondh is reflected in their claim as the descendants of Naimraja, their legendary ancestor-king. The background against which the villages stand is really picturesque. If one views a village from a distance he will find some low-thatched houses almost lost in greenness. Every Dongria Kondh village is a cluster of houses arranged in two rows and in each row the houses are continuous in a linear fashion. Between the two rows of houses runs the main street of the village. In majority of the villages, besides the Dongria Kondh, there are the Domb, the nearest and the most unavoidable neighbours of the Kondh. Although the Domb are considered untouchables by them on several socio-economic, political and religious occasions the Dongria Kondh and the Domb may unit together as one. Both simple and compound types of families are found among the Dongria Kondh. The compound families among them are either polygynous, a group consisting of a man and two or more wives and their children or a group formed by the remarriage of a widow or widower having children by a former marriage. Co-wives live in the same dwelling with the husband and their unmarried children. The Dongria Kondh organize themselves into territorial clan groups. Each clan is strictly exogamous. Cooperation and conflict between clans are the significant dimensions of the social structure of the Dongria Kondh. Each of the Dongria Kondh clans can be divided into four functional groups, namely, mondal, bismajhi, jani and pujari. Clan is called *kuda* and the functional group is called *punja*. They are basically swidden cultivators and they keep orchards. They grow banana, pineapples, turmeric and a number of varieties of cereals and pulse in the swiddens. Besides the swidden produce they depend upon forest resources for meeting the daily necessities of life. They raise livestock like goats, pigs and hens for meeting the demand of pre-stations and for their own use on ritual occasions. In every year between January and March they observe meriah festival at the level of clan territory and sacrifice buffaloes on the occasion and offer it to the earth goddess, dharni penu. Girls' dormitory is one of the interesting institutions to which young boys of the same village cannot enter. Young men from affinal clan villages attend the dormitory late in the evening and leave the place before dawn. Barter and exchange labour are essentially still in practice, and traditional labour cooperatives based on age and sex continue to be functional today. Characteristically they are one of the feuding tribes of India; wage feuds to keep peace.

Gadaba is one of the Munda groups of tribes found concentrated in Lamptaput, Similiguda, Pottangi and Khairput of Koraput and Malkangiri districts. As per 1991 census, they have a population of 67138. Their sex ratio is 972. In 1981 their literacy was 6.50 per cent. They speak gutab, one of the dialects of the Austro-Asiatic language family. They are divided into four broad sections, such as, *Bado Gadaba, Parenga, Olaro and Sano Gadaba.* Each group is again divided into a number of clans and lineages. The Gadaba prefer adult marriage and have the custom of bride price. Monogamy is the rule although in some cases polygyny is practised. In the Gadaba villages three types of houses are found. These are the *Mahad dien, the Dondul Dien and the Chhendi Dien.* The first two are rectangular and the third one is circular with a conical roof. A small portion of the house is set apart for the kitchen. The *Mahad dien* and the *Dandul dien* houses have verandahs in the front. The economic life of the Gadabas mainly centres around rice cultivation. It is supplemented by collection of forest produce, fishing and wage earning. The Gadaba extensively practised shifting cultivation in the past. A mixture of varieties of millets, pulses and Niger is sown in their swiddens. The Gadaba women are fond of wearing ornaments to adorn themselves. They are made up of brass, aluminium and gold. The women wear short strip of clothes traditionally known as kisali tied round the waist and another piece as apron. The men wear loincloth the end flap hanging down in front. In every Gadaba village the traditional council is headed by naik. The headman is assisted by a challan and a messenger called *barik.* The village meeting is held at a central place called *sadar,* a raised platform of stones under a big tree. The village priest, disari performs all religious rites. He also acts as a medicineman-cum-astrologers. Thakurani is their chief village deity. Thakurani is represented by a stone and is offered sacrifices by disari. The shrine is called hundi. The important festivals of the Gadaba are bandapana, Dusserah Parab, Pus Parab and Chait Parab. The Gadaba are fond of dance and music. They are famous for their characteristic dhemsa dance. In this dance the women wear colourful kereng saris. The men play musical instruments and the women dance in semicircles sidewise and forward movement of footsteps. After death the corpse is taken to the burial ground located a little away from the village settlement. The family members and kinsmen accompany the corpse wailing all along. After the dead body is disposed of all of them go to a nearby stream for a wash and catch fish. They cook fish and rice in separate pots and leave them half way to the cremation ground. On the tenth day a feast is arranged in the deceased's house partaken by kins only. Every three to five years the Gadaba observe gottar, the secondary burial ritual at the village level in which kinsmen from far and wide participate and commemorate the dead amidst lavish food and drinks.

Juang is one of the primitive tribal groups exclusively found in Orissa. In the past, they were being called Pattoas for wearing leaves. The word 'Juang' means "Sons of Man". They claim themselves to be the first humans on the earth, originating at the sacred Gonasika hills as descendants of their legendary ancestors, the risi couple. They firmly believe that they are the Thanyas, the autochthons of Keonjhar as compared to their brethren who have fled to the neighbouring Pallahara area in the long past, distinguished as Bhagudias, the emigrants. Linguistically Juangs are Munda speaking people (Munda being one of the Austro-Asiatic language families) and racially belong to Proto-Australoid stock. As per 1991 census their total population in 35665 and sex ratio is 1059. In 1981 their literacy was 8 per cent. Juang Settlements are scattered, hidden inside hills and forests of Gonasika region. The Hill-Juang eke out subsistence pursuing shifting cultivation and collecting minor forest produce. The plains-Juang earn their livelihood by pursuing small-scale settled cultivation and wage earning. The Hill-Juang villages of Gonasika area are grouped under four pirhas - territorially organized confederation of villages, traditionally being the maximal-socio-political units - named as Satkhand, Jharkhand, Kathua and Rebena which had received due recognition and patronage of the then rulers of ex-Keonjhar State. Each pirha is led by a traditional tribal chief designated as *sardar*. Each Juang village is an autonomous socio-political unit managed by a set of traditional leaders and a corporate body of village elders called *bhalabhai* or *barabhai*. The village community owns and manages all the productive and useful natural resources like swiddens, forests, grazing land, habitation sites etc. which lie within their village boundary. Another important feature of the Juang society is their traditional youth organization and dormitory, majang or mandaghar. The unmarried boys and girls become members of this institution. They are an well-organized group that carries out various public services and social and cultural activities for their community. Boys and girls together sing, dance and make merry in moonlit nights in front of majang. The majang, a rectangular house standing conspicuously in the centre of the village serves as a community house for the youth, court house for the elders and *barabhai*, guest house for visitors, cooperative store for storage of common grains, place for keeping musical instruments, a venue for communal rituals, cultural centre for dance and music and a museum of Juang art and craft. The other distinguishing features of the Juang are their strong kinship organization dividing them into kutumb, kins, and bandhu, affines. Most of the Juang villages have uni-clan composition; village exogamy is the rule.

Kandha is numerically the largest tribe of Orissa. Numbering 11,40,314 individuals in 1991 census, they constituted 17.5 per cent of the total tribal population of the State. The sex ratio is 973. In 1981 their literacy was 12.40 per cent. They are largely concentrated in the undivided Phulbani, Kalahandi and Koraput districts. They speak Kui and Kuvi, the dialects of the Dravidian language. The Desia section speaks Oriya. The tribe is distributed in various pockets of southern Orissa forming several endogamous territorial sections, namely, Kutia, Dongria, Desia, Sitha, Nanguli, Jhamia, Pengo, Jhuria, Malua etc. with the suffix Kandha. Each section is formed by territorial and exogamous clan groups called *Kuda* or Bons. The Kandha villages have linear settlement pattern. Jarkhiri, the altar of their earth goddess, Dharni Penu, lies at the centre of the village street in between two rows of houses. The dress pattern and adornments among them vary from section to section. Generally men put on loincloth and grow long hairs. Women wear pieces of cloth as skirts and approans. Now-a-days they wear coloured saris. The women put on tatoo marks. The institution of youth dormitory is called in various names, such as,

Dhangda-Dhangdi Basa, Dhangda-Dhangdi-Ghar, Dhanger, Idu etc. They acquire mates by negotiation, service, bride capture. Levirate and sorrorate practices are there. Brideprice is paid in cash and kinds. They follow both burial and cremation practices. Death pollution continues for ten days and purificatory rites are performed on the eleventh day. Their subsistence activities revolve round land and forest. Different sections of them earn their livelihood by pursuing shifting and settled cultivation, hunting, food gathering, animal husbandry, wage earning etc. The Dongria Kandha are expert horticulturists. Dharni Penu, earth goddess is their supreme deity. In the past, the Kandha used to make human sacrifices called *Meriah*. The British rulers had suppressed this custom and now it is substituted by buffalo sacrifice. Jatrakudi, village deity, Gungi Penu, stream deity, Bhima Penu, mountain god, Lai Penu, the forest god, Sita Penu, deity of wealth, Birna Penu, rain god etc. are propitiated by them. They also worship ancestral spirits, ghosts and other benevolent and malevolent sprits and firmly believe in the efficacy of black and white magic. Their mangico-religious activities are conducted by various specialists designated as Jani, Lamba and Pujari. Dishari, the astrologer, Beju, Bejuni and Kalisi, Sacrifice of Buffalo, goats, pigs, pigeons, chicks, cocks etc. is indispensable in Kandha rituals. Their important festivals are Kedu or Meriah and Chait Parab. The village functionaries are Saanta, Mondal, Jani, Bismajhi and Barik. At the regional level they have Mutha organization headed by Mandal, Majhi or Patro. Now, the traditional leaders are loosing their importance and replaced by democratically elected leaders.

Koya live in the southernmost part of Orissa, concentrated in Podia, Motu, and Malkangiri blocks. As per census 1991, they have a population of 141927 and their sex ratio is 919. Their literacy in 1981 was 4.90 per cent. Koya village settlements are unique having houses quite spread out. Typical palisade bamboo fencing all around is a distinguishing feature of Koya settlements. Very close to their settlements one notices stone pillars and wooden posts erected in memory of their dead ancestors. They have two important deities: Bijagudi, house deity and Gudimata, village deity. They grow tobacco, maize, beans, vegetables, mustard, millets etc. in their fields. The number of houses in village varies from ten to thirty. Each house, its courtyard and adjoining kitchen garden are nicely fenced by bamboo splits. They have mud houses beautifully thatched by a type of jungle grass. Houses are rectangular giving shelters to their pigs and fowls. Herds of cattle are put or tethered in front courtyard open air. The traditional village council used to be headed by pedda, the village headman, and perma, the priest. The posts of *pedda* and *perma* are hereditary. The shaman, magician-cum-herbal medicineman is known as *wadde*. Kotwal, hailed from the Domb scheduled caste community acts as the messenger. Well-to-do and influential Koyas used to acquire two or more wives. Their kins, kutumb, and affines, wiwalwand, are clearly distinguished. Koya society is divided into five broad social divisions, katta, such as, Kowasi, Sodi, Madkami, Madi and Padiyami. Each social division is further subdivided into several groups and sub-groups. Marriage is termed as *pendul*. Koya parents have the liberty to select brides. Marriages by service, intrusion, and exchange are also practised. The custom of bride price or bride wealth is prevalent. In some cases the wife is younger to the husband. Marriage negotiation starts at an early age. The children are considered as gift of God. They worship mother-earth as village deity. They observe a number of festivals like, Bija Pendu, Kota Pendu, Bumud Pendu, Idu Pendu, or Ikk Pendu, etc. Most of the festivals revolve round their agricultural calendar and associated with health and happiness of the family and the villagers. They offer sacrifices of eggs, pigeons, fowls, goats, and pigs, cows and buffaloes to their deities and spirits. They observe rites de passage; secondary burials ritual is observed most elaborately. They are basically rice cultivators and at the same time cattle herders. Seasonally they depend upon forest collections and fishing. They sell milk and milk products but do not relish them. In spite of impact of modernization, the Koya have retained their rich cultural heritage in different forms. The bison horn dances are characteristic among the Koya.

Kutia Kondh is one of the primitive sections of the Kondh tribe. They are found mainly in Belghar, Gumma, Lankagarh, Jhinipani Gram Panchayats of Tumudibandha Block and a few villages of Subarnagiri area of Kotagarh Block of Phulbani district. Some of there are also found in Lanjigarh Block of Kalahandi district. The Kutia Kondh of Belghar an Gumma are more primitive than their counterparts living in Subarnagiri and Lanjigarh. The total population of Kutia Kondh is 6479. The term kuti means a big hole on earth. They believe that they have emerged out of that hole and hence called Kutia Kondh. The Kutia Kondh live in small settlements. Houses are built in two rows separated by a broad street facing east-west. In every village there are dormitories separately for boys and girls. Girls' dormitory is called *kude*. The Kutia Kondh organize themselves into several clans. Clan is called *gochhi*. Each clan has its distinct name. There are 14 clans among them. Polygyny is in practice. They acquire mates by arrangement, capture, elopement and by service. Clan exogamy is strictly followed. They cremate the dead. Purification rite, dulki-arna, is observed either on the third or seventh day. Dharani Penu, earth goddess, is considered supreme. Besides Dharani Pennu they worship Sosu Pennu, Linga Pennu, Piju Pennu, Namli Penu and Jaka Pennu. Korubiha Dakina, otherwise known as meriah is the biggest festival observed by them. Some other festivals like, Burlang Kalu Dakina, Dedusina Dakina, Bicha Dakina, Takukalu Dakina, Badabina Dakina are also observed. All the festivals revolve round various phases of agricultural operations. Basically, they are shifting cultivators. In lenient seasons they work as labourers. Barter economy is still prevalent among them. The Kutia Kondh classify their land into: Padagiri, backyard land, Bada, Bata, up-land, Mera, low paddy land, and Netta, swidden land. Each Kutia Kondh village has a set of traditional village functionaries, such as Majhi, secular head, Jani, religious head, Gonda/Pesuni, Messenger and Kutaka, the spirit medium. These are hereditary positions. A person continue in the post until he/she enjoys the confidence of the villagers. The traditional functionaries and the village elders constitute the village council.

Lanjia Saora is one of the primitive groups of the Saora tribe. Apart from Orissa the Saora are widely distributed in many parts of central India, such as, Bihar, Madhya Pradesh, Andhra Pradesh, Maharashtra and West Bengal. In Orissa, the Lanjia Saora are concentrated in Rayagada and Gajapati districts. As per 1991 census the Saora population in Orissa was 403710. The growth rate (1971-81) was 8 per cent and the sex ratio, 1015. Their literacy was 14.15 per cent in 1981. In the absence of separate enumeration for the Lanjia Saora their exact population is not known. However, their population in two Micro Project areas is 7,587. They belong to Proto-Australoid racial stock and speak a dialect called Sora that comes under the Austro-Asiatic family of Munda group of languages. Traditionally, the men used to wear loincloth and women a skirt. The latter use ornaments to adorn their ear, nose, waist and ankle. The settlements are located in undulating terrain and houses remain scattered. Close to the settlements megaliths are erected to commemorate the dead kins. An ordinary house is a one-roomed thatched rectangular dwelling having stone and mud walls with high plinth verandah. The guardian deity of the village is represented by two wooden posts, called *Gasadasum* or *kitungsum* installed at the entrance of the settlement. The subsistence economy of the Lanjia Saora rests primarily on shifting cultivation and importantly on terrace cultivation. Occasional hunting, fishing and round-the-year forest collection supplement it. They exhibit a high degree of indigenous skill and technological out-fit preparing the terrace beds and in their water management system. Mainly rice is grown in terrace fields and mixed crop of minor millets, cereals and pulses in the swiddens. They have their traditional system of labour cooperative known as *ansir* which ensures smooth conduct of agricultural activities. In a way, it is the hallmark of Lanjia Saora economy. Their ordinary meal consists of rice or millet gruel. They enjoy alcoholic drinks and smoke tobacco. The aesthetic life of the Lanjia Soara is reflected through their colourful dance, typical music and the wall paintings, anital, in particular. The icons are so skillfully dreamt and drawn that these have made them famous among the scholars and artists of the country and aboard. The Lanjia Saora pantheon includes numerous gods, deities and spirits, benevolent and malevolent. They get worshipped with fear and anxiety. People offer sacrifice for safety and wellbeing of the family members. Most of the festivals revolve round agricultural cycle and lifecycle rituals. Guar is celebrated to commemorate the dead. Gomango is the secular head of the village. He is assisted by buya, the ritual head, Disari is the village astrologer. The other important functionary is the shaman called *Kudan*, male, and *Kudenboi*, female. The Saora society is divided into as many 25 subdivisions based on occupation, food habit, social status, customs and traditions. The Lanjia Saora is one of them. The family is mostly nuclear; the well to do practise polygyny. Birinda, extended family is characteristic of the Saora social organization. Women even after marriage continue to belong to the brother's birinda.

Lodha was known as a criminal tribe until the revocation of the criminal Tribes Act in 1956. They are found in a contiguous area stretching from northwest of the Chhotnagpur plateau to the southeast of the river basin of Subarnarekha. In Orissa, according to the 1991 census, their population is 7458 and sex ratio is 1043. In 1981 their literacy was 8.40%. They are mainly concentrated in Suliapada and Morada Blocks of Mayurbhanj district. It is widely accepted that the tribe derived its name from the word lubdhaka meaning the *fowler* or *trapper*. They claim their ancestry to Byadha or Kirata, the Savara king Viswabasu and consider Lord Jagannath as the supreme deity. They take pride in giving their identity as *Lodha Savar*. Apart from pursuing cultivation Lodhas eke out their living by rearing and collecting cocoons, selling firewood and preparing ropes out of sabai grass. The Lodha women are hard working and at the same time clever. Almost all Lodha men and women are adept in agricultural activities like transplanting, weeding and harvesting. They used to have one-roomed houses with raised verandah in the front. In side the house, close to the hearth there is a raised earthen platform called *isan*. This is said to be the seat of the family deity. A few household artifacts for multipurpose use are found in a Lodha house. They have exogamous totemic clans like Bhotda, Malik, Bag, Nayak, Dandapat, Paramanik, Ahori, Bhuria and Kotal. They practise clan exogamy. Child marriage is still prevalent among them. After marriage the ladies put vermilion mark on forehead and iron bangle around the wrist. The practice of brideprice is still in vogue in their community. They local people look at the Lodha with suspicion.

Parenga is believed to be a sub-tribe of Gadaba of the Munda Group. They are inhabitants of Koraput district. They are concentrated in Padwa area of Koraput Sadar Subdivision. They are synonymous with Parenga Paroja and Parenga Paraja. According to 1991 census their population is 5843 with sex ratio of 937. Their literacy was 11.5%, in 1981. The Parenga speak a dialect of their own called *Parenga bhasa* which belongs to the Munda family. Besides they speak Oriya and Telegu. Parenga family is nuclear, patrilocal, patrilineal and patripotestal. They are divided into a number of exogamous totemic clans viz. Antal (Cobra), Khara (Sun), Khilla (tiger), Pangi (Vulture), Khinbudi (bear), Machha (fish) and Golari (serpent) etc. Sorrorate, junior levirate and cross-cousin marriages are prevalent among them. Marriage by negotiation (Raibadi) is considered ideal and prestigious. Marriage by capture, elopement, exchange and by service is in vogue. Family is monogamous and remarriage of widow and widower and divorcee are allowed. Bride price costing around Rs. 2000/- includes a goat or a sheep, rice beer and food grains. Divorce is approved by the traditional council of the village elders. A pregnant woman is attended by a mid-wife (Sutrani) belonging to Dom community during child birth. Birth pollution is observed for seven days and on the 10th day name giving ceremony is observed. The first hair cutting is performed after one year. They have puberty rites. The first menstruating girl remains in seclusion for seven days. The Parenga practise both cremation and burial. Dom musicians beat the drum when the corpse is carried to the burial ground. They observe death pollution for 5 days. Their priest, Disari officiates in the rituals and a feast is given to the villagers, kith and kin on the 5th day. They perform the annual Barsikia or Badkum rites and like the Gadaba conduct Gottar rites for the deceased. Parenga are settled cultivators and wage earners. Their livelihood is supplemented by seasonal forest collections. Their staple food is ragi and maize. Occasionally they take rice. They also eat non-vegetarian items and are habituated to alcoholic drinks and smoking tobacco. Besides their own deities like Nissani, Nangseri, Budha Bhairab and Mangal Pura they worship different Hindu Gods and Goddesses, visit Hindu temples and observe Hindu festivals. They observe Pus Parab, Chaita Parab, Bandapana, Ammu (new mango eating) with dance and music. Naik in the traditional village headman. He is assisted by a Challan or Barik belonging to scheduled caste community Disari and Sisa, the ritual functionaries also assist the Naik in managing the village affairs. The regional head is called *Bhata Naik*. The institution of youth dormitory was in functional form. Now it is dwindling. However, they have preserved their rich tradition of dance and music. Their popular dance forms are, Dhemsa, Ghumura, Gottar and Lathidudia performed on various festive occasions.

Paroja is one of the major tribes of southern Orissa, largely concentrated in the undivided Koraput district and the adjoining Kalahandi district. According to 1991 census, their total population is 3,53,536. The nomenclature Paroja is derived from the local Oriya word Praja or Paraja meaning the common people who are tenants or subjects or citizens under ex-feudal lords or Raja. The tribe is divided into two broad sections: the Bada Paroja and the Sana Paroja. Each section further divided into two sub-sections: Bada Paroja or Sodia Paraja and Bada Jodia Paraja or Penga Paraja under the former, and Bareng Jodia Paraja and Konda Paraja or Selia Paraja under the latter. The major distinction between both the sections is that the Bada Paroja are more Hinduised than the Sana Paroja. The former do not take beef. They observe elaborate purificatory rites in the event of the death of a cow or buffalo in their household while the latter are said to be beef-eaters. Among all the four sub-sections the Selia or Chhelia who were goat-breeders in the past are given the lowest rank. Their dress and ornaments are more or less similar to those of the neighbouring tribes like the Kondh, the Gond, the Gadaba etc. Wearing of brass made nose rings and earrings, khagla, the silver neckband and khadu, the silver armlet and wristband is compulsory for married women. Tattooing is popular among women. The Paroja live in big and small settlements in the company of other communities. The villages lie in the plains, at the foothills and near forests in close proximity to hill streams. Inside the village there are two important spots - Berna Munda and Nissan Munda. The former is the seat of traditional village council. It is marked by a constellation of circular stone slabs at a central place, preferably in front of the headman's, Muduli's house. The latter is a monument made of a circular stone slab encircled by menhirs representing the seat of the village deity called *Hundi.* The Paroja observe birth pollution till the naval court of the newborn dries up. The name giving and first hair cutting rituals held during the first year. Disari, the astrologer chooses auspicious dates. The maternal uncle and grand parents play major role in the ritual. The puberty rites are observed for girls. The pollution period continues for seven days during which they observe several taboos. Youth dormitories for boys and girls, Dhangda Basa Ghar and Dhangdi Basa Ghar respectively were functioning till the recent past. The dormitories provide opportunity to both young men and women to meet, sing and dance together. The institution is now obsolete. The Paroja prefer adult marriage, monogamy, cross-cousin marriage and village exogamy following the rules of clan exogamy. Marriage by negotiation is relatively an expensive affair. Those cannot afford it resort to other means, such as capture, jhinka-utra, elopement, udlia, levirate, sorrorate, etc. They were practising shifting cultivation extensively in the past. Gradually they took up settled cultivation. Using simple implements, they grow a variety of cereals, pulses and vegetables in their dry and wet land and kitchen garden round the year. They are fond of raising livestock. They meet a part of their subsistence needs by collecting minor forest produce. Millet and rice and their principal food. Use of liquor is customary in all rituals. The affairs of a Paroja village are managed by a set of traditional leaders designated as muduli, the secular chief, jani, the priest, and challan, the messenger-cum-assistant. Other important magico-religious functionaries are disari, gurumai, gunia and bhatanaik. The most significant and colourful Paroja festivals are chait parab and pus parab observed with much pomp during December-January and March-April respectively. Their artistic talents find expression in Dhemsa and Dungdunga dances and laga songs.

Paudi Bhuinya belongs to the primitive section of the Bhuinya tribe. The Bhuiyan are widely distributed in many parts of Orissa, Bengal, Bihar, Assam and Chhotanagpur. Desh Bhuinya or Mala

Bhuinya is one of the sections of the Bhuinya represented mainly by Pauri Bhuinya. The Pauri Bhuinya distinguish themselves from other sections of the Bhuinya by adopting banghy, a wooden carrying level as their tribal emblem. Bhuinya is derived from a Sanskrit word Bhumi meaning land or earth. The tribe is variously found mentioned as Bhuiya, Bhuiyan and Bhuinya. The tribe belongs to the Munda group of tribes. They have no tribal language of their own; they speak Oriya. The Pauri Bhuinya inhabit the Bhuinya Pirh of Keonjhar district, Bonai Hills of Sundargarh district and Nagira Hills of Dhenkanal district. The population of the Pauri Bhuinya inhabiting the Micro Project areas (as the tribe is not enumerated separately) is 10,510 (1993-94) survey approximately. The Pauri males and females dress just like the caste neighbours. Pauri women adorn themselves with a number of bangles, nose rings, ear rings, toe rings, anklets made of brass alloy and cover their neck and chest with multi coloured bead necklaces. They have scattered settlements. They pursue shifting cultivation, called koman or dahi. The new village site is inaugurated by ceremoniously affixing a carved wooden post, khunta, representing gaisiri, the village deity, in the centre to ensure protection and blessings of ancestor gods. The Pauri houses re without windows having only one door. The tutelary deity of family is placed in one corner near the hearth. They make regular offerings there. The Pauri Bhuinya have dormitories for the unmarried boys that serve as a guest house, elders' meeting place and granary of the village. Pauri Bhuinyas are mainly shifting cultivators. Some families pursue dry and wet rice cultivation. Forest collections add to their subsistence. Their lineal kins as kutumbs at a bigger level form a corporate group called khilli. They follow khilli exogamy. Marriage by capture, ghicha, is the most common type and other types include marriage by elopement, dhripala, and love marriage, phulkhusi. Bride price is prevalent and it varies depending on the status of the family. The Pauris believe in many gods and goddesses. Dharam Devta, Sun god, and Basukimata, earth goddess, are regarded as their supreme deities. They also worship the spirits of hills, rivers for their territory called pat and the common worship of these pats reflects their tribal solidarity. Dihuri is their priest. The Pauri Bhuinyas observe a series of festivals which mark the turning points in the annual round of their economic life such as distribution of forest land for cultivation, felling trees, eating new crops, etc. Some of their festivals are: Magh Podoi, Ama Nua, Katha jatra, Boram Devata, etc. The Pauri Bhuinya dances have a social and religious significance. Women dance while the men play Changu, drums and sing songs. Besides, their essential events of life like birth, marriage and death are observed ceremoniously. The village council includes all the adult members of the community headed by naik or pradhan. At inter village level, a group of Pauri villages of a territory form a confederacy called bar or pirh headed by a sardar.

Pentia is otherwise called Penthia and Pentiya, Holva, Holuva or Halba (Thurston, 1909). The Pentia are inhabitants of undivided Koraput district and some parts of Mayurbhanj and keonjhar districts. They are said to be betel leaf sellers and Oriya cultivators of Vizagapatam Agency (Madras Census report, 1901). Mr. C. Hagavadan Rao reported that pentia have migrated from Bastar State and settled as agriculturists in Petikona area and hence were designated as Petikonaya or Pentia denoting the place they inhabited. According to 1991 census, the population of Pentia is 11,399 and their percentage of literacy was 24.8 per cent in 1981. They had their own dialect, Haluva in the past. Now they have adopted local Oriya as their mother tongue. Pentia family is generally nuclear, patrilocal, patrileneal and patripotestal. The tribe is divided into two endogamous sections i.e. Bada and Sano which have several exogamous totemic septs like Surya (Sun), Mankar (monkey), Bagh (tiger), Nag (cobra), kurum or kachop (tortoise), etc. marriage through negotiation is regarded as most desired mode of acquiring mates; cross cousin marriage is permitted. Few cases of junior sorrorate and junior levirate are reported. Though polygyny is not disallowed monogamy is commonly practised. Remarriage of widow, widower and divorcees is permitted. Bride price both in cash and kind is paid on the date of solemnization of marriage. Other modes of marriage are elopement and capture, where parental consent and payment of bride price is not easy to come. The Pentia observe name giving ceremony for newborn babies, and follow puberty rites for adolescent girls. Pollution period in case of puberty is observed for nine days and the pubescent girl is segregated for 9 days till she takes purificatory bath. The Pentia practise both burial and cremation. They observe death pollution for a period of ten days. During this time the family members are tabooed against taking non-vegetarian foods. Services for Hindu Barber and Brahman are utilized during observation of mortuary rites. Finally, the bereaved family hosts a feast for the kinsmen and villagers. The Pentia are generally settled cultivators and agricultural labourers. They produce paddy and some minor millet. Besides, they collect different edible roots, tubers and other forest produces. They are non-vegetarians. Rice is their principal diet. Most of them are addicted to country made liquor. Pentia religion is admixture of Hindusim and local beliefs and traditions. Besides their own deity, Nissani and Tahkurani, they worship Hindu deities like Gupteswar, Jagannath and celebrate festivals like Nuakhia, Amm Nua (new mango eating), Pus punei and Diwali with dance and music. Pentia have their own traditional village council headed by Naik and an inter-village council headed by Bhata Naik or Kul Naik that settles intra- and inter-community disputes. The other office bearers who assist the Naik are Dissari, Pujari, Bhandari, Dhoba and Challan (messenger).

They are fond of dance and music during various festive occasions. They claim a better position in the social hierarchy than their neighbours, like, the Kandha, the Gadaba, the Paraja and the Koya, for they get the services of Brahman, Barik (barber) and Dhoba (washer man).

4. Madhya Pradesh

With a view to giving special attention to certain tribal groups looking at their backwardness the concept of declaring certain tribal groups as special primitive tribal groups was evolved by Government of India. The Government of India issued directives vide their letter No. 20018/5/81-TDA dated 27th April, 1980 for the identification of primitive tribal groups.[8]

Three criteria for the identification of the primitive tribal groups have been evolved. These are as follows (i) use of technology, which is of pre-agricultural level, (ii) low level of literacy, and (iii) population which is stagnant or diminishing. Based on these criteria following tribes have been identified as Primitive tribal groups:-

(1) Abhujhmaria, (2) Baiga, (3) Bharia, (4) Birhor, (5) Pahari Korwa, (6) Kamar and (7) Saharia.

Having identified the primitive groups an exhaustive programme for them has been formulated. Primitive groups are to be distinguished from the impoverished as the very concept of poverty may be unknown to them. Hence, special programmes will have to be taken up as a part of general development in the area.

The organization of a society under SFDA/TDA model will be beneficial in the programming for primitive tribes. The society should have specific perspective plans for each of the communities so that continuity of the work to be conducted can be provided.

This programme can only succeed when a group of sensitive personnel is appointed to the task. The appointments cannot be made on functional basis, as the programmes relate to a small group numbering about 50 to 100 or 200 families. The officer will have to be school teacher and an agricultural extension officer rolled in one with adequate authority to take liaisons. They can be compensated for lack of social services or special pay can be given to them ranging between 25-50 per cent depending on the location of their headquarters.

The Project

Top priority should be given to provide protection for the existing economic activities of this group. External predatory forces sniping at their produce and leaving them bare should be warded off so that the members of the group are in position to fully enjoy the fruits of their labour. Restoration of land should be given top priority.

The project in each group must cover the entire gestation period so that the project should come to an end only when the group has become a viable one.

In settlement programmes generally some subsistence allowance is given without any labour input which can be demoralising and misused. A mechanism has to be found where by the community should be given the feeling that they are earning their subsistence and nothing is being paid to them exgratia.

A programme providing working opportunity for a period of 300 days in a year on minimum wages should be formulated. The principle of converting the manpower of the group into capital assets has to be followed. Thus, the entire land reclamation work can be taken up by the beneficiary group itself.

Irrigation programmes can be taken up provided bulk of the land belongs to the primitive tribes. In the plantation programme the approach has to be to give the ownership of the trees to the tribals while the land may continue to belong to the state. Bee-keeping and similar other cottage industries may have a good potential. It may be possible for the state Government to give the contract of fishing in the tank to the tribal co-operative development corporation which can organise co-operatives of fishermen in the areas. Co-operatives for the supply of raw-materials to the primitive tribes should be arranged, which will also undertake marketing of the finished goods.

The fuel collectors are the weakest group in any community. It will be useful if a programme for fuel wood collectors is taken up which should include organization of co-operatives, provision of consumption credit and planting of special fuel wood series.

Among the primitive groups the first problem is that of health. The entire primitive tribal community should be medically checked up by a team organized by the Health Department and they should be given medical care according to a time schedule.

The tribal groups under consideration have to be equipped mentally and psychologically so that they are able to withstand the depradation among them by external agencies. This can be done by educating them in a way which does not erode their distinct personality and cultural individuality. They need to include education of a sort different from the conventional type. A suitable incentive for attendance may be given as an indirect compensation to the parents for the loss in the earnings of a family as a result of the child going away to the school. At primary level the assistance has to be mostly in kind, school uniforms, text-books and exercise books. It would be desirable to work out a system whereby children also get some nourishment.

A substantial adult education effort should be made amongst the primitive tribes. In the first instance reading material should be prepared, keeping in view their own local situation and their problems.

The above instructions were issued by the Ministry of Welfare, Government of India during the year 1977 to the state governments. The Government of M.P., however identified these groups and launched four groups of schemes, viz., Family oriented economic, community infrastructure and human resources development programmes on the subsidy and loan basis. The loan component was kept only 20 per cent and subsidy upto 80 per cent. The subsidy portion was more as compared to normal tribal groups which is only 50 per cent.

The economic development programmes included Integrated Rural Development Programme, the development of agriculture and allied activities, self-employment and family oriented income generating schemes based on subsidy and loan basis.

The community Development programmes included distribution of uniforms and text-books, provision of health facilities, establishing agricultural farms, provisions for the ashrams, contour bunding, sericulture, bamboo plantation, distribution of iodized salt, provision of soap, employment training programmes. The infrastructure development programme include approach road, bridges and culverts, stop dam, nishtari tanks, construction of school building, hand pump and well construction and community buildings. Under Human Resources Development programmes all the educational and training programmes are included which help in equipping a person for getting suitable employment.

During the year 1992, however, a new approach was adopted wherein Five Year Development Plans based on the actual socio-economic surveys of these groups were prepared taking into account their aspirations.

With a view to providing a very dynamic and effective administrative and financial structure separate agencies were registered for each primitive tribal group. While Kamar, Bharia, Abhujhmaria, and Birhor are located in an area of a single district, the Baiga, Saharia and Pahadi Korwa are located in more than one district - the Baiga in five districts and Saharia in all the six districts of Gwalior and Chambal divisions. It was found difficult to ensure effective administration of schemes from one place of all the districts. Even the distribution of funds was disproportionate in all the districts-giving more funds of the district in which an agency was situated.

It was decided therefore to establish an agency in a district in which the population of primitive tribal group was 20,000 or more. In fourteen districts such agencies have been established. It has also been decided to nominate a member of the primitive community concerned, as the Chairman of the agencies and persons as members. The idea is to empower the members of the community themselves so that they can decide the mode of their development.

One very important measure has been taken to issue family identity cards to each primitive tribal group family so that they can get advantage of development works easily.

In this background the spread of the primitive tribal groups and amount spent for them is outlined below. The population, as per special survey conducted during 1992 of these groups is 6,11,710 which is 3.96 per cent of the total population of Scheduled Tribes in the State. The district wise spread is as follows:

Sl. No.	*Name of the Special Primitive Tribal Group*	*Total Population*	*Total Families*	*District*	*Blocks*	*Villages*
1	2	3	4	5	6	7
1.	Abhujhmaria	17016	4327	Bastar	1. Narainpur 2. Orchha 3. Dantewada 4. Bijapur	235
2.	Baiga	134357	27531	1. Mandla 2. Shahdol 3. Balaghat 4. Bilaspur 5. Rajnandgaon	30 blocks	1197
3.	Bharia	2012	238	Chhindwara Tamia		12

1	2	3	4	5	6	7
4.	Birhor	935	281	Raigarh	1. Lailunga 2. Dharma Jaigarh 3. Tamnar 4. Patthalgaon 5. Bagicha 6. Kunkuri 7. Kansabel	249
5.	Korwa	27019	6142	Raigarh Surguja Bilaspur	16 blocks	320
6.	Kamar	13310	2867	Raipur	1. Gariaband 2. Mainpur 3. Chhura 4. Nagri 5. Sihawa	249
7.	Saharia	417171	60997	Gwalior Morena Bhind Datia Guna Shivpuri	26 blocks	1159
	Total	6,11,710	1,02,383			

Quite a sizeable amount has been spent on various developmental programmes for these groups. The details are as follows:

Since Fifth Year Plan till 1994-95 the amount spent on these groups is as follows.( )

Out of a total of 1,02,383 special primitive tribal group families 63935 families of 62.44 per cent of the total received some kind of benefit or the other.

With a view to providing special employment opportunities the requisite qualifications for the recruitment to certain posts was relaxed as per GAD Order No. F NOC-3-17/86/3/1 dated 26 August, 1986. As such 17 Teachers and 44 peons got recruited in Pahadi Korwa area, 3 teachers and 6 peons in Birhor area, in Baiga

Agency Area 210 Asstt. Teachers and in Bhaira, 2 Assistant Teachers got recruited.

(Rs. in Lakh)

Sl. No.	Agency	Amount Received	Expenditure on Programmes				
			Family oriented economic development	Community development	Infrastructure development	Establishment	Total
1	2	3	4	5	6	7	8
1.	Kamar	250.56	42.87	165.87	19.38	-	228.12
2.	Bharia	120.95	20.87	27.47	34.12	25.22	107.68
3.	Abhujmaria	313.45	49.36	110:15	129.22	-	288.73
4.	Baiga	1274.42	238.60	718.11	175.28	-	1131.99
5.	Pahadi Korwa	300.00	78.33	61.35	117.38	-	257.06
6.	Birhor	68.00	19.34	17.14	21.36	-	57.84
7.	Saharia	533.41	84.45	239.88	133.38	-	457.71
	Total	2860.88	533.82	1339.97	630.12	25.22	2529.13

5. Note on Andaman and Nicobar Islands

The Union Territory of Andaman and Nicobar Islands is comprised of 306 Islands with a geographical area of 8249 sq. kms. is situated in the South East part of Bay of Bengal. The Andaman Group of Islands is delimited as Andamans Districts, the area of which is 6808 sq. kms., while the Nicobars Group of Islands is taken to constitute the Nicobars District, area of which is 1841 Sq. kms. The total population of A&N Islands is 2,80,661 out of which 26,770 belong to Scheduled Tribes constituting 9.54 per cent of the total population.

Andaman and Nicobar Islands have two ethnic (racial types of autochthons, viz., Mongoloid and Negrito, former stock has two tribes Shompens and Nicobarese inhabiting Nicobar Islands and latter has four tribes - Onge, Great Andamanese, Jarawa and Sentinelese inhabiting the Andaman Islands. These six tribes are categorised into two groups on the basis of level of their technology viz. the primitive and non-primitive, former comprising the Shompen, Onge, Jarawa, Great Andamanese and Sentinelese and later the Nicobarese. According to 1991 Census the population of Nicobarese is 24,853. who live in 156 villages in the district. The population of Shompenes is estimated at 214 and the population of Negrito Tribes is estimated at 400.

The Nicobar district has been constituted into ITDP and most of the schemes adopted in the Tribal Sub-Plan are implemented in that district for the socio-economic development of the Tribes there. To monitor the implementation of the schemes, one Project Officer is posted in the Nicobar district while a Research Cell has been created in the Directorate of Tribal Welfare at the Union Territory's capital.

An autonomous body, viz., Andaman Adim Janjati Vikas Samiti' fully financed by the Government of India is functioning at Port Blair to look after the welfare of the primitive tribes.

The primitive tribes of the A&N Islands are hunters and gatherers. Their hunting and gathering area with wide range of wild food resources is reduced due to the occupation of territory by the mainstream people under various schemes like colonization, rehabilitation and regularisation of the encroachments.

POPULATION CHANGE DURING DIFFERENT CENSUS PERIODS AMONG THE SCHEDULED TRIBES IN ANDAMAN AND NICOBAR ISLANDS

Sl.	*Tribe*	*1951*	*1961*	*1971*	*1981*	*1991*
1	Nicobarese	11902	13903	17874	21172	24853
2	Shompens	20	71	92	223	180(E)
3	Onges	150	129	112	97	101(E)
4	Great Andamanese	23	19	24	26	38(E)
5	Jarawa	50(E)	500(E)	NE	200	200(E)
6	Sentinelese	NE	50(E)	NE	80	100(E)

E-Estimated by U.T. Administration.
NE-Not estimated.

POPULATION CHANGE AMONG ABORIGINES SINCE 1901

Name of Tribe	*1901*	*1911*	*1921*	*1931*	*1951*	*1961*	*1971*	*1981*	*Present (1988)*
1	2	3	4	5	6	7	8	9	10
(a) Shompen	(348)	(375)	(375)	(200)	20	71	92	212	(135)
(b) Onge	(672)	(631)	(321)	(250)	150	129	112	-	98
(c) Great Andamanese	(1882)	(1317)	(786)	(460)	23	19	24	-	28
(d) Nicobarese	5962	7991	8032	9589	11902	13903	17874	-	21172
(e) Jarawa	-	-	(114)	(70)	(50)	(500)	N.E.	N.E.	(200)
(f) Sentinelese	-	-	(117)	(50)	-	(50)	N.E.	N.E.	(100)

**Source*: Census of India 1931: Andaman and Nicobar Island Vol: II, Census of India, 1951, Vol. XVII Appendix A

1. Figures in parenthesis indicate the estimated population.
2. N.E. - not enumerated.

Factual Note on the indigenous tribal people of the Union Territory of Andaman & Nicobar islands, with special reference to the Onges, Sentinelese and Jarawas

The Andaman & Nicobar Islands have six indigenous tribes of which four are located in Andaman District and belong to the Negrito group, while two are located in the Nicobar District and Belong to the Mongoloid group. Of the six tribal groups, the Nicobarese are the largest in number and their population was estimated to be about 26,000 at the time of the census of 1991. The Nicobarese are the most advanced of the six tribal groups, and they inhabit 12 islands in the Nicobar Group. The second tribe in the Mongoloid group are the Shompens who are located only in Great Nicobar Island over 500 kms to the south of Port Blair.

Great Andamanese

Reverting to the Negrito tribes in the Andaman District, the Great Andamanese were considerably numerous and estimated to have been of the order of over 10,000 towards end of the last century. Their number began diminishing not only with the arrival of the British, but more so with the establishment of penal settlements in 1858, to the extent that their numbers had diminished to only 19 by the mid 1960s. With a view to saving this tribe from complete extinction they were resettled in Strait Island in 1969. Over the last three decades their number, has gradually increased and is now reached 41. They are administered by a body dedicated to the welfare of primitive tribes established in 1976 known as the Andaman Adim Janjati Vikas Samiti (AAJVS), through the establishment of a Cooperative Society called the Great Andamanese Multipurpose Coop. Society located in this island. Educational facilities have been established and the most literate among the Great Andamanese is a student who has reached the fifth standard. The total number of students in the school is 11. Some of them have also been given Government employment in the police.

Onges

The Onges, who also belong to the Negrito group, have traditionally been located in Little Andaman in an area called Dugong Creek and South Bay. Since they were scattered over Little Andaman, with the resettlement of East Bengal refugees on this island in 1974, two Onge settlements were created at Dugong Creek and South Andaman in this island, and they were regrouped and settled here. Today their number is 97. Here again the Andaman Adim Janjati Vikas Samiti administers a cooperative society known as the Onge Multipurpose Coop Society for their welfare. A Primary School has been established in Dugong Creek, and Onge children are admitted to this school located there itself, and they have reached the 3rd Standard. The Onges are engaged on a coconut plantation raised by the Administration and administered by the Andaman Adim Janjathi Vikas Samiti. They also hunt wild pigs, turtles and are engaged in the collection of honey.

Both the Great Andamanese and the Onges (like the Mongoloid Nicobarese and Shompens) are registered on the voters list and have voted in last year's General Elections.

Sentinelese

The Sentinelese, the third tribe in the Negrito group, have traditionally been based only in North Sentinel Island. The

Sentinelese continue to be a hostile tribe and contacts with them had been few and far between, even with the contact policy of the Administration previously being followed. The only known friendly contact with the Sentinelese took place in 1991 when a team led by the Director of Tribal Welfare, Shri SA Awaradi was able to land on this island without any resistance from the Sentinelese and they accepted gifts of coconut. After this, there were infrequent expeditions upto the year 1996, but these were not friendly expeditions, in that, articles were merely left on the beach, and thereafter the team left the place without seeing the Sentinelese. A few years ago two vessels had run aground in the vicinity of North Sentinel island. One of these was a Panamian vessel called M.V. Primrose, while the other vessel was M.V. Rusley. Since these could cause serious navigational hazards, the Shipping Department of the Administration had arranged for the dismantling and disposal of these vessels and this activity necessitated landing on the island for sometime. After the year 1995 the A&N Administration has not sent any contact expedition to the North Sentinel Island and no one has been permitted to go to the island for the last 4 years. However, given the incidence of poaching by foreigners from South East Asian countries in the waters around the Andaman and Nicobar Islands, the Navy and Coast Guard have been patrolling the waters around North Sentinel Island from time to time, and this is strictly a defence oriented measure and not a contact with the Sentinelese. Since there has never been any survey of the Sentinelese population, the precise number of Sentinelese tribesmen is not known. They do not figure in the voters' list.

Jarawas

The Jarawas, the fourth tribe in the Negrito group, have also been regarded as a hostile tribe. Here, it should be mentioned that all the tribal areas in the Andaman and Nicobar Islands are protected by the Andaman & Nicobar Islands (Protection of Aboriginal Tribes) Regulations, 1956. Under this Regulation no non-tribal can enter any tribal area without a permit/pass issued by the Deputy Commissioners concerned. In so far as the Jarawa areas are concerned, no such permit/pass is issued to a non-tribal as a matter of Government policy. In case of the Onges and Great Andamanese, permit is issued on a very restricted basis and only to allow the Andaman Adim janjati Vikas Samiti and medical personnel, as also those seeking to conduct studies, to visit these settlements. (In so far as the Nicobar District is concerned, tribal area pass is issued on a very restricted basis in the shompen area to medical personnel and those conducting studies. AS for the Nicobar area, tribal pass is issued by the Deputy Commissioner, Car Nicobar for the purpose of executing developmental works through APWD and other government agencies, who may bring in outside labour for limited durations. The Andaman Adim Janjati Vikas Samiti do not have any jurisdiction over the Nicobar areas).

Almost every year, barring this year so far, there have been incidents of killing of non-tribal people by the arrows of Jarawas in the dry months of January, February and March. Such incidents occur due to occasional attempts at encroachment by non-tribals in the forest. Otherwise the fear of the Jarawas among non-tribals has traditionally been the best insurance, not only in the preservation of the Jarawas themselves and in ensuring protection from non-tribals seeking entry into their areas, but also of the thick tropical forests in South and Middle Andaman Islands. This Administration has always considered it important for the Jarawas to live in their traditional habitat deep inside the forests. It may be relevant to mention that the Jarawas occupy an area of 649 sq. kms in the reserved forests along the west cost in South Andaman and Middle Andaman Islands, and they are also found in a few smaller islands such as Spike Island bordering the west coast. The length of the territory inhabited by the Jarawas in the tropical forests extends to a distance of nearly 120-130 kms. along the west coast of the aforesaid two major islands.

There has never been a detailed study of Jarawa society by the Anthropological Survey of India or any other scientists, either foreign or Indian, based on primary data gathered through long residence in Jarawa habitations and recording of observations. Since they are regarded as hostile tribes there have been no such studies, so far. (This is also the case with the Sentinelese). As a result, the precise number of Jarawas can only be approximately estimated, based on visual identification whenever teams from the Administration undertake contact expeditions. This estimate varies between 350-400.

While there are no detailed chronicles of contacts with Jarawas in British times, except prejudiced accounts which describe them in the most derogatory terms, the first recorded non-hostile contact with Jarawas by the Administration in post-Independence times took place in 1974. Thereafter, over the last 25 years, the Administration's contact groups have been in periodic touch with the Jarawas in day time only, on days close to the period of the full moon. These contacts had been limited to gifting them with coconuts, bananas and red cloth.

In order to ensure minimal contact with Jarawas and the non-tribals in South and Middle Andaman Islands, the Administration has established a chain of police check posts inside the forests known as the *Jarawa Protection Police Posts*. At present these number 26. In British times these used to be known as the Bush Police. These outposts inside the reserved forests are built with the help of readily available minor forest products, and no modern materials have been used for construction. However, such cane and bamboo outposts have often been subject to Jarawa arrow attacks at night, even injuring policemen, from time to time.

In order to assist the Jarawas in staying inside the forests on the one hand, and also improving their capacity for self-reliance on the other, the Administration have, over the Years, imparted instruction to them to go in for dispersed horticultural cultivation inside the forests focussing on coconut, jack-fruit, papaya, Mango, etc. This has had only limited success, and barring jackfruit cultivation which they have indulged in inside the forests, other crops have not really prospered. Such dispersed cultivation was made along the west coast or in openings in the thick forest canopy. Other assistance has been in the nature of occasionally introducing some pigs (disease free) into the jungle, which the Jarawas hunt and relish. Also some efforts have been made in teaching them sea-ranching so as to enrich marine resources in their areas. Molluscs have also been broadcast in shallow waters and creeks in which sometimes, Jarawas, both adults and children, have also participated. Both in South and Middle Andamans, use of fish nets has also been taught to a few Jarawas. As already explained earlier, the Jarawas had remained hostile till a year ago. In fact killings by Jarawas of non-tribal persons took place in South Andaman Island as recently as the first quarter of 1998.

The Enmay Factor

In the month of May, 1995 a Jarawa boy called Enmay was found injured at Kadamtala in Middle Andaman Island with a leg fracture. He was initially treated at the Primary Health Centre and thereafter transferred to the GB Pant Hospital in Port Blair where he remained under treatment for nearly six months. This is the first case in post-Independence times of a Jarawa tribesman having actually lived in a non-tribal settlement, although for the purpose of medical treatment. After '.eatment he was returned to his tribal habitat. However, as a result, he did become a source of information foe his fellow tribesmen on the outside world, and this has manifested itself during the last one year in that large number of jarawas began appearing at non-tribal locations at Uttara Jetty in Middle Andaman, and from August, 1998 onwards in Tirur Police Post in South Andaman Island. On all such occasions they were returned to the forest, after giving them gifts such as coconuts and bananas. In the month of September, 1998 nearly 15 Jarawas including women and children were found at Middle Andaman in seriously sick condition. Some of them appeared to have respiratory problems, while others had acute dehydration problems. These sick Jarawas were transported to the GB Pant Hospital in Port Blair and treated for nearly three weeks. Once, they were restored to normal health, they were escorted back to their habitat in the forests. Alter these two incidents of medical treatment, no other attempt at fraternisation of the Jarawas was initiated by the Administration except for the contact teams periodically visiting their areas as has been the practice over the last 25 years. It may be mentioned here that Shri Enmay and Smti Enmay had also been introduced to the Hon'ble Prime Minister Shri Atal Behari Vajpayee at Port Blair on 31st December, 1998 and again on 1st January, 1999.

From the month of September, 1998 onwards large numbers of Jarawas, including women and children began to appear at Tirur outpost in South Andaman, and also along the Andaman Trunk Road (ATR) in South and Middle Andaman Islands (the

ATR which runs along the length of South Andaman, Baratang Island in the Middle Andaman group, Middle Andaman Island and a portion in North Andaman, is the only link between Chidyatapu, the southern most point in South Andaman, and Diglipur in North Andaman, a distance of about 350 kms. In between the road is cut by the Middle Strait separating the South Andaman from Baratang Island, Humfray Strait separating Baratang from Middle Andaman, and Austin Strait separating Middle from North Andaman Island. This road is not a recently constructed one, and was actually commenced in the 1960s and completed in the late 1970s. It was built by the Border Road Organisation (Yatrik). For a distance of about 120 kms. it runs along the periphery of the Jarawa reserve. In the last three to four months the Jarawas have been appearing in large numbers at a time along the ATR. Their interaction with non-tribal settlements on the periphery of the ATR have not been hostile but one of aggressive curiosity. On a few occasions the Jarawas have also entered non-tribal settlements which are well away from the forest, usually at night and aggressively demanded various household articles, arousing resentment among those in the settlements. The Jarawas do not, as yet have a clear understanding of ownership and right to property, and therefore tend to snatch articles.

This is a new development and the Administration has created a task force of officers including the Inspector General of Police, Principal Chief Conservator of Forests, Director (Tribal Welfare), some local experts who are long time residents of these islands with experience of working on Jarawa related schemes, Director of the Anthropological Survey of India Dr. P.K. Bhattacharjee (based at Kolkata), the local representative of the Anthropological Survey of India, Shri Kanchan Mukherjee, Director of Health Services and officers of the Andaman Adim Janjati Vikas Samiti to study the present situation and suggest, a modified strategy to deal with the matter. A research and development cell dedicated to analysing Jarawa behavioural patters and evolving both short term and long term strategies has also been created. Teams of officers are visiting areas frequented by the Jarawas in South and Middle Andaman Islands. Some of the steps already taken by the Administration are as follows:

(1) Vehicles along the Andaman Trunk Road are being allowed to move only in convoys escorted by police, so as to prevent fraternisation between those in the vehicles and the Jarawas.

(2) One of the possible reasons identified for Jarawa insecurity in the jungles is the incidence of foreign poaching along various parts of the west cost for which joint patrolling by the Navy, the Coast Guard and the Andaman Nicobar Police is being intensified.

(3) This year, so far, not a single hostile case involving Jarawas has been reported and there have been no killings of non-tribals in the dry season. The contacts involving offer of food items, fruits and coconuts, by the Administration are being maintained.

This Administration are misplaced and based on erroneous information. This Administration would advise the Central Government to investigate the sources of such misinformation on the mainland, who are believed to have communicated over the Internet to various foreign NGOs. The ostensible concern of the latter for the well being of the indigenous tribals of these islands through an orchestrated campaign of addressing letters and Fax messages to the Lt. Governor and the Central Government should be probed. For its part this Administration is only encouraging continued residence of the Jarawas in their traditional forest habitats. At the same time we do not accept the argument that the Jarawas should be severely confined to the jungle indefinitely and not promote any process of gradual integration at all. This Administration believes in gradual integration as opposed to assimilation over an indefinite period which would stretch to several decades. Whatever is done, will be done without reducing the self-reliance and independence of the Jarawas or abandoning their culture, which has traditionally imparted to them a feeling of self-esteem and confidence, even if at times they are hostile. The Administration is against any scheme on the lines of the Onge resettlement, because both this and the Great Andamanese resettlement programmes, while no doubt, preserving these two indigenous tribes from extinction, and in fact contributing towards their increase in numbers over the last two to three decades, appear in retrospect, to have diminished their self-reliance, independence and self-confidence.

What the Administration is doing at present is

(a) to understand the spoken dialect of Jarawas. The Central Institute of Indian Languages, Mysore has worked in this direction and a dictionary has already been prepared;

(b) to enrich the Jarawa area by teaching the Jarawas to plant fruit trees etc. to which they are used to;

(c) to teach them fishing by use of nets;

(d) to prevent their mixing with local population and to this end we have teams of social workers and police who take them to staging huts in their area when they come. and after some work has above they are given food items and sent back to their habitat.

The Administration keeps in touch with experts of anthropology, sociology and tribal welfare for modulating its approach.

In so far as the Sentinelese are concerned, the present policy of discontinuing contact with them since 1994-95 is proposed to be maintained. At the same time this would be done in a manner consistent with such safeguards as patrolling by Navy, Coast Guard and the Andaman and Nicobar Police, as felt necessary for the security of the isolated Sentinel Island. Patrolling of the waters around North Sentinel shall continue from time to time as this is an important ingredient of national security.

The above explanatory note should clarify the position adequately. There is no intention at present, nor has there been in the past, of imposing urbanisation on the indigenous tribals.

Comments of Government of India on Urgent Action Bulletin which appeared in the Survival of February 1999, regarding Indigenous Tribal Communities of Union Territory of Andaman and Nicobar Island

In the Urgent Action Bulletin which had appeared in the Survival of February' 1999 it had been alleged that there was a serious danger to the human rights of the Jarwa and Sentinelese tribes of Andaman and Nicobar Islands. It was also alleged that the Indian Government was seeking to embark on abolishing of settling and assimilating people of these communities, thereby repeating the mistakes of British authorities during the colonial period which led to the genocide of Great Andamanese. It was suggested that Jarwas rights to the ownership of their land must be protected from encroachment and poaching. As a minimum the Jarwa reserve must be restored to its 1957 limits and all settlers and forest camps within the area relocated. Similarly, the Sentinelese should be left alone.

Under the Constitution (Andaman & Nicobar Islands) Scheduled Tribes Order, 1959 promulgated by the President of India on 31st March, 1959, six Communities have been notified as Scheduled Tribes for their special treatment, of which three are jarwas, Sentinelese and Onges. These communities are located in Andaman District and belong to Negrito group. Since independence it has been the policy of the Indian Government that the tribal people should develop along the lines of their own genius and nothing should be imposed on them. Further their areas should not be over administered and Government programmes should work through and not in rivalary to their own social and cultural institutions. The tribals have a specially protected status under the Indian constitution. The Article 19 (5) of the Constitution empowers the State to impose certain restrictions on the fundamental rights of Indian citizens for the protection of Scheduled Tribes. All the tribal areas in the A & N Islands are protected by the A & N Islands (Protection of Aboriginal Tribes) Regulation, 1956. Under this Regulation no non-tribal can enter any tribal area without a permit/pass issued by the Deputy Commissioners concerned.

At the outset Government of India categorically denies the reports alleging imposition of urbanisation of aboriginal tribes of A & N Islands. The expression of concern by various Organisation in United Kingdom criticizing or questioning the policy of Government are misplaced and based on erroneous information.

Jarawas

The Jarawas occupy an area of 649 sq. kms in the reserved forests along the west coast in South Andaman and Middle

Andaman Islands. They are also found in a few smaller islands such as Spike island bordering the west coast. The length of the territory inhabited by the Jarawas in the tropical forests extends to a distance of nearly 120-130 kms. along the west coast of the aforesaid two major islands. It has been the policy of the Government that Jarawas should live in their traditional habitat i.e., deep inside the forest. In order to ensure minimal contact with jarawas and the non-tribals in South and Middle Andaman Islands, the Administration has established a chain of police check posts inside the forests known as the Jarawa Protection Police Posts. At present these number 26. In British times these used to be known as the Bush Police. These outposts inside the reserved forests are built with the help of readily available minor forest products, and no modern materials have been used for construction. However, India being a democratic welfare State it becomes the duty of Government to provide some basic minimum needs to all sections of the society including the tribals. It does not subsrcibe to the policy of isolation followed during the colonial rule in respect of socio-economic development of tribal communities. That is why the Government do not accept the argument that the jarwas should severely confined to the jungles indefinitely and not promote and process of gradual integration at all. The Government believes in gradual integration as oppose to assimilation over an indefinite period which would stretch to several decades. Whatever is done, will be done without reducing the self-reliance and independence of the Jarawas or abandoning their culture, which has traditionally imparted to them a feeling of self-esteem and confidence, even if at times they are hostile. Therefore, since 1974 occasional contacts are being made with the Jarwas in day time only, on days close to the period full moon. These contacts have been limited to gifting them with coconut, bananas and red cloth.

In order to protect the interest of Jarawas, the Government has taken following steps:-

(i) Vehicles along the Andaman Trunk Road are being allowed to move only in convoys escorted by police, so as to prevent fraternisation between those in the vehicles and the Jarwas.

(ii) One of the possible reasons identified for Jarawa insecurity in the jungles is the incidence of foreign poaching along various parts of the west coast for which joint patrolling by the Navy, the Coast Guard and the Andaman Nicobar Police is being intensified.

(iii) It is the endeavour of the Government of extend to them medical assistance whenever this is felt to be necessary. This aspect cannot be ignored and shall continue.

(iv) People in the non-tribal settlements on the periphery of the protected areas are being imparted instruction on the importance of preservation of the Jarawa way of life, without any intrusion from the civilised world.

(v) To enrich the Jarawa area by teaching the Jarawas to plant fruit trees etc. to which they are used to.

(vi) To teach them fishing by use of nets.

(vii) To prevent their mixing with local population, teams of social workers and police have been constituted who give them food items and send back them to their habitats.

Sentinelese

The Sentinelese, who also belong to the negrito group, have traditionally been based only in North Sentinel Island. The only known friendly contact with the Sentinelese took place in 1991. The Government is maintaining presently the policy of discontinuing contact with this tribe since 1995. However, given the incidence of poaching by foreigners from South East Asian countries in the waters around the Andaman and Nicobar Islands, the Navy and Coast Guard have been patrolling the waters around North Sentinel Island from time to time and this is strictly a defence oriented measure and not a contact with the Sentinelese.

Onges

The Onges, who also belong to the Negrito group are found in Little Andaman in an area called Dugong Creek and South Bay. Since they were scattered over Little Andaman, with the resettlement of East Bengal refugees on this island in 1974, two Onge settlements were created at Dugong Creek and South

Andaman in this island, and they were regrouped and settled here. The Andaman Adim Janjati Vikas Samiti administers a Cooperative Society known as the Onge Multipurpose Coop. Society for their welfare. The Onges are registered on the voters list and have voted in last General Elections.

Twelve

Primitive Tribes of Jharkhand

A Brief Note

1. Name of the Tribe: Asur

2. Area of Habitation

The main concentration of Asur tribe is in the district of Gumla, Lohardaga, and Palamu of Jharkhand.

3. Population of the State

The total population of Asur tribe is 7783 as per 1981 census.

4. Characteristic of the Tribe

The main sources of livelihood of Asur tribe is agriculture. They also collect forest minor produces and work as mining labourers for wages. Hunting and fishing are practised as subsidiary occupations.

The Asurs are divided into three main categories:

(i) Bir Asur (ii) Birjia Asur (iii) Agaria Asur.

Most of Asurs belong to nuclear family consisting of mother, father and unmarried children. The Asurs have patrilineal, patrilocal and patriarchal family. Their clan system is strong. Their totemic clans are frog, fish, Toppo, Deer, lion etc. The Asurs were traditionally iron smelters.

The Asurs use some indigenous herbs in the treatment of various diseases and for the control of unwanted birth.

The Asurs believe in Sing-Bonga, Marang Bonga and other Bongas also. They also celebrated festivals like Sarhul, Phagua, Karma, Nawakhani etc.

They also believe in witchcraft and consult witch-doctors

(Sokha). Wherever the Asurs have some problems they consult mati and Ojha.

The Tribal Welfare Department of Government of India and State Government also initiated many welfare activities through Government agencies for the development of Asurs.

1. Name of the Tribe: Birhor

2. Area of Habitation

The Birhors confined mostly in forest region of Ranchi, Hazaribag, Giridih, Gumla and Lohardaga districts of Jharkhand.

3. Population of the State

Birhor is one of the most primitive tribes of Jharkhand with total population of 4377 as per 1981 census.

4. Characteristic of the Tribe

Basically Birhor is nomadic, food gathering and hunting tribes.

Ethnically the Birhor belongs to proto-Austroloid race and linguistically to the Austro - Asiatic Mundari group. They also speak sadari. The Birhor tribe is divided into migratory Birhor (Uthlu) and the settled Birhor (Jangli). Recently a third type of Birhor has emerged from Uthlu Birhor known as semi-nomadic Birhor (Baslu Birhor).

The band organisation is one of the most important features of the Birhor. They live in small bands (Tanda). Their houses (Kumbha) are temporarily typically made of leaves. The Birhor recognises clan. Tanda is partilineal and patrilocal.

The Birhors do not marry with persons related to father or mother. The marriage is fixed on bride-prices. Jocking and avoidance relationship is found among them.

The Birhor economy is traditional and mainly revolves round the forest. Forest is the hub of their life.

Their main source of livelihood is collection of different types of edible roots, fruits, flowers, leafy vegetable, mushroom etc., round the year from forest, while they trap hares which they sell in the village market. They also collect different types of indigenous raw materials, from the forest with which they make rope made articles. Besides in a few of them collect honey from the forest and sell it. Occasional the women make mat and broom some Birhors have got good knowledge of indigenous herbal medicines. The sun is considered as higher God. Pahan, Bhagat, Ojha and Naya are considered to be the religious specialist. There are many festivals celebrated by them. The important festivals are Soharai, Holi, Dusshera and Diwali.

1. Name of the Tribe: Parahiya

2. Area of Habitation

The Parahiya tribe is found mainly in the district of Palamau and Hazaribag of Jharkhand State.

3. Population of the Tribe in the State

According to 1981 census, the total population of Parahiya tribe is 24012 in combined Bihar.

4. Characteristic of the Tribe

The ecological setting of the Parahiya country provides the foundation of their economic life. In their economic life, forest root and fruit collection continues to play a key role, but their economy also depends upon bamboo work, lac cultivation ard farming. Even today the Parahiya earn a part of their living by collecting and selling forest products like fruit, roots, honey, leaves, bamboo and others. The proportion of income derived from forest products varies according to the density of the forest and the demand for these products. The parahiyas exchange their forest products partly for cash and partly for grain. When they sell in the weekly market they receive cash, whereas in the villages they exchange for grain only.

On the whole a parahiya recognizes and social affiliation with the terms Bhat and Chatal. This means that range of a Parahiyas social connection extends upon the point where he accepts Bhat and Chatal (caste rice and caste mal).

Broadly speaking the Parahiya kingship comprises two sets of relationship viz. Dhaiyoia (consanguineal relationship) and sanahi (affinal relationship) members as Hill Kutum. Marriage always takes place outside the Dhaiynia. At the time of birth, marriage and death the Dhaiynia kinsmen are remembered and are the main participants.

The parahiyas habitually group their closer relatives into five major categories. Aparsa which includes Ajakur (Progeny of the same grandfather), Bapkur (Progeny of the same father), Dhadaniya (Progeny of the son) and putania (Progeny of the daughter). The next is the Ghutagari which includes Nankur (Progeny of other father) Manusuaku (Progeny of mothers sister) and Phuphkur (Progeny of fathers sister). They use as broad terms for these two categories of relationship. Pitia and Hitia respectively. Pitias are more kind and indulgent, whereas Hitias are more friendly and cordial.

Marriage among the parahiyas is the process by which the lineage group obtains females as partners for its members and by which new elementary families are brought into being. As regards restrictions on marriages the parahiyas have certain principles of exogamy and endogamy. Firstly, a parahiya should not marry outside his parental Dihwar or spirit parahiya belonging to particular Dihwar must find his match within this limit. Further, the Parahiyas maintain a very strict principle of lineage exogamy.

The parahiyas strongly believe that their entire life is controlled by super natural powers, which are all pervading and infinite. These supernatural powers are embodied in deities and spirits. They can inspire both animate and ananimate objects such as trees, earth, rivers and stones. The parahiyas also recognize that these various supernatural powers have different functions and the capacity to influence human beings. The parahiyas have classified some of the deities as benevolent powers. Some as malevolent and some having both molevolent and benevolent powers.

The new order of land tenancy has brought a great change in lineage organisation. The lineage and the village no longer play important role in the individual sphere in the past little could be done without taking the lineage into consideration. Now everything can be done without any reference to the lineage. This has destroyed the former power and privileges of the head of the lineage.

1. Name of the Tribe: Mal Pahariya

2. Area of Habitation

The Mal paharia constitutes a distinct tribe in the Rajmahal hills and along its adjoining areas. Their concentration occurs in Dumka, Pakur and Sahibganj districts of Jharkhand state.

3. Population of the Tribe in the State

The total population in 1971 census was 48,636 but in 1981 census, it was 79,322 showing an increase of 30,686. This increase does not appear to be credible. The census enumeration could not distinguish between Sauria Paharias and Mal Paharias.

4. Characteristic of the Tribe

The Mal Paharias have a patriarchal family system, which recognizes the male dominance. Widow marriage with the deceased brother is permitted through mutual consent. However divorce is allowed. Polygamy is permitted in the Mal Paharia society.

The Mal Paharias are predominantly agricultural labourers, working on the fields which are mostly owned by the Santhals and others. A small section of the Mal Paharias do have some agricultural lands where the method is primitive subsistence type. This is called "Kurao, a kind of shifting cultivation. They normally produce paddy, barbatti, maize and other coarse grains which hardly seem to be sustainable.

It is become of the poverty that the system of bonded labour is found among them.

Over 90 per cent Mal Paharias are Hindus, a few of them have faith in the Christianity. They mostly observe Hindu religious festivals. Their strong faith in Karma is indicative of animism in their religious faith as their Chief deities are the sun and the Earth worship (Bhi Deo Pujaj) is widely practised in the Damin area with the belief that the worship brings in peace and good harvest. The worship is done by the village priest which is hereditary in nature. The earth worship is occasionally marked by sacrifice of animals.

Totem is very much prevalent in the Mal Paharia Society.

They believe the every observable feature has life, hence it must be worshipped.

Apart from their own traditional rituals, the Mal Paharias also observe the Durga Puja, Kali Puja, the Holi with great enthusiasm and fervour. The females observe the jitia festival.

1. Name of the Tribe: Hill Kharia

2. Area of Habitation

Hill Kharia mainly resides in the different blocks of East Singhbhum district of Jharkhand.

3. Population of the tribe in the State

The total population of Hill Kharia tribe is 12,387 according to 1981 census in Jharkhand.

4. Characteristic of the Tribe

The Kharia has three sections, viz. The Dudh, Dhelki and Hill Kharia, representing different grade of culture. Among the three sections, the Hill Kharia are still in the primitive stage of economic culture and lead a hand to mouth existence by the collection of forest products and occasionally by shifting cultivation. They depends upon forest products viz. collection of honey, edible fruits, roots and herbs. Besides this they work as agricultural labourers in the forest throughout the year.

The Hill Kharias are most primitive community. A Hill Kharia house consists of only one room which is used as bed-room store-room, kitchens and guest-room.

Family is the central part of social organisation in the Hill Kharia society. Most of the families of this tribe are nuclear. The Hill Kharias have patrilineal, Patrilocal and patriarchal family. Among them clan system is strongly prevalent. They cannot eat or hunt their totemic objects. These totems may be animals, birds, fish, tree or even inanimate objects. The names of clans among Hill Kharia are Gulgu (Sal fish), Bhuiya (fish), Jaru (Rat), Badya (Tuber), Test (Bird), and Hembrom (Bettlement). Clan plays a vital role in the marriage negotiation. Marriage within the same clan is strictly prohibited. The Kinship organisations of the Hill Kharia is of the classificatory type. The bride-price is an essential part of the marriage of this tribe. All the activities of the Hill Kharias are associated with religious beliefs. They worship numerous. Gods and spirits their religious head is called Dihuri by the Hill Kharias. This is a hereditary post. The Hill Kharia worship the Gram Deota' They celebrate the Indra Parab. Their main festivals are Sohrai, Karma, Indra etc.

The Hill Kharia have been settled by the state government in East Singhbhum for their economic and material development they feel secure in the forest and hence decry the facilities for rehabilitation.

1. Name of the Tribe: Korwa

2. Area of Habitation

The main concentration of Korwa tribe in Jharkhand in the districts of Palamu, Garhwa and Gumla.

3. Population of the Tribe in the State

According to 1981 census total population of Korwa is 20,950 in the state.

4. Characteristic of the Tribe

The Korwa word is derived from the Kodawas meaning diggers of earth. They are branch of Kolarian tribe. The Korwa are generally of short stature. Their dialect belong to the Mundari branch of the Austric family of language. This tribe also speaks Hindi, Sadri and other local dialects. The tribe has two subtribe known as Pahari Korwa and Dihari Korwa.

The main sources of livelihood of Korwa tribe is food gathering, hunting and minor forest products collection. They collect minor forest product like mahua, gum, tendu leaves, amla, honey etc. In rainy season, they gather some forest roots, leaves and other vegetables. Now-a-days, they do cultivation but their technique is very primitive. Fishing and hunting are practised as subsidiary occupations. The Dihari Korwa who have no land work for other tribal cultivators as labour.

The village site is usually chosen on the top of a hill or on a owned covered with tick forest. Most of the families of Korwa tribe are nuclear. The kinship system is still the basic sub-structure for them. Some strict relationship taboo separate relatives from each other among the Korwa. A person cannot marry a member of the same clan or outside the tribe. Like the other tribes of Jharkhand the bridegroom has to pay the bride-wealth to the brides people. The Korwa have patrilineal, patrilocal and patriarchal family. Each named after some animals, plants or other object with which the ancestor of the clan may have had some association in the remotest past. Each of their totemistic clans from an exogamous group and so the marriage between the members of the same clan (killi) is prohibited.

The Korwa, worship many deities, of which the most important ones are the Bhagwan Pat deotas, village deities. They worship god and goddess for recovery from illness, better crops, safety and protection against natural calamities. They believe in magic and witchcraft. The magician are the tribe is known as 'Baiga'. Their main festivals are Deothan which is observed on the full moon day of Pus and all their gods are worshipped. The Nawanna or harvest festival, Holi, Dusshera are also celebrated.

1. Name of the Tribe: Sauria Paharia

2. Area of Habitation

The main concentration of the Sauria Paharias is in Rajmahal Godda and Pakaur districts of Santal Paraganas of Jharkhand. In Santal Paraganas, they are concentrated in Rajmahal hills their villages are situated on the hills within Damin-i-koh area which is a Government estate.

3. Population of the State

The total population of Sauria Paharias is 39,269 as per 1981 census in combined Bihar.

4. Characteristic of the Tribe

The Malto language of Sauria Paharia are similar to the Kurukh language or oraon as both belong to the dravidian language family. The main sources of Sauria livelihood are agriculture, forest products, wine making, live stock and occasional labour for wages. The physical environment has greatly influenced their economic life. The availability of the things in their environment has led them to depend upon forest products hunting and shifting cultivation for their livelihood.

The cloths worn by the Sauria are purchased from the market. The upper ornaments of the Sauria of males consists of a shirt and Ganji turbans of red colour are used by very few saurias. Their lower garments are Dhoti, Pant and Lungi. Pants and lungies are worn mostly by the Christian saurias. The upper garment for women are blouse and piece of cloths called topwar.

The sauria use various source of ornaments which they obtain from market. Their ornaments are mostly brass. Their common ornaments are hairpin (erpin), earring (kad-b-e-angli) nose ring (muan angli) etc. A jungle flower, an arrow, aspear and the stars are liked by them as tatooing mark.

The saurias dance and bring mostly during marriage and festivals or when they take rice bear or country liquor. Their musical instruments consists of violin (Banam) flute (Bansli) drum (Khailu) etc.

In sauria society, the family may be nuclear or joint family, they have no clan system, in the absence of which kinship is taken into consideration in marriage negotiation. They do not marry with the relatives up to three generation from parents sides. They have a classificatory type of kinship system. The saurias are endogamous. They are monogamous but polygamy is practised. The marriage negotiation is started through the help of intermediaries called 'Sithu'. Among the saurias a girl may marry a boy of her choice, the bride price is paid in cash and kind, the sauria bury their dead.

Sauria Paharia observe certain festival on different occasions. Among them, barbati, gangi, mare festival are of local importance and of little tradition. Bandna and some Hindu festivals like Durga Puja, Deepawali and Mahadeo Puja are also observed by them and these are of great tradition. Among all the festivals bandna is very important and lasts for four days. All the activities of the sauria are associated with religious rituals. The worship numerous gods and spirits.

1. Name of the Tribe: Birjia

2. Area of Habitation

The main concentration of the Birjia tribe in the district of Gumla, Lohardaga and Palamu of Jharkhand State.

3. Population of the State

The total population of Birjia tribe is 4,057 are per 1981 census in combined Bihar.

4. Characteristic of the Tribe

The main sources of livelihood of Birjia tribe is plough cultivation. A few among them still smelt iron, practice slash and burn cultivation and also prepare bamboo khadi craft materials for sale. Occasionally they become forest labourer under private contractors. They are also agriculture labourers.

They lead a forest life. They make their houses on the spurs of the highest hills, where two or three families will be found living together in wretched little gram huts, hardly big for pig with a decent sized litten.

The Birjia are divided into different totemistic groups. These are also two cross division. According to the first, they are divided into 'senduria' and 'telia' and according to the second they are divided into 'Dudh' and rash Birjia. The sendurias use vermilion in solemnization of marriage. For the 'Dudh Birjias' beef is taboo. But not for the Rash Birjia.

The Birjia have community Panchayat, consisting of the communing elders, under the Baiga. The Panchayat looks after the traditional customs and practices.

They believe that death occurs due to malevolent act of evil spirit. The deed are burnt as well as buried and death in the family brings pollution which can only be removed after due ceremonies. The Birjias observed all the festivals observed by the Asurs. Ancestor worship among them is observed. Religion plays a vital role in each and every sphere of their life.

1. Name of the Tribe: Savar

2. Area of Habitation

The savars, a minor Scheduled Tribe in the state of Jharkhand are concentrated in the districts of Singhbhum, Ranchi and Hazaribagh.

3. Population of the State

The total population of Savar tribe is 3,014 as per 1981 census.

4. Characteristic of the tribe

The Savars now residing in Dhalbhum, might have originally come from Orissa tributary states. They still have marriage alliances in those tributary states. They are divided into four sub-tribes of which could tell the name of three only viz. Jhara, Basoo and Jaytapati. All the four sub tribes are endogamous. Out of the four sub tribes only Jhara sub tribe are the savar is living in the Dhalbhum.

The main sources of livelihood of savar tribe are labour for wages, collecting ediable roofs, herbs and fruits from the Jungle, agriculture and wine making. They are landless. They cultivates small 'baris' which are found near the house. These baries where settled on them by the government and are their private property. In inheritance is patrilineal. They do not have their own plough and cattle and hence they hire them from their neighbours, they do not practise shifting cultivation. They work as labourer through out the year on daily wage basis.

The family of the savars are nuclear type. Consisting of father, mother and unmarried children. As soon as they are married, the children set up their own families. The savar are monogamous but polygamy is not unknown to them. Their family structure is patrilineal.

The savar have no clan system. In Dhalbhum area, the marriage is regulated through kinship. The marriage does not take place between relative up to three generations above the parents.

The kinship system of the savars of Dhalbhum of the classificatory type.

The Savar have a traditional panchayat presided over by a village ahead called 'Pradhan'. He is assisted by a Gorait who acts messenger. Their offices are hereditary. They have own traditional laws and customs which control the social behaviour of the savar.

In the savar community widow marriage is permitted. The life cycle of an individual ends with death. They carry the corpse on a wooden bier or on a cot upside down for cremation to 'Sasan'.

The savar worship a female divinity, the proto type of the Hindu Kali. They also worship Mansa Devi.

Thirteen

U.P. and Uttaranchal

In Uttar Pradesh two Scheduled Tribes, viz., Raji and Buksa were declared as primitive tribal group by Govt. of India. After the partition of the State and creation of new State Uttaranchal only Buksa primitive tribe remained in the present State which is found in Bijnor district only. According to 1991 census the population of Buksa tribe in U.P. is as follows:

District	*Tehsil*	*Population*
Bijnor	Kotwali	1329
	Nazibabad	351
	Afjalgarh	180
	Total	1860

Buksa's are Mongoloid. They follow the patraleneal & Patriarchal society and village pradhan is known as 'mukhia' which is said to be head of the village and made to be responsible for all the social and cultural activities of the tribe in the village.

The tribe is divided into many clan and inter-clan marriage is prohibited among them.

Buksa are fond of rice, dal and fish like Tharus the other Scheduled Tribe of U.P. and use liquor also. The Buksas are mainly agriculturists but most of them are marginal farmers the sow crops like wheat, rice, gram, barley etc. Animal Husbandry is their subsidiary occupation which they adopted recently. The development measures of the government and education changed the traditional living cropping and agricultural pattern of Buksas as well as their life style. Now, they grow cane and collect minor forest produce also. Bee keeping is also prevalent among them.

The changing pattern of their occupation has developed the economic condition of the tribe.

A Primitive Tribal Development project is running at Nazibabad, Bijnor for this tribe on the cent per cent grant of Central Assistance. In this project Self-Employment, Agriculture development etc. scheme are running.

In the year 2000-01 Rs. 0.60 lacs were spend among 10 beneficiaries under Self-Employment Scheme and Rs. 0.50 lacs among 50 beneficiaries under Agriculture Development scheme. It is proposed to spend Rs. 1.20 under Self-Employment Scheme and Rs. 6.80 lacs under Agriculture Development, Safe Drinking Water, Housing Vocational Training etc. schemes during 2001-02.

Buksa's are Mongoloid. They follow the patraleneal and Patriachal society and village pradhan is known as 'mukhia' which is said to be head of the village and made to be responsible for all the social and cultural activities of the tribe in the village.

The tribe is divided into may clan and inter-clan marriage is prohibited among them.

Buksa are fond of rice, dal and fish like Tharus the other Scheduled Tribe of U.P. and use liquor also. The Buksas are mainly agriculturists but most of them are marginal farmers the sow crops like wheat, rice, gram, barley etc. Animal Husbandry is their subsidiary occupation which they adopted recently. The development measures of the government and education changed the traditional living cropping and agricultural pattern of Buksas as well as their life style. Now, they grow cane and collect minor forest produce also. Bee keeping is also prevalent among them. The changing pattern of their occupation has developed the economic condition of the tribe.

Fourteen

Primitive Tribe of Manipur

Introduction

The Maram tribe of Manipur is the only declared primitive tribal group in the State. People belonging to this tribal group inhabit parts of Tadubi and Kangpokpi Block/Sub-Divisions under the Senapati District. A recent survey - conducted by the Department for Development of Tribals and Scheduled Castes, Manipur indicated that there are 23,957 persons with 3134 households scattered in 28 nos. of villages. There are 4 nos. of villages inhabited by this group under the Kangpokpi Sub-Division and the remaining 24 nos. of villages under Tadubi Sub-Division. Since the inception of the Maram Primitive Tribe Project under the Special Central Assistance to Tribal Sub-Plan during the year, 1981-82, there have been considerable improvement in the living condition of the people belonging to this group. Nevertheless, further improvement in the living condition is still imperative as they are behind the rest of the tribal groups in the State.

1.1. On the economic front the Marams still depend solely on pre-agricultural method of cultivation. Shifting cultivation is rampant. Permanent cultivation has not been taken up at large scale due to absence of infrastructural facilities like Minor irrigation etc. There is an acute scarcity of potable water in the Maram tribe inhabited villages. Animal Husbandry in commercial scale has so far not been adopted for lack of resources and technical know-who except for some small domestic uses. Almost 95 per cent of the Marams are dependent on agriculture of which about 90 per cent still practice - the age old method of shifting cultivation for their livelihood. Topographical condition of the villages inhabited by this group does not permit well and tube well facilities and as such almost all the people depend on stream water. A few villages are taken up by the State P.H.E. Department for providing safe drinking water which are being commissioned. There are again some villages where perennial source of water flows down below from where it is very difficult to lift water to the villages without installing pumps etc. Therefore, systematic infrastructure development is required for the overall development of the people belonging to this tribal group.

1.2. This primitive tribal group is vulnerable to all forms of diseases as there is neither adequate facility of medical institution nor trained medical personnel. A few P.H.S.Cs are there in areas inhabited by the people of this group, however, adequate medicines and trained personnels are not available resulting to depriving health care facilities.

1.3. Education level, the backbone of any modern civilised life, is at a very low key among the people of this Primitive Tribal Group. Except for few private schools run by Missionaries, no other educational institution worth mentioning is available in the area. The literacy rate as per survey (1997-98) conducted by the Department are indicated below:—

Total	28.25 per cent
Male	37.87 per cent
Female	19.25 per cent

The State literacy rate was 59.89 per cent with 71.63 per cent for Male and 47.60 per cent for Female (1991 census). The Scheduled Tribe literacy rate as per 1991 census were 53.63 per cent with 62.39 per cent for male and 44.47 per cent for Female. The State literacy rate as per 2001 Population Census (Provisional) is 68.87 per cent (Male - 77.87 per cent and Female - 59.70 per cent). The decadal increase in the Literacy rate is higher than the national average. While the same for the Maram Primitive tribe is marginal. Hence, there is need for educational development for the children belonging to this primitive tribal group.

1.4. Facts and figures enumerated above indicates that even though there are considerable development attained by the people belonging to the Maram Primitive Tribal Group, there is still dearth of certain amenities which require special attention. Facilities for medical and health care, provision of water in the villages, setting of educational awareness camps, special coaching centres, setting up of educational institutions, construction and repairing of inter-village roads, suspension bridges, etc. are still lacking in the areas inhabited by this tribal group.

Development Programmes Undertaken

The Maram Primitive Tribe Project was first set up during this year, 1981-82 with a token sanction of an amount of Rs. 1.00 lakh by the Government of India, under the Special Central Assistance to Tribal Sub-Plan. Since then, an amount of Rs. 132.41 lakhs were earmarked for the development of this tribal group till the year, 1999-2000. Against this allocation, an amount of Rs. 124.94 lakhs was spent during the same period. With the availability of this amount, a total of 2300 nos. of persons belonging to Maram Primitive tribal group were financially assisted to take up various developmental programmes under Agriculture/Horticulture, Animal Husbandry, Village and Small Industries sectors alongwith running and maintenance of the Training Centre at Maram wherein 12 nos. of trainees are trained in each of the Tailoring and Weaving trades. On successful completion of the training, each trainee is awarded with a Sewing machine under tailoring trade and a weaving loom under weaving trade to enable them to start business under their respective trade. Under the Maram Primitive Tribe Project, a total of 13 villages were taken up for improvement of inter village roads and repairing works for 6 (six) nos. of School buildings and 1 (one) hostel building situated in the areas inhabited by this primitive tribal group. Details of programmes taken up by the Department under the Maram Project since its inception in the year, 1981-82 to the year, 1999-2000 are indicated in the enclosed statement as Annexure-A.

2.1 During the year, 2000-01, an amount of Rs. 18.00 lakhs was earmarked for taking up developmental works as per details given below:

(a) Running and maintenance of the training centre at Maram	Rs. 3.86 lakhs
(b) Rearing of bulls	Rs. 4.20 lakhs
(c) Financial assistance for opening of small grocery shops.	Rs. 5.00 lakhs
(d) Land reclamation programme.	Rs. 4.94 lakhs
Total	Rs. 18.00 lakhs

However, only an amount of Rs. 46,332/- for procurement of materials for the Training centre at Maram, could be encashed during the last financial year, 2000-01 due to late authorisation by the State Finance Department and also due to ban on transaction imposed by the Reserve Bank of India. However, the process for revalidation and re-authorisation of the balance amount of Rs. 17.54 lakhs have already been taken up for implementation of the programme as approved by the Work Advisory Board for Maram Primitive Tribe in the Department during the year, 2000-01 for implementation during the current financial year, 2001-02.

2.2 Apart from implementation of developmental programmes under the Special Central Assistance to Tribal Sub-Plan, there are yet another two sources for funding the development activities taken up in the areas inhabited by the Maram Primitive Tribe viz. i) fund under the central sector scheme for development of Maram Primitive Tribe under N.G.O. sector and ii) Central sector scheme for development of Maram Primitive Tribe under Tribal Research Institute sector.

Under the N.G.O. sector an amount of Rs. 9.73 lakhs was released during the year, 2000-01 for the implementation of programmes like, Special Coaching for students belonging to Maram Tribe, Educational Awareness programme, Health camps in the villages inhabited by Maram People and economic development programmes for Maram people. All these programmes are being implemented by the concerned N.G.O. Under the Tribal Research Institute sector, an amount of Rs. 26.00 lakhs was sanctioned by the Ministry of Tribal Affairs, Government of India during the last financial year, 2000-01. However, this amount could not be utilised during the said year due to late receipt. With the availability of this amount of Rs. 26.00 lakhs, 10 villages will be covered under the construction/improvement of Inter-village roads amounting to Rs. 20.00 lakhs and another amount of Rs. 6.00 lakhs is earmarked for the construction of one Suspension Bridge covering two Maram villages. These programmes are being implemented shortly. Required Utilisation Certificates for the amounts released under the Central Sector Scheme of development of Primitive Tribal Groups for the amount of Rs. 9.73 lakhs under N.G.O. and Rs. 26.00 lakhs under T.R.I. will be submitted soon.

STATEMENT SHOWING THE ACTUAL EXPENDITURE AND ACHIEVEMENT UNDER MARAM PRIMITIVE TRIBE PROJECT FROM ITS INCEPTION

(Rs. in lakhs)

Plan period/ Year	*Outlay*	*Expenditure*	*Achievements*
1	*2*	*3*	*4*
6th Plan (1980-85) (w.e.f. 1981-82)	10.70	10.57	(i) 167 families (ii) Establishment of Training centre at Maram. (iii) 11 villages under communication.
7th Plan (1985-90)	27.77	27.76	(i) 1034 families (ii) Maintenance and running of training Institute. (iii) 2 villages under communication.
Annual Plan (1990-91)	11.25	11.79	(i) 142 families (ii) Maintenance and running of training Institute. (iii) Construction of Staff Quarters - 2 nos.
Annual Plan (1991-92)	8.54	8.51	(i) 93 families (ii) Maintenance and running of training Institute. (iii) Repairing of School building-6 nos. and Hostel building-1 no.
8th Plan (1992-97)	41.15	40.36	(i) 628 families (ii) Maintenance and running of training Institute. (iii) Construction of Rest House.
Annual Plan (1997-98)	9.00	7.30	(i) 84 families (ii) Maintenance and running of training Institute.
Annual Plan (1998-99)	12.00	11.43	(i) 92 families (ii) Maintenance and running of training Institute.
Annual Plan (1999-2000)	12.00	7.22	(i) 60 families (ii) Maintenance and running of training Institute.
Total	132.41	124.94	(i) 2300 families (ii) 13 villages under communication, repairing of 6 nos of school and 1 (one) hostel building. (iii) Running of Training Institute and Maintenance of training centre. (Due to RBI ban fund could not utilised the same programme will be available during the year, 2001-2002).

Suggestions

To improve the living condition of the people belonging to Maram Primitive Tribe of Manipur, a lot of development activities are still required to be undertaken. While the family oriented income generating programmes could be taken up under the Special Central Assistance to Tribal Sub-Plan and the N.G.O.'s sector, the infrastructure development programme on the other hand could be continued under the Central sector scheme for the development of Maram Primitive Tribe under T.R.I. and N.G.O. sectors. Infrastructure development in the hill areas are very important even for the successful implementation of the family oriented income generating programmes. The Government of India in the Ministry of Tribal Affairs may therefore consider the continuance of the Central Sector programmes for the Development of Maram Primitive Tribe for at least another period of 5 (five) years both under N.G.O. and T.R.I. sectors for attaining sustainable improvement in the living condition of the people belonging to the Maram Primitive Tribe of Manipur.

Fifteen

Kerala

Kurumbar

The Kurumbar subsist on shifting cultivation, forest labour and minor forest produce collection. Out of 16 Kurumbar hamlets, 10 are situated in the Reserve Forests and the rest in Vested forests. The number of households in a hamlet varies from 5 to 45. The hamlet land is owned communally but cultivation is done independently by each family on separate plots. They cultivate at a time one fifth of the hamlet land. The remaining area is left follow. At a time, a particular plot is used for two to three years consecutively and then they shift to another plot. Finally, they may return to the first plot after 12 to 15 years by which time it would have regained its lost fertility. They cultivate mixed crop which include ragi (Elusine coracana), avara (Dolichos lab-lab), Chama (Panicum miliaceum) and red gram. The Kurumbar also collect varieties of roots, tubers, nuts, mushrooms from neighbouring forests during scarcity periods.

The Kurumbar collect minor forest produces such as soap nut, dammer resin, cardamom, gooseberry, oil seeds, honey, bee wax etc. The peak collection period are from October to December and from March to June. It is assessed that forest produces worth Rs. 2,500 are transacted annually by 90 per cent of the Kurumbar families with the Kurumbar Girijan Co-operative Society. They are adapted to poultry rearing and goats rearing. They rear cattle for milk products and they fatten it for sale too.

The Kurumbar traditionally dwell in linear structures which are compartmentalised and a conjugal family is accommodated in each apartment. There are such two or three linear dwelling structures to accommodate all the families. During agriculture season they erect small huts at the centre of the individual's cultivated plots. They guard they crops by staying in these huts, shifting home articles from the permanent hamlet. The cultivation period which coincides with post monsoon and cold seasons lasting for 5 to 6 months, i.e., from September to February. After harvest, they abandon these temporary huts and return to regular hamlet life after an annual repair. They draw water from nearby streams and springs.

The total population of Kurumbar is 1820 (1991 census) with 955 male and 865 females.

The Kurumbar society is politically acephalous. Hamlet (ooru) is the minimum socio-political unit. The headman of a hamlet is called oorumoopan. It is he who presides over all the social, political and religious functions. He also act as the representative of the hamlet people for inter hamlet disputes and in dealing with the Government officials and visitors. He is assisted by other social functionaries viz., bhandari, kuruthalai and mannookkaran. The bhandari is the treasurer of the socio-political functions and the kuruthalai assist the oorumooan in carrying out the social and religious functions. He also plays the role of "messenger". The mannookkaran is the soil expert and determine the agricultural activities. The role of social functionaries is hereditary.

Their society is divided into eight exogamous clans. In a hamlet various social functionaries are from different clans. The Kurumbar are patrilineal in descent and inheritance. Their residence is patrilocal and their family is nuclear. Bride price and pre-marital courting are the peculiarities of their marriage. Widow, widower and diverse re-marriages are allowed. Menstrual birth and death pollutions are observed. The kurumbar do have marriage alliance with Mudugar a tribal community living in the lower valley.

The Kurumbar worship ancestral spirits with elaborate burial and post-burial rites which eat up their savings of years together. The Kurumbar also worship a legion of Hindu deities, gods and godlings along with their Karadaivam (earth god). They also propitiate clan deities and ancestral spirits. The Kurumbar are known for their expertise in witchcraft and magical manoeuvrings such as odivekkal, mayyivekkal etc. They are feared by other tribal communities in the area. Among Kurumbar there are specialist herbal therapists who are widely sought by tribes and non-tribes.

Kadar

Introduction

The Kadar (Kadan-singular, Kadar - plural) one of the primitive tribes of Kerala are known in anthropological literature as 'Kadars of Cochin'. According to the 1991 Census, the population of Kadar was 2021. The Kadar language is a form of Tamil with Malayalam elements. They subsist mainly on *non wood forest produce* (nwfp) collection and forest labour. The Kadar live in the Parambikulam, Kuriyarkutty, Nelliampathy and Kodassery forest areas coming under Chittoor taluk of Palakkad district and Vazhachal, Poringalkuthu and Sholayar forest areas of Mokundapuram taluk of Thrissur district. They are also found in the adjoining Anamalai hills of Coimbatore District of Tamil Nadu.

Distribution of population

The distribution of Kadar settlements in accordance with the Forest Range during 1999 March are given below.

A. Palakkad District

	Name of settlements	*No. of families*	*Name of Forest Range*
1.	Kuriyarkutty	70	Orukomban Range
2.	Parambikulam dam site	9	Parambikulam Range
3.	Parambikulam earth dam	32	Karimala Range
4.	Thekkady	15	Kollangode Range
5.	Kalchadi	17	Nemmara Special Range
6.	Cheruneeli	7	Nelliampathy special Range
7.	Thaliyakallu	36	Nelliampathy Special Range
8.	Malakkappara	50	Sholayar Range
9.	Sholayar power house	21	Sholayar Range
10.	Anakkayam	14	Sholayar Range
11.	Vachumaram	39	Vazhachal Range
12.	Poringalkuthu	22	Vazhachal Range
13.	Pokyilappara	19	Kollathirumedu Range
14.	Vazhachal	60	Cherpu Range
15.	Anapantham	49	Velhhaiangara Range
	Total no. of families	460	

The Kadar territory is situated at an elevation of about 1000 feet to 3500 feet above MSL. The forests were once very rich in timber and nwfp. The area is now covered largely by monoculture teak plantations and polyculture forest trees plantations. The region receives both southwest and northeast monsoons. A few Kadar hamlets are located inside the wild life sanctuaries. The forest is abundant with wild life and the Kadar abode of Palakkad district include the Parambikulam wild life sanctuary Elephants, Sambur, varieties of deer, primates etc. are a common sight. The area is also rich in medicinal herbs.

The Kada - Cultural Profile

Material culture

Earlier accounts on Kadar state that they lived in kingroups of three to ten families and lead a nomadic life in the forests. While camping in forests, they erected small leaf shelters. Some Kadar of Nelliyampathy area are found occupying rock shelters during their collection pursuits. Their hutments are usually located on a slope near a water source. Currently, it is observed that except in Kalehadi hamlet of Nelliyampathy Special Forest Range, in all other areas, the Kadar lead a settled life during major part of the year. Within a settlement the houses are distributed haphazardly. The huts are flimsy structures erected on poles raised on a mud platform in a roughly rectangular shape and looks like a shed. The walls and rafters are made of bamboo. The roof is generally thatched with reed leaves. Hearth is in a corner near the entrance. A little away from the dwelling structures one can note seclusion huts here and there. In olden days kadar used to desert their huts the death of all important member of the family.

They used to carry water in bamboo internodes. Now-a-days, earthen and aluminium vessels are used. They sleep on cora grass mats. Iron hand axe digging sticks, choppers and knives are inseparable items from a Kadar. In former days fire was produced with the help of bamboo saw. A few earthen pots for cooking and containers made of bamboo internodes can also be seen in the huts.

The custom of chipping incisor tooth, both upper and lower into sharply pointed ones was prevalent. The sign of it can be sparingly seen among elders even today. This is done with a chisel of billhook by a member of the tribe on boys at the age of 18 and girls at the age of 10. Leaf and bark clothes were used in former days. The Kadar woman who inhabit the interior forests put on a loin cloth and blouse while those living near non tribal quarters around dam sites are seen wearing sari and blouse, during ceremonies and festivals. Boys are often seen putting on shirts and shorts and girls, skirts and blouses.

The staple food of Kadar is rice. This is also supplemented with roots and tubers. These roots are consumed either after boiling or roasting. Among animals they hunt for food include wild boars, sambur, deer, black monkey, mongoose, rats etc. Fishing is also an important source for food. Beef and buffalo meat are taboo. They drink toddy, arrack and smoke beedi.

Economy

As stated earlier, the Kadar economy revolves mainly on collection of *non-wood forest produces* (nwfp) and forest labour. Nwfp collection is known among them as thettam. The evergreen upper ghat forests of the Kadar habitat is rich in nwfp. It is especially true of evergreen forests around hamlets viz kuriyamutty, Parambikulam earth dam site colony, Thaliyakallu, Kalchadi, Vachumaram, Malakkappara etc. Thelly (dammer), honey, wax, soap nut, maramanjal, pathripoo, pulinjlka incha bark, mutty, aralithiri, muttipal, kanjirakuru (nux vomica) arrow root, gooseberry are the main items collected.

The roots and tubers collected for consumption include noorai, thali nara, chandra, chukanmera, chaval and vettila. They also collect fruits like wild jack and mango. These are collected during season. They are also expert in hunting, fishing, and rope making. Rope making out of bark is done during rainy season.

Social life

The society and policy of Kadar is acephalic. The hamlet headmen is called *moopan* and he controls the socio-political matters of a hamlet. In olden days, they were installed by the royal family of Kochi and hence the *moopans* wielded much powers in the community. Without his consent no marriage, puberty ceremony, funeral and death rites could be celebrated. It is true that the *moopans* do not wield the same authority now, as in the past.

The Kadar clans are known as *Jati*. It is named after the original settlement or pathi. There are seven such clans among the Kadar. They are anamalyil, kodakalayal,.patinharayal, thekeddiyal, taliyil, kottarayal, and kalluchadiyil. The kadar society is monogamous and hamlet exogamy prevails. Cross cousin marriages are preferred. Levirate and sororate are now-a-days reported though these were not conventionally approved by the society. Instances of rare cases of polygynous and polyandrous marriages have been noticed. Marriage by service is very common. The custom of bride price is prevalent. It is paid in cash. The Kadar follows a bilateral system of inheritance to which patrilineal and matrilineal inheritance and succession pattern have permeated to an approvable degree. It is noted these days that among Kadar, patrilineal inheritance is the dominant feature.

Confinements generally take place in huts erected for the purpose. Birth pollution is observed for 91 days and menstrual pollution for 5 to 7 days. Onset of menarche is celebrated. Those who can afford may arrange a feast for the members of the settlement. The dead among the kadar is buried. All the implements and articles used by the dead are buried along with the corpse. Death pollution is observed for 16 days. The chief mourners are the eldest nephew and eldest son. The Kadar worship Hindu deities, sylvan and ancestral spirits. These deities are worshipped during March - April just prior to the season for the collection of minor forest produces. Fire walking is performed in order to appease deities after ritual fasts. The oracle is called *thaivamali*. Onam and Vishu are the two important festivals celebrated by the Kadar.

Cholanaicken

Ecological and Cultural Scenario

The Cholanaicken inhabit the evergreen recess of the forests of the Ghat section of the Nilambur Valley, Ernad taluk, Malappuram district, Kerala State. They were leading a life with very limited contact with society at large. They subsist on food gathering, hunting and the collection of minor forest produces. Population above 16 years are totally illiterate and are shy and elusive. Their total population estimated to be 350 in 1979 at the Chungathara I & II (179) and Karulai (171) ranges. The survey conducted for the preparation of this plan, estimated the population of the Cholanaicken as 365.

The Cholanaicken lead a nomadic life in the forests. They dwell in rock shelters (allai) or in open camp sites making instant leaf shelters (mana). It is estimated that there are more than 65 rock shelters and a number of open camp sites. The Cholanaicken are distributed in various regions of the forest in territorial groupings, consisting of 2-7 primary families. The territory over which the kingroup wields its economic rights and other privileges is called chemmam. The families of a particular chemmam do not trespass the rights of other chemmam. Each chemmam invariably constitute a particular river basin. For instance, the karimpuzha chemmam is known after the Karimpuzha river. As there is vast areas in between two chemmam, interaction of the Cholanaicken with those of another is very limited. They generally meet each other when they visit the bartering centres for the transaction of minor forest produces.

The cholanaicken society is politically acephalous. The chemmakkaran, the headman and officiating priest of a chemmam is the decision maker regarding the socio-political, religious and economic matters. The role of chemmakkaran descend from elder son or to an younger brother. Nuclear family is the basic socio-economic unit. The Cholanaicken generally follow patrilocal residence and chemmam rights.

The Cholanaicken have deep attachment with their respective territories. Any attempt for taking out the Cholanaicken family of a chemmam from their respective chemmam in the name of colonization, housing, agriculture etc so far met failure. They are highly reluctant to come down to the lower valley for settling down in colonies envisaged by the Tribal Development Department. The territorial affinity of the Cholanaicken have to be taken in its true spirt and cultural significance while preparing this Action Plan.

Economy

The main source of outside money for the Cholanaicken is derived from *minor forest produce* (mfp) collection. They have the potential to collect annually around 5000kg of honey, 15-25 tonns of soapnut, 5000kg of dammer resins and a number of other highly sought forest produces. The Cholanaicken are the members of the Kalkulam Girijan Service Co-operative Society, which operates in the Cholanaicken area. The society has its jurisdiction - Nilambur south and North Divisions. The forest ranges comes under this Divisions are Karulai, Kalikavu, Nilambur, Vazhikadavu and Edavanna. The Society collect minor forest produces from Cholanaicken by opening collection sheds at different locations of the forest, during seasons. The Cholanaicken complaint that Society collect mfps at a low price when compared to private agencies. The Society couldn't establish sufficient number of collection sheds. All the mfp items available in the habitat such as medicinal plants, roots/tubers, oil seeds etc. are not collected by the Society. Because of these failures, the society couldn't function effectively and the Cholanaicken are reported to be permanently indebted to the Society.

Streamlining of the existing co-operative Society is a must for the Cholanaicken development. This Girijan Service Co-operative society should concentrate mainly in the collection of minor forest produces and in the supply of necessary provisions to Cholanaicken. Tribal communities viz., Kattunaicken, Pathinaicken, Paniyan and Aranadan are also inhabitants of the area. These tribal communities too collect mfps and transact with the above society. The strengthening Kalkulam Girijan Service Co-operative Society also will be beneficial to these communities too and this will ensue total collection and elimination of private agencies.

Health

During the last two decades, the population had occasional exposure to allopathi treatment. Spread of viral fever was found highly dangerous to the life of the Cholanaicken during 1977-79. Such episodes of death have not repeated so far. But sexually transmitted diseases, TB and leprosy (only three) are reported sparingly, among them. They do not isolate TB and leprosy patients from the camp sites. Common ailments found among them are toothache, fever and headache, scabies, lice infestation, purulent sores, fungal infections, early loss of tooth etc. The members of the tribe living in the disturbed habitats of Nilambur North Division are found suffering from ailments caused by malnutrition in contradistinction to those living in relatively undisturbed areas of Nilambur South Division. Due to the nomadic life of the Cholanaicken, the feeding centres started for the pre-school children, pregnant and lactating mother couldn't bring any desired impact.

Result of Drawing Cholanaicken for a Settled Life

Attempts were made in late 1980s and early 1990s for drawing Cholanaicken for a settled life by establishing colonies at Myladipotti, Alakkal etc. Initially some temporary sheds made up of bamboo were erected for the Cholanaicken of the Karulai Range at Myladipotti. Coconut seedlings were planted and coffee cultivation attempted. Elephants attack caused severe damage to the colony, hence trenches were dug around the 15 acre plot. Later twenty pucca houses were built. It is observed that at no time all the houses were occupied by the Cholanaicken. A collection store of the Co-operative society, a Balvijnan Kendra, a pucca building for the housing the Tribal Extension Officer are the other capital inputs in the colony.

Tough the beneficiaries were identified with the allotted houses, they stay in these houses, whenever they visit the collection shed and store for transacting the minor forest produces collected. Their stay is very short in the colony and they have taken least interest in the proper keeping of the houses. Because of the poor construction and inattention, the houses got damaged and dilapidated. The impact of the colonisation is virtually zero. The Cholanaicken of the Karulai and Kalikavu Ranges continue to roam inside the forest. On the other hand, the Cholanaicken of Alakkal have responded relatively better to colonisation. Here also, the houses are unattended for the major part of the year and the houses need annual repair for the stay.

Education

Most of the Cholanaicken parents were interested in their childrens' education whenever they are lured with residential school facilities. Though the attendance were irregular it gave them an impression that their children need education. About 80 per cent of the children have attended Balvijnan Kendra started at Myladipotti and Punchakolli. The starting of an Ashram School at Manjeri for the Cholanaicken and Kattunaicken of Malappuram district, indeed was a book for their educational aspirations. The Cholanaicken parents are finding it difficult to take the children to the schools during the school opening after vacations like mid-summer, onam, pooja, christmas etc. Similar is the case with taking children home (habitat). They require financial assistance for the above aspect. Many of the Cholanaicken children are now studying at this residential school. It is expected that by 2001 AD there will be a dozen SSLC passed Cholanaicken boys and girls. There is already a student who is studying in twelfth standard (science group). However it is noted that the semi-namadic nature of the Cholanaicken is the major detriment to their childrens' education and health.

Koraga

The Koraga are inhabitants of Kasaragod district. It is the northernmost district of Kerala. The Koraga are also seen in adjoining areas of Karnataka State, which lies contiguous to Kasaragod district. In both the States the Koraga are treated as a Primitive Tribal Group. Census of 1961, 1971 and 1981 record Koraga population as 544, 724 and 1098 respectively. The survey undertaken in 1998 for the preparation of this action plan estimate their population as 1330. It constitutes 646 males and 684 females consisting of 407 nuclear families living in 284 house. Sex ratio among them is 1059. The total population of Koraga according to 1991 census is 1651 (826 male and 825 Female).

The Koraga live mostly in rural areas. They were compelled to lead a segregated life from the immediate multi-ethnic, multi-religious neighbourhood till a few decades back owing to the severe untouchability prevailed in the region. In earlier days they aged to remove carcasses and ate carrion. There were no inter-dining, no sharing of drinking water wells with non-Koraga. The caste Hindus and other non-tribal population treated them as untouchables, unapproachables and bestowed them slavery. The Koraga remain socially, economically and educationally extreme backward. They speak a language of their own, close to Tulu and Kannada. The multi-lingual population of the area rarely interact with them and their socio-economic ties with the neighbouring population are limited.

The Koraga community is divided into two endogamous sub-divisions viz. Kuntu Koraga (living in plans) and Chappu Koraga (living in the forest). The Chappu Koraga are reported to be found in Karnataka State. The Kuntu Koraga covers two endogamous sections viz., Badiyadka group and Pulikoor group. In addition to this, there are 88 Koraga families living in Pavoor colony, whose forefathers embraced Christianity and is known as Christian Koraga. The Kuntu Koraga's economic and educational condition are not different from that of Christian Koraga.

In Kasaragod district, Koraga live in 43 hamlets, distributed in Kasaragod and Manjeshwar blocks (Annexure-1). Thee are two hamlets in Kasaragod block, one each in Kasaragode panchayat (Vidhyanagar colony) and Madhur panchayat (Pulikur colony). In Manjeswar block, these are 41 hamlets, distributed in the following *panchayats, viz.*, badiadka (6), Meencha (5), Vorkady (6), Paivalige (9), Puthige (3), Mangalpadi (2), Bellur (1), Ednmagaje (5) and Kumbala (4).

The Koraga Population are seen in pockets or colonies. Most of these colonies are Govt. established. The houses are mostly clustered. Families of a hamlet are bound kinship ties. The Koraga eke out their livelihood from agriculture labour and basketry. Untouchability denied them participation in other economic activities of the area. The depletion of forest cover in the area has resulted in the scarcity of wild creepers, bamboo for basket making.

The social and religious head of a hamlet is called *Gurukara*. They are monogamous. Polygyny and polyandry are not in vogue. Widow, widower, divorcee remarriage permitted. The Gurukara head the socio-religious functions such as marriage, death rites, worshipping of deities and ancestral souls. Only one intermarriage with non-tribal is reported, that too by a Christian Koraga. But there are cases of stray Koraga women. Elder and invalid among them are leading a totally dependent life to non-tribals. The traditional social control mechanism becomes ineffective. The Koraga self-esteem is reported to below.

Rice is the staple food of the Koraga. They generally takes the left over of the previous night in the morning itself. The Koraga cook mainly the evening meal. It is also seen that while they work at hamlet premises, they cook afternoon meals too. The Koraga are non-vegetarians. Besides meat they also consume fish either fresh or dried. Roots and tubers are collected by the Koraga from the nearby jungles to supplement their diet. A considerable section of the community is addicted to alcohol and a major share of their earning is spent on that. They are also habituated to betel chewing. Menfolk smoke profusely.

Kattunayakan

The Kattunayakan are one of the primitive tribal communities of Kerala. Kattunayakan (both singular and Plural) has a population of 12155 (1991 Census). 84.5 per cent of this tribe live in Wayanad district. Rest of the kattunayakan are found in Malappuram and Kozhikode Districts. In Malappuram district the Kattunayakan are known as Pathinaicken and Cholanaicken. The Cholanaicken are identified as a separate PTG of Kerala. They live in the forest regions of the three districts.

The Kattunayakan subsist mainly on food gathering collection of non wood forest produces, forest labour and agricultural labour. They speak a language, which is close to Kannada. The Kattunayakans were forest nomads till a few decades back. They are now in a process of settling down in permanent abodes. The Kattunayakan settlements are seen distributed both inside the forests and also in the revenue lands.

A Kattunayakan settlement is known as *kudi*. The average household in hamlet is 10.6. The maximum number of houses found in the hamlet is 22 and the minimum is 4. It is learned that in the earlier days, they have had relatively smaller sized huts. Some of the present large size Kattunayakan hamlets are formed by attracting Kattunayakan from different parts of forests to a colony site. Because of the propinquity to forest, the Kattunayakan could maintain their traditional forest oriented economic life. A few Kattunayakan families are found cultivating ginger, plantain and vegetables in their household plots.

The Kattunayakan are found benefited by various housing schemes 60 per cent of the families are found living in Government built tiled or asbestos roofed houses. The traditional huts are flimsy structures devoid of any raised platforms, the walls are made of bamboo wattle work with mud plastering inside and roof made of bamboo and reed poles, thatched with grass. The household articles are meagre. Usually, they sleep they sleep on floors on grass mats.

Economy

The Kattunayakan economy can be grouped as follows(a) Food gatherers and collectors of minor forest produces (b) Landless agricultural labourers (c) Small scale cultivators and (d) those who work in forests as mahouts, fire watchers etc. The kattunayakan have a hand to mouth existence. Those who live inside and near forest subsist mainly on food gathering and collection of nonwood forest produces. They gather a variety of roots, tubers, edible fruits, piths, greens etc. from forests. They collect minor forest produces like honey, wax, gooseberry, fungus obtained from certain tree bark, damper, soap nut, wild turmeric, ginger, pepper etc. These are sold to Girijan Co-operative societies or sold to the needy. There exists a complaint that the Girijan Co-operative societies do not pay them as much as the others. The tribals who collect minor forest produces are having forest 'entry pass' permitting entry to forests for collection.

Social Organisation

The Kattunayakan till 50 years back lead a nomadic life in the forest bands. Now, they are in the process of settling down in small hamlets. Head of the padi or hamlet is called *Moopan* by them. But outsiders address him as mothali. Moopan has an important role to play in all the religious and social functions of the hamlet. When the Moopan dies the position is developed and is transferred to his son and in his absence to the eldest son of his brother.

The Kattunayakan are an endogamous community. Clan identity has not so far evolved to a discernible level. Marriage is prohibited within identified relationship and also within the kudi. The marriage negotiations generally involve the amount of bride price to be paid by the grooms family to the bride's parent. Among ruralised Kattunayakan any one can initiate the negotiations for marriage and the bride price is fixed at the highest. The bride price is agreed at the very outset and has to be paid before the actual ceremony. Eating together and feeding one another are the important part of the ceremony. The exchange of betel leaves, nut for chewing are also considered important aspects. The 'tali' is made of string of beads and shells. Marriage can take place at the hut of either of the family. When it is in the boy's hut his parents or friends visit the bride's house and give presents to the bride's mother who escorts them to the boy's hut to participate in the ceremony. During the marriage ceremony they perform a dance called "vattakkali" accompanied by music of drum and pipe.

Divorces/desertions do occur among them. If family get broken up owing to the misbehaviour of wife her family must repay the bride price. The bride price must be returned should the wife die before children are born to her. Occasionally as pointed out earlier, a Kattunaickan may have more then one wife, in that case the first wife have no special status. The Kattunayakan I think that all wives should be treated equally. A form of levirate is practised among Kattuynayakan in the event of man leaving a surviving wife and children. Normally younger brother of the deceased takes over the responsibility of the wife and children.

A kind of avoidance rule is observed. Father is generally prohibited from seeing his son's wife. He will not eat food cooked by son's wife. Similarly a Kattunayakan cannot see his mother-in-law face to face nor can be accept water, food from his mother-in-law directly. For marriage and divorce the consent of the *'mothali'* is a must, It is reported that marriage by elopement are also in vogue. In this kind of marriage, if they boy and girl happened to like each other, they elope to forests or to a distant hamlet for a couple of weeks. After a lapse of time, the couple may go back to the house of either the groom or the bride and later they gain accomplice of the society. It is mostly now purchased and marriage by service are also taking place. Now, the general practice is marriage after attaining puberty. In the past if a Kattunayakan woman happened to have sexual relationship outside the community she was subjected to ex-communication.

Religion

The Kattunayakan worship ancestral spirits, sylvan deities and certain local Hindu godlings. They undertake an annual ancestral propitiation worship during the commencement of nwfp collection season. Their post burial rites and associated feasts are postponed for a better day. The Kattunayakan pay obeisance to local Hindu temples consecrated to deities such as goddess Bhagavathy, Goodlikan etc. The local Hindu temple festivals are well attended by them. They worship the Sun and the Moon. In all the traditional hamlets a small sacred hut called *Daivamana*. Inside the shrine a small wooden stool (peedom) covered by red cloth is kept. On top of it very small icons are placed. It includes images of a man holding sword, man sitting on an elephant, tiger etc. The sacred spot is always kept neat and tidy. The Mothali who also act as the priest alone is entitled to enter the shrine. For warding of evil spirits, for divining the root cause of calamities and disease afflictions. The Mothali enters the shrine, takes the beed (gourd shell filled with seeds of Kunni), and rattles the beeda and invoke the guardian spirits. In the trance state he answers the questions put forth for solutions, rectification's and warding of and remedies for curing illnesses etc. Annually the hamlet shrine is renewed. If they shift the hamlet to a different location a new hut is erected for the purpose.

Sixteen

Tamil Nadu

1. Introduction

Tamil Nadu, one of the major states of the southern zone in India, consists of important tribal groups. There are thirty six (36) scheduled tribes of varying numerical strengths in the State. Based on pre-agricultural level of technology, low level of literacy and small population, six (6) scheduled tribal communities, in Tamil Nadu, have been identified Primitive Tribal Groups (PTGs). They are namely:

1. Kattu Naickans,
2. Kotas,
3. Kurumbas,
4. Irulas,
5. Paniyans,
6. Todas,

All these Primitive Tribal Groups are referred as hill tribes where most of them live in hilly and remote areas. The Kattu Naickans, Kotas, Kurumas, Paniyans and Todas are exclusively living in Nilgiri District of Tamil Nadu where as Irulas are living throughout Tamil Nadu.

II. Population of PTGs

According to 1981 census, the tribe wise total population of Primitive Tribal Groups in Tamil Nadu was as follows:

1. Kattu Naickans	26383
2. Kotas	603
3. Kurumbas	4353
4. Irulas	105757
5. Paniyans	6091
6. Todas	874
Total	144061

Tribe wise census of 1991 is not available and was not published by the Census Report 1991.

The Tribal Research Centre has taken the census Primitive Tribal Groups living in Nilgiri district in the year 1999. As per the TRC census 1999 the PTGs of Nilgiris district population is as follows:

1. Kattu Naickans	1565
2. Kotas	1984
3. Kurumbas	7995
4. Irulas	7250
5. Paniyans	7480
6. Todas	1480
Total	27754

It is to be noted here that the total population of Kattu Naickans and Irulas who are living outside Nilgiri district are not included in the Nilgiri district PTG population.

III. Ethnographic details of Primitive Tribal Groups;

1. Kattu Naickans

In Nilgiri District, the KattuNaickans are found only in Gudalur Taluk. The Government of India identified them as Primitive Tribal Group. They are also known as Kadu or Shola Nayakans and Jenu or Teen Kurumans. Their name correctly connotes that they are the Nayakans (chiefs) of the Kattu or Kadu (forest). They claim to be autochons of the Western Ghats. They are also believed to be the modern representatives of the ancient Kurumbas (Pallavas) who dominated the South of India till they were defeated in the 7th century by the Chola, Konga and Chalukya Kings. They speak a Kurumba dialect mixed with Kannada, Malayalam and Tamil words. Kattu Naickans village is called, Padi represents five to ten huts in a hamlet. They are short, black in colour with protruding foreheads, Men wear short dhotis and half sleeved shirts and women tie a long single piece of cloth round their body just below the neck, leaving the shoulders and arms bare. They are non-vegetarians.

The Kattu Naickans do not have sub-groups or divisions and they do not know about their early clan divisions and rules.

They are patrilineal with patrilocal residence. Child marriages were common but now-a-days girls marry after attaining puberty. Monogamy is most common form of marriage. Their life cycle rituals are simple at par with their customary norms. They bury the dead near their habitation and thereafter it was customary to desert that locality and even carefully avoid visiting. There were reports that the hut in which death occurred is destroyed. Kattu Naickans were hunters and food gatherers. Now-a-days besides gathering the minor forest produce, they are employed by the Forest Department as mahouts and watchers. Some of them used to cultivate small patches of land on hill slopes. They are experts at collecting wild honey and wax. A few have become wage labourers in tea Estates. They have the institution of the Muttan (headman) who is obeyed and respected. They were animists and totemists who worshipped trees, snakes and animal but now most of them claim to be Hindus and use popular Hindu names. They worship Lord Shiva under the name 'Bairavan'. They are fond of music, songs and dance.

2. The Kota

The Kota are known by several names like Koter, Kothewars and Kohatur. They are found only in Nilgiri district and distributed only in seven settlements. The Government of India identified the Kota as one of the six Primitive Tribal Groups of Tamil Nadu. The derivation of the name Kota, according to Aiyappan (1948; 118), is from the Gauda-Dravida root 'Ko' or 'Ku' meaning mountain. The Kotas belong to the Guardian branch'. The Kota speak 'Kota dialect', an old dialect of Kannada mixed with Tamil words. Very little is known about the origin and migration of the Kotas. Kota village is called a Kokkal, represent a linear type, thirty to sixty houses, with two or three localities called 'Keris'. The Kota people are light skinned, having a copper colour, tolerable height and strong built. The Kotas tradition is that a man is not shorten or shave off his hairs. Male dress consists of a shirt and mundu (ling) and a woman's dress consist of single piece of white coarse cloth called Kir. Their traditional garment is known as 'varad, a white bed-spread cloth, is thrown around the body by men and women. Kadk (ear-rings) are used by both men and women. They are non-vegetarians.

The Kota have no broad sub-division but the most striking feature is their 'Keri system'. Keri, means a street, acts as an exogamous unit, and is descent is unilineal in the male line, which regulates the marriage pattern. Monogamy is the most common form of marriage. Child marriages were common. A token fee of 25 paise coin is to be given by the boy's parents to the girl for binding the alliance. The life cycle rituals are marked with purity and pollution. They cremate the dead body and sacrifice a male buffalow at the funeral. They follow the male ultimo-geniture mode of inheritance. The Kotas are the only artisan community on the hill of the Nilgiris. According to Rev. Metz (1864), "Kotas in the olden days were the only one of all the hill tribes who practiced the industrial arts and they were therefore essential almost to the very existence of the other tribes and castes of the Nilgiris". Kotas have been smiths in gold and silver, they are carpenters, blacksmiths, potters and musicians. Agriculture is new to them. The Kota women are experts in pottery work. The Kota were living in symbiosis with other communities, viz. the Todas, the Badagas and the Kurumbas. Their tribal council, called as "Koot, maintains customary norms in the community. The Kota follow Hindu religion and worship their deities, Kambatrayan and kambatiswari in the names of Ayyanor and Ammanor, and later identify them with Lord Shiva and goddess Parvathy. As said elsewhere (Parthasarathy: 1991 : 174), the Kota women are interested for change in the status and roles.

3. The Kurumba

The Kurumba of Nilgiri hills are entirely different from other names like Kuruman, Kuruban or Kuruba. There is a confusion of names in regard to this tribe, that is the reason, Government of India, recognised them under the name "Kurumbas" and to avoid confusion, it declared that, those Kurumbas who are living only in Nilgiri district are categorized as Scheduled Tribe and included them in the list of Primitive Tribal Groups. Luiz (1962: 116) stated that, "It is possible that their name originated from the Tamil word "Kurumbo (mischief), because in their savage state they were very arrogant and mischievous". Kapp (1985) identified seven district Kurumba tribes in the Nilgiris on the basis of region of residence. They are Alu Kurumbas, Palu Kurumbas, Mudugas, Betta Kurumbas, Jenu Kurumbas, Mullu Kurumbas Urali Kurumbas. The Alu Kurumbas speak Tamil dialect mixed with more Kannada words. The Kurumba settlement is called a 'Mottam', represents cluster of 15 to 25 houses or huts in small hamlets. The Kurumba people are dark skinned, well built and of moderate height. Men usually wear mundu (lungi) and towel and women wear blouses, sarees, bangles and coloured beads. They are non-vegetarians.

The Alu Kurumbas are divided into two exogamous phratries, which are further divided into clans. They practice cross-cousin marriage. Their life cycle rituals are simple and they follow rigid pollution. They follow the custom of burial with elaborate funeral rituals which differ according to sex, age and rank. They follow the partilineal rule of succession. The Kurumbas were hunters, shifting cultivators, effective sorcerers, now a few of them became cultivators, laborers and basket wavers. They recognise a village headman called 'Maniagara' who presides the Kurumba tribal council. They were animists, now believe Hindu religion and worship goddess 'Kurupada Tayi'. Kapp and Hockings (1989-232) lamented that "It is certainly ironic that while the Kurumbas were the first Nilgiri community to become known to scholars, they were the last to be studied at all closely".

4. The Irulas

Irulas are one of the major tribes of Tamil Nadu, and are distributed in ten districts which includes the Nilgiris. The Irula are known by several name like Irular, Iriligaru, Iiliga, Iuvan, Villiar, Kadu Pujaris etc. The name Irula is supposed to be derived from the Tamil word, 'Irul, meaning darkness, which may refer to their black skin complexion. The Government of India, identified the irula as one of the six primitive tribal groups of Tamil Nadu. They speak 'Irula, which is a South Dravidian Language of the Tamil-Malayalam sub group. Irulas settlement is called as "Aral, represent many houses or huts built contiguous to each other. Man wears a short piece of cloth around the waist and a towel on their shoulders, women wears tundu (a piece of cloth) around the waist in combination with the modern blouse. They are non-vegetarians.

The Irula of Nilgiris are also known as Mudumars (Southern Irulas), Kasabas or Kasabas or Kasuvas (northern Irulas) and Urali Irulas. They are divided into seven exogamous groups, called 'Kuams'. They practice cross-cousin marriages. Monogamy is the common form of marriage. Child marriages are common. They are rigid regarding taboos connected with child birth, puberty and death. They bury the dead and observe pollution period of fifteen days. They follow the male equigeniture mode of inheritance. Irulas are hunters and food gatherers. Shortt (1868 : 62) wrote that, "Irulas collected wild fruits, herbs and roots to appease hunger along with beeswax, drugs, dyes, gum, honey and medicinal herbs. The gathered products were exchanged with lowlanders for cloth or food". Now most of the Irulas are wage labourers working in Tea Estates. The Irula have headman called 'maniyakara', who presides over their tribal council. The Irula are partly Hinduized, but have their own autochthonous-indigenous religious system. An Irula priest performs rituals at famous Rangaswamy temple in Nilgiri hills. As mentioned elsewhere (Parthasarathy: 1988:248), Irulas are suffering because of much interference of non-tribal into their aesthetic, social and cultural needs. According to some scholars (Zvelebil 1982; Hockings 1980) the Irula of the Nilgiris afford a case for the study of modes of adaptation, acculturation and modernization.

5. The Paniyan

In Nilgiri district, the Paniyan are found only in Gudalur taluk. The Government of India identified them as one of the six Primitive Tribal Groups of Tamil Nadu. The term 'Paniyan', literally means a worker, is the modified form of the Malayalam word Panikkar (labourer). They resemble the African tribes in their curly hair and thick lips. There are numerous speculations regarding the origin of the Paniyans, Luiz (1962: 318: 219) mentioned that, "Some are of the opinion that they are an African tribe that came into India after a shipwreck of the West Coast. Their cephalic and nasal indices indicate a resemblance to the long-armed African Negroes and Kapiries....At one time in the past they were the principle stock in trade for slave trade on the West Coast, and it is possible that they were imported from Africa and sold in malabar. It is reported that the Paniyan found in Gudalur Taluk were brought over long ago from Wynaad region (Kerala state) by the mandatan Chettis as agricultural labourers. The Paniyans speak 'Paniya basha, mixed with Malayalam and Tamil words. The Paniyans settlement is called as Paddi, represent a few houses or huts built in rose in one corner of the agriculture farm. The Paniyan are black in colour being short, strong built and curly haired. Men wear a mundu (a piece of cloth) around their waist and long towel around their body, women tie a white cloth wound around twice over the abdomen like a belt. The women wear base metal bangles and bracelets in their wrists and they embed leaves and seeds into the dilated ear lobes. They are non-vegetarians.

The Paniyans do not have sub groups among themselves but they have different lineages known as 'illams', which is traced in the paternal line. Monogamy is the most common form of marriage. Child marriage were common but changed to adult marriages. They observe strict taboos and rituals during child birth, puberty and death. They bury the dead and celebrate funeral rites elaborately with the help of their priest, 'attall; Rules of inheritance among the Paniyan is 'marumakkathayam, i.e., the right of inheritance is restricted to sister's children. Their chief occupation is agricultural labour. They subjected to a subtle form of bonded labour by the local non-tribal land owners. Most of them are employed in the agricultural farms owned by the Chettis (Hindus), Moplahs (Muslims) and Syrin Christians, Government run farm. The Paniyan tribal council called 'Kottani' is a permanent body with a group of elderly Paniyans called 'muppanmars'. They follow the religious cult of animism and worship goddess 'Kattu Bhagabathy'. A few paniyan embraced to Christianity. As mentioned elsewhere (parthasarathy: 1992 : 14-15). "The paniyans are becoming the true survivors of the disappeared Malabar Civilization. They are still searching the old meanings of the malabar culture and primitive ethos. The freedom of Paniyan women became a movement for civilized modern women, who dream of Paniyan style of life".

6. The Todas

The Toda are known by several names like Tudas, Tudavans, Toras and Todar. They are found only in Nilgiri district. The

Government of India identified the Toda as one of the six Primitive Tribal Groups of Tamil Nadu. The name Toda is supposed to be derived from the word 'tud', the sacred tud tree (Meliosma simplicifolia) of Todas). The Linguist Emeneau (1958 : 47-50) said that, "Toda dialect is an independent language of the Dravidian family affiliated with Tamil-Malayalam. The uniqueness of their half-barrel shaped houses given speculations regarding their origin ranged from Rome to Sumeria. The Toda village is called a mund, means a herd or a cattle pen. It is usually a collection of three or five half barrel shaped huts each 18 feet by 9 feet high with a small doorway measuring only 32 inches by 18 inches. Besides the hut, the mund has another hut with a smaller doorway called 'Tirieril or dairy temple. In the vicinity of the mund is the cattle pen. Toda people are white (fair) in colour, being tall, strong built and well shaped. The striking feature of the women is the arrangement of their hair which is dressed in ringlets and flows waving down to the shoulders. The traditional garment of a toda of known as put-kuli, is of thick white cotton cloth with red and blue strips which is embellished further embroidery by the Toda women is thrown around the body by men and women like "Roman Toga". Jewellery is worn by both men and women. They are traditionally lacto vegetarians.

The Toda community is divided into two endogamous divisions known as 'tharthazoll and 'thevelioll, which are further divided into exogamous patrilineal clans, besides every Toda belong to an exogamous matrilineal clan. In the past, the Toda followed the polyandrous form of marriage. Toda were in the habit of killing the female children. The rite of defloration marks a girl's entry into woman blood. The life-cycle rituals are markedly different from other rites. During the dead body cremation, they sacrifice number of buffaloes. Rules of inheritance restricted to the sons only. The property of Todas consists of the house, household materials, jewellery, buffaloes and cultivable lands. The Toda were purely a pastoral people. The care of buffaloes and the duties connected with the dairy formed the sole work of the Todas. Agriculture is new to them. The Toda women are experts in embroidery work. The Toda tribal council is not a permanent body but only a group of elderly Toda males selected by common consent for a particular dispute. Their principal deity. A few Todas have embraced to Christianity. As mentioned elsewhere (Parthasarathy: 1991 : 24), Toda women with their low status serve the Toda society as 'culture survivors'. According to some scholars (Mandelbaum : 1982 : Anthony R. Walker: 1986), a great many other ways, the Todas changed.

Since the tribal Sub-Plan strategy was initiated in Tamil Nadu, Special Central Assistance (SCA) was given to undertake welfare schemes for the development of Primitive Tribal Groups. Adi Dravidor and Tribal Welfare Department, Tribal Development Division, Government of Tamil Nadu is implementing various schemes for the development of PTGs without destroying their culture and traditions and trying to brought them at pare with other Scheduled Tribe Communities.

Annexure I

LIST OF APPROVED PRIMITIVE TRIBAL GROUPS

1. Andhra Pradesh	1. Bodo Gadaba 2. Bondo Poroja 3. Chenchu 4. Dongaria Khonds	5. Gutob Gababa 6. Khond Poroja 7. Kolam 8. Kondareddis	9 Konda Savaras 10. Kuttiya Kondhs 11 Parangiperja 12 Thoti
2. Bihar	13 Asur 14 Birhor	16 Hill Kharia 17 Korwa	19 Paharias 20 Sauria Pahariya
3. Jharkhand	15 Birjia	18 Mal Pharia	21 Savar
4. Gujarat	22 Kathodi 23 Kotwalia	24 Padhar 25 Siddi	26 Kolgha
5. Karnataka	27 Jenu Kuruba	28 Koraga	
6. Kerala	29 Cholanaikayan (A section of Kattunayakan)	30 Kadar 31 Kattunayakan	32 Kurumbas 33 Koraga
7. Madhya Pradesh	34 Abujh Maria 35 Baiga	37 Hill Korwa 38 Kamar	40 Birhor
8. Chhattisgarh	36 Bharia	39 Sahariya	
9. Maharashtra	41 Katkaria (Kathodi)	42 Kolam	43 Maria Gond
10. Manipur	44 Maram Naga		
11. Orissa	45 Birhor 46 Bondo 47 Didayi 48 Dongria-Khond 49 Juang	50 Kharia 51 Kutia Khond 52 Lanjia Saura 53 Lodha 54 Mankirdia	55 Paudi Bhuyan 56 Saura 57 Chuktia Bhunjia
12. Rajasthan	58 Seharias		
13. Tamil Nadu	59 Kattunaickans 60 Kotas	61 Kurumbas 62 Irulas	63 Paniyans 64 Todas
14. Tripura	65 Reangs		
15. Uttar Pradesh	66 Buxas	67 Rajis	
16. West Bengal	68 Birhor	69 Lodha	70 Totos
17. A & N Islands	71 Great Andamanese 72 Jarawas	73 Onges 74 Sentenelese	75 Shompens

Annexure II. see p. 183-194.

Annexure - III

LITERACY RATES OF STs; THE GAP BETWEEN ST AND GENERAL POPULATION

Indicator	(1971)			(1991)		
	Total	ST	Gap (Col. 2-3)	Total	ST	Gap (Col. 5-6)
(1)	(2)	(3)	(4)	(5)	(6)	(7)
Total Literacy	**29.5**	**11.3**	**18.2**	**52.2**	**29.6**	**22.6**
Male	39.5	17.6	21.9	64.1	40.7	23.4
Female	18.7	4.9	13.8	39.3	18.2	21.1
Gross Enrolment Ratios						
Classes I-V		*(1990-91)*			*(1999-2000)*	
Total	100.1	85.9	(-)14.2	94.9	97.7	(+)2.8
Boys	114.0	101.3	(-)12.7	104.1	112.7	(+)8.6
Girls	85.5	68.2	(-)17.3	85.2	82.7	(-)2.5
Classes VI-VIII		*(1990-91)*			*(1993-94)*	
Total	62.1	32.2	(-)29.9	58.8	58.0	(-)0.8
Boys	76.6	42.3	(-)34.3	67.2	70.8	(+)3.6
Girls	47.0	21.9	(-)25.1	49.7	44.8	(-)4.9
Drop-out Rates						
(Classes I-VIII)		*(1990-91)*			*(1993-94)*	
Total	60.9	78.6	(+)17.7	60.5	77.7	(+)17.2
Boys	59.1	75.7	(+)16.6	58.3	75.4	(+)17.3
Girls	65.1	82.2	(+)17.1	63.5	80.9	(+)17.4

Source: Selected Educational Statistics, 1990-91 and 1998-99, Department of Education, Government of India, New Delhi.

Annexure - IV

STATEMENT SHOWING STATE-WISE LITERACY PERCENTAGE FOR THE YEARS 1961, 1971, 1981 and 1991 (ESTIMATE)

Sl. No.	States	Identified Primitive Tribes	1961	1971	1981	1991 (Estimate)
(1)	(2)	(3)	(4)	(5)	(6)	(7)
1.	Gujarat	1. Kathodi		2.80	11.12	
		2. Kolgha		7.76	10.38	
		3. Padhar			6.57	
		4. Kotwalia		1.20	17.08	
		5. Siddi			23.04	
2.	Karnataka	1. Jenu Kurubas	6.60	15.50	17.50	
		2. Koraga	8.70	8.00	18.30	
3.	Kerala	1. Cholanaickan				
		2. Kurumbas		12.58	12.58	
		3. Kadar		14.19	14.19	
		4. Kuttunayakan		1.95	1.95	
		5. Koraga		10.71	10.71	
4.	Madhya Pradesh	1. Abujhmarias				
		2. Baigas				
		3. Bharias				
		4. Pahadi Korwas			4.06	
		5. Kamars				
		6. Seharias		1.20	2.74	4.30
5.	Rajasthan	1. Saharia		3.44	6.06	
6.	Tripura	1. Reangs	3.76	7.79	12.70	
7.	Orissa	1. Bonda			3.6	4.79
		2. Didayi			3.72	39.93
		3. Juang			8.0	12.24
		4. Lodha.			8.4	22.66
		5. Mankirdia			1.1	27.71
		6. Hill Kharia			3.1	
		7. Soura				13.86
		8. Langia Soura				22.55
		9. Paudi Bhuyan				42.77
		10. Dangaria Khond				43.70
		11. Kutia Khond			12.4	20.77
		12. Birhor				
		13. Chuktia Bhunjia				8.1

(Contd...)

(Annexure IV (Contd.)

(1)	(2)	(3)	(4)	(5)	(6)	(7)
8.	Andhra Pradesh	Gadaba	2.52	3.43	10.59	
		1. Gutob Gadaba				
		2. Bodo Gadaba				
		Poroja	1.82	2.39	2.88	
		3. Bondo Poroja				
		4. Khond Poroja				
		5. Parengi Poroja				
		Khonds	1.01	0.92	1.26	
		6. Kutra Khond				
		7. Dongria Khond				
		8. Kondasavara				
		9. Thoti	12.09	12.99	17.94	
		10. Chenchus	5.95	6.59	9.71	
		11. Konda Reddi	1.85	4.25	7.77	
		12. Kolams	0.94	1.36	3.46	

Annexure - IV

A FEW SOCIO-ECONOMIC CHARACTERISTICS OF PTGS OF NOR TH ZONE EASTERN GHATS

Sl. No.	Name of the Tribe		Groups	Totems	Linguistic/ Racial Group	Economic Activity			Environment/ Habitat	Other Tribes in the same habitat(?)	Population in the notified State	Population in other States	Remarks
	Sub-Tribe	Main Tribe				Main	Subsidiary	Artisan (?)					
(1)	(2)	(3)	(4)	(5)	(6)	(7)	(8)	(9)	(10)	(11)	(12)	(13)	(14)
01 02	Bodo Gadaba Gutob Gadaba	Gadaba	Bodo, Parenge, Olarc, Kalayi, Kapu, Kathivi, Jurunu, Gutob.	Kora (Sun), Nag (Cobra), Bhag (Tiger), Kera (Parrot), Gollori (Monkey), Kettera (Scissors), Kukur (Dog).	Dravidian Telugu Austro-Asiatic Gutob	Shifting Cultivation	Wage workers	Basket, Mat Making	Korput, Ganjam, Kalahandi and Sundargarh District of Orissa Srikakulam, Vizianagaram & Visakhapatnam Districts of AP	Bhagata, Poroja, Khond, Kotia, Mali, Valmiki.	OR-56,911 AP-7,732 Ch-3,254	Ch-3,254	Land owning (Partly)
03 04	Dongria Khond Kutia Khond	Khond	Dongria, Kutia, Desi, Penga, Malwa, Jhuria, Tikiria, Yenity, Kodi.	Milleku (Peacock), Mandenga (Tiger), Moosaka (Ape), Tadinga (Snake), Sirika (Fly).	Dravidian Kuvi	Shifting Cultivation	Animal Husbandry Hunting-Gathering	Agricul. Tools	Phulbani, Koraput and Kalahandi Districts of Orissa Srikakulam, Vizianagaram & Visakhapatnam Districts of AP	Bhagata, Poroja, Kotia, Nooka Dora, Mali, Valmiki.	OR-989,342 AP-39,408	Ch-1,670 BI-1,264 WB-639 MH-406	Land owning (Partly)

(Contd...)

(Contd...)

(1)	(2)	(3)	(4)	(5)	(6)	(7)	(8)	(9)	(10)	(11)	(12)	(13)	(14)
05 06 07 08	Khond Poroja Parangi Poroja Bondo Poroja Didayi	Poroja	Sodia, Bodu, Barengi, Jodia, Bada, Jodia, Penger, Kondi, Seila.	Bagh (Tiger), Nag (Cobra), Mandi (Cow), Kachim (Tortois), Bouda (Goat), Nagam (Dog), Godhi (Bengal Monitor), Pondi (Dove).	Dravidian Parji	Plough agricul-ture Shifting Cultiva-tion	MFP Collec-tion Hurtting-Gather-ing Agricul-ture labour	Basket, Mat Making	Koraput and Kalahandi Districts of Orissa Visakhapatnam District of AP	Bhagata, Gadaba, Konda Dora, Khond, Kotia, Mali.	OR-267,185 AP-16,479	MP-1,408 MH-806	Land owning (Partly)
09 10 11	Konda Saora Langia Saora Saura	Saora	Jati, Arsi, Jadu, Kindal, Kumbi, Langia and Sudha	About 25 totems	Austro-Asiatic Saora	Shifting Cultiva-tion Terrace Cultiva-tion	MFP Collect-ion Hunt-ing Gather-ing	Agricul. Tools	Ganjam, Koraput other adjoining Districts of Orissa. Srikakulam and Vizianagaram Districts of AP	Gadaba Jatapu	OR-370,055 AP-82,101	MP-63,773 WB-37,247 BI-3,014 MH-301	Saora Paint-ings Land owning (Partly)

(Contd...)

(Contd...)

(1)	(2)	(3)	(4)	(5)	(6)	(7)	(8)	(9)	(10)	(11)	(12)	(13)	(14)
12	Bondo	Bondo	—	Ontol (Cobra) Killo (Tiger)	Austro-Asiatic Bondo	Shifting Cultiva-tion Plough agricul-ture	MFP collec-tion Hunting Fishing Animal Hus-bandry	Weaving Bead making Agricul. Tools	Malkangiri District of Orissa	Dom	OR-5895	—	Orna-ments and naked-ness Land owning (Partly)
13	Konda Reddy	Konda Reddy	—	—	Dravidian Telugu	Shifting Cultiva-tion Plough agricul-ture	MFP collec-tion, Agricul-ture labour	Agricul. Tools	East Godavari and West Godavari Districts of AP	Koya, Konda Kammara.	AP-54,685	TN-31,525 KA-1,064	Land owning (Partly)

Bibliography

Elwin, Verrier, 1944, 'The Aboriginals', Oxford University Press

Grigson, W.V. 1944, 'The Aboriginal Problem in the Central Provinces and Berar' Oxford University Press.

Elwin, Verrier, 1958, 'Philosophy for NEFA', NEFA administration

Elwin, Verrier 1960, Report on the Committee on Special Multipurpose Tribal Blocks. Government of India, New Delhi.

Panikkar, K.M. 1962, 'A Survey of Indian History.

Das, Amal Kumar and S.K. Banerjee, 1962, Impact of Industrialisation on the life of the Tribal of West Bengal, Bulletin of the Cultural Research Society, No.1, Calcutta.

Bhowmick, P.K. 1963, Lodhas of West Bengal, Punthi Pustak, Calcutta.

Das, Amal Kumar 1964, The Koras and Some little known community of West Bengal, Bulletin of the Cultural Research Institute, No.5, Calcutta.

Majumdar, R.C., 1967, 'An Advanced History of India, 'Macmillan & Co. Ltd.

Banerjee, A.K. 1968, West Bengal District Gazetters, Medinipur, Government of West Bengal.

Dalton, E.T. 1973, Tribal History of Eastern India, Cosmo Publications, New Delhi.

Singh, K.S., 1978, 'Colonial Transformation of the Tribal Society in Middle India.

Bajpai, S.R. Dr., 1982, 'Methods of Social Survey and Research', Kitab Ghar.

Sarkar, Sumit, 1983, 'Modern India (1885-1947)' Macmillan India Ltd.

Basu, D.D., 1989, 'Introduction to the Constitution of India' Prentice Hall International.

Bhowmick, P.K. 1992, Chenchus of the Forest and Plateanx. ISRAA Calcutta.

Bhowmick, Pradip K. 1993, Dynamic of Tribal Development Practices in India. M.D. Publications, New Delhi.

Bhowmick, P.K. 1994, Primitive Tribal Groups in Eastern India Welfare and Evaluation Gyan Publishing House, New Delhi.

Bhowmick, Pradip K. 1994, Rural and Tribal Development Practices in India. M.D. Publications, New Delhi.

Bhowmick, Pradip K. 1994, Level of Participation and involvement of Tribal communities in development programmes.

Singh, Dr. Bhupinder, 1999, Antiquity to Modernity, Edited by Dr. S.C. Dubey, I.C.S.S.R., Published by Inter-India Publications, New Delhi-15.

Russell, R.V. and Raibahadur, Hiralal, 'Tribes and Castes of the Central Provinces of India', Cosmos Publications.

Government Publications

Roy, S.C 1912, The Mundas and their country, Ranchi.

Planning Commission 1951, Draft Report of First Five Year Plan, Government of India, New Delhi.

Planning Commission 1956, Draft Report of Second Five Year Plan, Government of India, New Delhi.

Planning Commission 1961, Draft Report of Third Five Year Plan, Government of India, New Delhi.

Dhebar, U.N., 1961 'Report of the Scheduled Areas and Scheduled Tribes Commission,' 1961.

Planning Commission 1969, Draft Report on Fourth Five Year Plan, Government of India, New Delhi.

Planning Commission 1969, Committee on Plan Projects, 'Report of the Study Team on Tribal Development Programme'.

Ministry of Home Affairs, 1969, Government of India, New Delhi, 'Report of the Study Team on Tribal Development Programme'.

Sengupta, S.K. 1969, The Portrait of Mahali Economy in Medinipur, Calcutta.

Singh, Kumar Suresh, 1972, Tribal Situation in India, Transaction of Indian Institute of Advanced Study, Simla.

Singh, K.S., 1972, 'State Formation in Tribal Society: Some Preliminary Discussion,' Journal of the Indian Anthropological Society, Vol. VI.

Planning Commission, 1974, Draft Report on Fifth Five Year Plan, Government of India, New Delhi.

Ministry of Home Affairs, 1975, Government of India, New Delhi, 'Tribal Development in the Fifth Plan (some basic policy papers) Vols. 1 and 2.

Ministry of Home Affairs, 1975 Government of India, New Delhi, 'Preparation of Sub-Plan for Tribal Regions'.

NICD, Hyderabad, 1975, 'Perspective on Tribal Development and Administration'.

NICD Hyderabad, 1975, Integrated Tribal Development Planning' (ed. V.R.K. Paramahamsa).

Ministry of Home Affairs 1977, Approach to Tribal Development in the Sixth Plan, A Preliminary Perspective, Occasional Papers on Tribal Development No. 71, p. 98.

Ministry of Home Affairs, 1978, Government of India, New Delhi, 'Report of the working group on Tribal Development during Medium Term Plan 1978-83.

National Commission for Scheduled Castes and Scheduled Tribes, 1978, 'Historical background, Functions, General information'.

Directorate of Tribal Area Planning, Bhopal, 1979-80, 'Draft Medium Term Plan, 1978-88 and Annual Plan 1979-80'.

Planning Commission 1980, Draft Report on Sixth Five Year Plan, Government of India, New Delhi.

Sharma, B.D. 1984, Planning for Tribal Development, New Delhi.

Planning Commission 1985, Draft Report on Seventh Five Year Plan, Government of India, New Delhi.

Ministry of Home Affairs 1985, Tribal Development A Statistical profile, Background Paper on Tribal Development No. 12, Government of India, New Delhi.

Ministry of Home Affairs, 1990, Government of India, New Delhi, 'Annual Report of the Commissioner for Scheduled Castes and Scheduled Tribes'.

Ministry of Home Affairs, 1990, Government of India, Tribal Development Division, 'Compendium of Circulars/Guidelines of Tribal Development.'

Planning Commission 1990, Draft Report on Eighth Five Year Plan, Government of India, New Delhi.

Report of the Working Group. 1990, Development of Scheduled Tribes during Seventh Five Year Plan, New Delhi.

Ministry of Home Affairs 1997, Government of India, New Delhi, Approach to Tribal Development in the Sixth Plan., A Preliminary of Perspective.

Index